ReThinking
SYNAGOGUES

A New
Vocabulary for
Congregational Life

Rabbi Lawrence A. Hoffman

For People of All Faiths, All Backgrounds

JEWISH LIGHTS Publishing

Woodstock, Vermont

ReThinking Synagogues:
A New Vocabulary for Congregational Life

2006 First Printing
© 2006 by Lawrence A. Hoffman

Library of Congress Cataloging-in-Publication Data
Hoffman, Lawrence A., 1942–
Rethinking synagogues : a new vocabulary for congregational life / Lawrence A. Hoffman.
p. cm.
Includes bibliographical references.
ISBN-13: 978-1-58023-248-7 (quality pbk.)
ISBN-10: 1-58023-248-5 (quality pbk.)
1. Synagogues—United States. 2. Judaism—21st century. 3. Synagogue 2000 (Project) 4. Community—Religious aspects—Judaism. 5. Spiritual life—Judaism. I. Title.
BM563.H64 2006
296.6'50973—dc22
2006013536

Manufactured in the United States of America
Cover Design: Sara Dismukes

Published by Jewish Lights Publishing
A Division of LongHill Partners, Inc.
Sunset Farm Offices, Route 4, P.O. Box 237
Woodstock, VT 05091
Tel: (802) 457-4000   Fax: (802) 457-4004
www.jewishlights.com

For Sally,
without whose constant love and support
none of this would have been possible.

Contents

1. The Theory in Short　　　　　　　　　　　　1

2. Thinking Spiritually　　　　　　　　　　　23

3. Telling the Story　　　　　　　　　　　　51

4. Crafting the Vision　　　　　　　　　　　83

5. Sacred Community　　　　　　　　　　　117

6. Sacred Culture, Sacred System　　　　　　146

7. Synagogues in Context: The Larger Picture　　183

　Acknowledgments　　　　　　　　　　　212

　Notes　　　　　　　　　　　　　　　　217

1
The Theory in Short

I write detective stories, not arguments to a jury. Instead of giving opening statements that summarize my conclusions in advance, I build my case slowly and steadily, hoping the reader will stay the course until the end. But then, I am a professional scholar who can afford the luxury of lingering over details before the summary payoff: scholars write that way; other scholars expect it.

In this case, however, too much is at stake. My topic is the future of the American synagogue. I go so far as to wonder on occasion if there even is a future for the American synagogue, a topic that ought to alarm Jewish leaders in droves, but instead barely piques their interest. I believe that significant Jewish existence in North America depends on our ability to sustain Judaism as a religion, rather than a last hurrah of ethnic nostalgia. And the only way to do that is to sustain a synagogue where religion is taken seriously. By religion, I mean more than outward demonstrations of ritual observance. I mean a combination of spirituality and ethics. The theme of this book is that synagogues must become spiritual and moral centers for the twenty-first century.

Synagogues are not exactly in trouble: membership is stable, even rising somewhat. But what does "being out of trouble" mean? Public education is also not in trouble, if by that we mean that classrooms are mostly full of children who mostly graduate and mostly move on to jobs and life. But no one seriously thinks that schools are successfully maximizing deep, learned, and lasting commitment to cultural competence and democratic debate. It may be too early to dial 911 for synagogue help—synagogues are doing many things exceptionally well. But it is not too early to think about putting 911 in our phone directory. This book is about synagogues now, so we won't have to dial 911 later.

The Jewish People in America is also doing reasonably well. No 911 required. But population surveys properly raise concerns about what "doing reasonably well" means. Already in 1990, while the American population grew, our numbers remained stagnant. In an article entitled "Zoroastrians Turn to Internet Dating to Rescue Religion," the *Wall Street Journal* chronicles heroic measures by "one of the world's oldest religions" to avoid oblivion—frantic warnings against intermarriage and appeals to Zoroastrian women to have more children.[1] American Judaism is a whole lot better off than Indian Zoroastrianism, but the parallels are striking. I do not really worry that we will disappear. But if "Jewish People, USA" were a stock, I wonder how many people would invest in its growth—without some steps taken to retool its product, American Judaism. This book proposes such a retooling: not Judaism by default, but Judaism with purpose. I ask synagogues to make that purpose manifest.

My observations derive from a decade of experience with Synagogue 2000 (now relabeled Synagogue 3000), a project dedicated to synagogue transformation. While there, I worked directly with close to a hundred synagogues. But this is not an official report. It is my own personal "take" on things. I support my position with facts and figures when they are available, but I consider my argument philosophical in its essence. I think ideas that matter cannot fly in the face of fact, but they cannot limit themselves to empirical experience either. They have to challenge the facts, suggesting that if we think differently enough, other facts are possible.

But new ideas presuppose new conversations. As philosopher Richard Rorty says, we make progress not by arguing better but by talking differently, finding endless redescriptions that move our projects forward.[2] Redescriptions require new sentences, and new sentences need new words to string together in promising and provocative ways. This is a book about changing congregational culture by redescribing what synagogues are all about; it is a book about thinking and talking differently.

Given the religious-theological nature of my redescriptions, I worry that people who consider themselves "cultural Jews" may misconstrue my intent and be tempted to close the book before even beginning it. I hasten, therefore, to reassure such readers that I neither minimize nor denigrate Jewish culture—just the opposite. I believe it rich, wise, deep, and compelling. I am also a Zionist by commitment, upbringing, and maybe even neurosis; I identify firmly with the Jewish People. What I oppose is not Jewish culture but a particular form of vapid ethnicity that once sustained Jewish life here but cannot do so any longer. What then is the difference between Jewish culture and Jewish ethnicity? Why should Jewish religionists and Jewish culturalists care about our synagogue future?

CULTURE, ETHNICITY, AND RELIGION

By Jewish culture, I mean the totality of wisdom, practices, folkways, and so forth that constitute what we choose to remember of Jewish experience. That experience is simply too massive for anyone to remember it all, so every generation selects part of it (reinterpreting it as necessary) and leaves the rest behind. Leaving behind does not mean losing it forever, however. The parts of Jewish culture that do not get selected in any given generation remain in the cultural reservoir, as it were, to be recovered someday by others.

The reason the cultural reservoir remains so fertile is the remarkable fact that Judaism demands study of even the most arcane material, the stuff that generations haven't lived by for centuries. This insistence on studying everything, not just what is immediately pertinent, is basic to Jewish culture, making Jewish culture its own best argument for itself, in that it insists on its own intrinsic importance. Jewish study differs from the kind of analysis that occurs in a secular university, where Judaism as a culture might also be pursued, but without regard to its relevance. What matters here is the Jewish People meeting "virtually" over a discussion of Talmud, a shared identification with a Jewish novel, passion for the State of Israel, attention to headlines about Jews in foreign countries, enjoyment of Jewish music, and just plain coming together as Jews, in a Jewish setting, and for Jewish purposes. Jewish culture is reflected, borne, and furthered by the conscious choice to be part of these meetings.

Since my topic is synagogues, and since I argue for them on religious grounds, I must be quite clear that I by no means disparage Jewish culturalists who support Israel, defend Jewish rights, use Jewish values in raising children, go to Jewish concerts, read Jewish novels, and so forth, without demonstrating concern for Judaism as a religion. I do, however, believe that because America is a religious country, Judaism as a religion will flourish, whereas the purely cultural agenda will not be as successful. I hope I am wrong. I hope both approaches to Judaism prove winning. I hope religionists round out their religious attachment with due appreciation for Jewish culture. Equally, however, I hope culturalists will appreciate the centrality of the sacred within Judaism and the role that the synagogue as sacred center must play in a vital future for North American Jews.

My argument is not with Jewish culture, but with Jewish ethnicity, by which I mean something altogether different, something best illustrated by the tale of how Synagogue 2000 came into being. Ironically, it originated in a dying ethnic center, the Concord Hotel in the New York Catskill Mountains. Once upon a time, it had been a mecca for New York ethnic Jews. It is now defunct.

It was there that Ron Wolfson and I met, at the behest of Rabbi Rachel Cowan, the grants officer at the time for Jewish causes at the Nathan Cummings Foundation. Ron had requested seed money to study synagogues. As my student some years back, Rachel remembered my own wish list for synagogue reform (no one used the word "transformation" yet); I had even sought a Cummings grant years earlier—in vain, at the time—to apply spiritual thinking to synagogues. As a specialist in people-synergy, Rachel put Ron and me together. We later shared with each other (and with Rachel) the fact that we had come to the meeting purely as a favor to her. By the end of what became a two-hour conversation, we agreed not only to ask for the seed grant together, but also to collaborate in spending it.

The Concord closed officially shortly after we met, but the shape of the coffee shop at the time suggested it had already died but didn't know it. It had a frayed look; we were the only customers. Old signs remained up from the people who had come the week before: a convention of Polish Americans celebrating their ethnic identity. The dying coffee shop and the signs celebrating old-world ethnicity proved omen-like (though not ominous) for the project we hatched there. At stake was the imminent demise of Jewish ethnicity.

"Ethnic" comes from the Greek *ethnos*, meaning "nation" or "people." In the Septuagint (the Greek translation of the Bible), it replaces the Hebrew *goy*, meaning "nation," and through early Christian usage, it comes to denote those who are neither Jews nor Christians, that is, pagans. It eventually gets twisted into the word "heathen." But everyone belonged to an all-embracing *ethnos* of some sort, so sociologists adopted the word without its negative connotations to describe any group with a common cultural tradition and unique identity as a subgroup within society as a whole.[3] To the extent that Jewish ethnicity reflects Jewish Peoplehood and represents the commitment to build thriving Jewish community, I applaud it.

But "ethnicity" has a less positive connotation: a nostalgic yearning for Jewish folkways that once sustained us as a people apart, but can no longer do so. Ethnicity in this sense is doing what we think Jews have always done, whether or not they have always done it, and whether or not it is even authentically Jewish. It is behaving by social habit, "doing what comes naturally," but with no transcendent purpose. Philip Roth illustrates this kind of ethnicity when he says he grew up knowing little about Judaism except that Jews were "we" and everyone else was "they." Ethnic Judaism is psychological Judaism, the psychological penchant for being with other Jews who have the same ethnic memories, but not, say, with Jews by choice, who (ethnic Jews think) "can never really be fully Jewish"—as, indeed, they cannot, if Judaism is the residue of growing up Jewish with little or no concern for Jewish religion and culture. Freud was such a Jew. All Freud's friends were Jewish; he belonged "faithfully" to B'nai B'rith, but would not allow his wife to light Shabbat candles; he told Karl Abrahams, one of his many Jewish disciples, that Jung was not smart enough to grasp psychoanalysis because he wasn't Jewish.[4]

My use of "culture" here is admittedly biased. I can fairly be charged with emphasizing elite, not folk, culture. In its broad sense, Jewish culture does include behavior governed by shared ethnic moments of the past—borscht belt humor, for example, or lox and bagel breakfasts. But the borscht belt is dead—its humor now embarrasses more than it entertains—and lox and bagels are American, not Jewish, staples. "Lox and bagel" culture has no staying power. It evaporates into nostalgia.

The argument here is that synagogues ought to be religious in their essence. But even though Judaism is indeed a religion, it is not purely a faith, in the Protestant sense of being a "confession." It includes elite Jewish culture, which is defined by the real and virtual gatherings of Jews intent on enjoying, interpreting, and staking a claim on Jewish texts, music, novels, history, and so on. Jewish culture looks forward, Jewish ethnicity backward. Jewish culture changes and grows; Jewish ethnicity peters out and dies.

It is of mild interest, for example, that Greco-Roman Jews in the first couple of centuries CE enjoyed festive meals in which men (mostly) ate hors d'oeuvres, then reclined on couches to eat and drink heavily, and discussed gentlemanly Jewish topics of one sort or another. That much is ancient ethnicity, easily mistaken for being Jewish, when in fact it is simply Greco-Roman with a Jewish slant. It is of permanent significance, however, that one such meal became a Passover seder with a script that invests the ordinary festive food with Jewish meaning.

> Jewish culture looks forward, Jewish ethnicity backward. Jewish culture changes and grows; Jewish ethnicity peters out and dies.

Similarly, although it is interesting, no one much cares in any serious way about the fact that northern European Jews, who had no spring greens at Passover time, substituted potatoes for lettuce, or that Mediterranean Jews, who had all sorts of produce by that time of year, made *charoset* out of dates, almonds, and other fruits that grew naturally in their backyards. It does matter, however, even for Ashkenazi Jews who never eat it, that the dates and almonds recipe was interpreted culturally as honoring the special produce of the Land of Israel, in an effort to keep that Land foremost in Jewish consciousness—a lesson that every viable form of Jewish civilization has retained in one way or another.[5]

Ethnic things get forgotten if they do not enter cultural consciousness. Historians may sometimes dig them up, but they can usually do so only because culture-conscious Jews saw fit to write about them, and not just as curios, but as cultural symbols that point to something higher.

Immigrant Yiddish humor, for instance, that the Concord Hotel once featured is pure ethnicity. In 1952, Nathan Ausubel collected a lot of it in *A Treasury of Jewish Humor*, a popular book of its time, but hardly read by anyone anymore. That self-effacing humor is now an ethnic dinosaur. As for gastronomic Judaism, never mind the lox and bagel breakfasts; what about the ubiquitous Chinese restaurant in Jewish neighborhoods? Shall we identify that as Jewish just because for some period of time Jews in some locales have tended to meet there while their neighbors ate Christmas dinners?

By contrast, I applaud Jewish culture as lasting. Insofar as it depends on Jews who celebrate it with other Jews, it appears to be ethnic, but there is a huge distinction between Jewish storekeepers who would habitually meet for a corned beef sandwich lunch and Jews who gather for a Jewish folk or film festival. The former is a bit of nostalgia for a romanticized touch of eastern Europe. The latter is an inchoate quest for the glue that binds Jews together into virtual Jewish community.

I am in favor of Jewish culture, then, as I am committed to the need for a Jewish community that logs time together pursuing it. Long ago, Emile Durkheim, a founder of sociology and a Jew himself (though hardly a practicing one),[6] saw the positive correlation between logging regular and sustained time together and the growth of shared communal sympathies. If ongoing Jewish community requires Jewish culture, it is equally true that Jewish culture demands ongoing Jewish communities. So I support Jewish community in and of itself, without which neither Jewish religion nor Jewish culture will survive.

But my concern for Jewish community is not ethnic. It is religious. Mordecai Kaplan, the founder of Jewish Reconstructionism and a disciple of Durkheim, thought Jewish community needed no justification beyond itself. Every people requires community, so any community that exists for the good of its members (and not to the detriment of others) has an absolute right to exist. But Kaplan was a staunch advocate for Jewish culture, not just Jewish survival for its own sake, and he knew also that Jewish culture has never been successfully divorced from religion. He described Judaism not just as a civilization, but as a *religious* civilization.

Decidedly irreligious culturalists are actually a phenomenon of a very small swath of Jewish history, the late nineteenth and early twentieth centuries, and they are nowadays just that—history. When, for example, Czarist politics announced a threefold Jewish solution—one-third killed, one-third emigrated, and one-third assimilated—Jews responded with two ideologies: Zionism and territorialism. Zionists, even nonreligious Zionists, demanded a return to the religiously significant homeland of Israel. The territorialists, by contrast, sought to carve out a Yiddish-speaking land in Czarist Russia, like those of other ethnic groups in the Russian orbit. Religion was to have no place in their territory. Zionism is still a live topic; territorialism is dead.

The culturalist commitment to Jewish Peoplehood is itself religious. If Jews who arrived here from 1881 to 1924 ate Lower East Side food and laughed at Catskill humor, other immigrant groups had their own culinary and jocular favorites. But they did not see anything transcendent in the people to which they belonged, while Jews did. Religionists may describe it as our covenant with God; nontheists may prefer thinking of the role Jews play in human history. In any case, there is something transcendent and, therefore, religious about it. Joel Hoffman, an academic linguist and passionate Jew in his own right, is fond of saying that some people never leave home without a gun; he never leaves home without a pen and a book. Jews have contributed mightily to the growth of the human spirit; we represent a notable share of the list of Nobel Prize winners; we invented vowels to make reading possible.[7] Many Jews see these accomplishments as the unfolding of a Jewish mission in the evolution of human affairs.

Like all things historical, both culture and ethnicity are contingent. But ethnicity is contingent on forces that inevitably die out, whereas culture depends on historical chance, human will, and, perhaps, divine intervention. Of the three, human will alone is ours to control. That is why we elect to study culture over and over again. And that is where the obligation to worry about synagogue change enters in. History places us in a country and time where religious institutions matter, but where our own such institution, the synagogue, is threatened. Unable to count on God to come to our rescue, we need to manufacture the will to redescribe the synagogue in a newly compelling way.

I plead for a revival of Jewish culture as religiously important, and I plead for the reinvention of the synagogue as the sole institution with the capacity for reviving it. To be sure, I believe also in other institutions—JCCs, Federations, and the like. Ultimately, my plea is for a reshaped Jewish community altogether (chapter 7). But I firmly believe that any North American Jewish community that hopes to be around in a hundred years must have religion at its center, with the synagogue, the religious institution that best fits North American culture, at its very core.

So much for "culture" and "ethnicity." I should now explain what I mean by "religion" and "synagogue." I will be clearer about "religion" in a moment, when I discuss spirituality and the sacred. For now, I need only say that I do not identify religion as any single variety of what any particular kind of "religious" Jew practices. I mean by it any serious and ongoing interpretation of the theological claim of Jewish ultimacy (I am comfortable using traditional "God language" for it). Not every interpretation of Jewish religion will be seen in retrospect to have worked. (Christian Jews, for instance, eventually became Jewish Christians, and then just Christians, substituting the story of Jesus of Nazareth for the tale of Jews leaving Egypt.) But, by the same token, no one knows in advance just which definition will turn out to count, and part of my claim will be that American culture is kind to Jews because it allows us free reign to experiment with many forms of what we think Jewish religion ought to be. By "religious," then, I do not mean "Orthodox" in the sense that many Israelis understand the word, even though I fully appreciate modern Orthodoxy as a valid religious option. I say the same of Reform,

> *Religion is a moving theological target. Religious Jews are those who keep trying to hit it somewhere rather than give up Jewish archery altogether. Synagogues should at least hand out bows and arrows.*

Conservative, Reconstructionist, and Renewal Judaism. Religion is a moving theological target. Religious Jews are those who keep trying to hit it somewhere rather than give up Jewish archery altogether. Synagogues should at least hand out bows and arrows.

I asked earlier, why should both Jewish religionists and Jewish culturalists care about our synagogue future? The answer is now clear. Since America is a religious country, it is likely that Judaism as a religion, not just a culture, will flourish. Religion in America means churches for Christians and, therefore, synagogues for Jews.

I recognize the cultural vagaries that have informed the evolution of synagogues, so I do not necessarily argue for every neighborhood synagogue that we now have. On the contrary, the synagogue is at a new set of historical crossroads. This book makes the case for synagogue transformation, not the retrenchment of yesterday's synagogue forms.

It is a case, moreover, that I hope the people charged with synagogues will read. It is directed at synagogue boards, denominational leaders, seminarians, cantors, rabbis, executive directors, educators, and all the others who make synagogues their passion. I assume, however, that these people are not fools. Jews may be the most learned sector of North American society. Of Jews aged thirty-five to forty-four, 88 percent have been to college, 68 percent have a college degree, and 33 percent have a graduate degree as well. Of those who are synagogue members, the numbers are even higher: 93 percent, 77 percent, and 42 percent.

The last thing I want to do, then, is dumb down a topic that already suffers from a dearth of serious conversation. The whole point of the book, after all, is to provide a new and exciting vocabulary that will facilitate equally new and exciting conversation. While not technically academic, then, this is hardly a quick and easy read. It is meant for people with intellectual curiosity who know their discussions about synagogues do not measure up to the depth and seriousness that they expect in other areas of expertise—legal, business, and medical journals, for example.

I write my critique as the individual Jew I am—I have no choice but to do that—but also as a thoughtful and creative Jew who has been privileged to work alongside other thoughtful and creative people in a ten-year experiment called Synagogue 2000 (S2K). Although it is now renamed Synagogue 3000 (S3K), I will refer to it by the older title, the one it enjoyed during the period I am reporting on. But given the need for synagogue seriousness, it is more than a field report on what works and what does not. It is a work of theory intertwined with practice—what philosophers have called "critical theory."

CRITICAL THEORY

"Critical theory" is a technical term describing a philosophical movement that emerged in Weimar Germany, known also as the Frankfurt School. With the rise of Hitler, its members, mostly Jews, relocated to New York. Like so many Jews, they had begun as Marxists, only to be appalled at the way Marxist thought had crystallized into real-world politics—first and foremost, Stalinism, but also civil war between Stalinist and independent socialists in Germany following World War I, which allowed the German state to do them both in.

In the light of practical defeat, the Frankfurt School set about redefining the theory, but this time verifying it empirically as they went along, the idea being that theory should explain the possibility of social transformation but that it should also prove practical in terms of actually working toward the predicted transformative end. The word that came to be used for the combination of practice and theory is "praxis."

Theory should explain the possibility of social transformation, but it should also prove practical in terms of actually working toward the predicted transformative end.

Synagogue 2000 was an experiment in praxis: theory that explains transformation while bringing transformation about. This book, then, is neither theory nor practice independently. It is praxis, the kind of interweaving that prohibits practice from going unexplained and prevents theory from lapsing into fantasy.

The central idea is that ideas count. They provide ways of thinking about what we want to change, such that we can imagine what it is we want to become. What was striking, as we considered synagogue transformation, was the absence of any conceptual framework with which to imagine it. Critical issues like funding, boards, and the space that synagogues inhabit were treated just as "funding, boards, and space"—they were givens, as if they could be critiqued or altered without first having some prior idea from which to entertain the critique or design the alteration. It would be tantamount to speaking about arms, legs, and intestines as making up a body, but having no notion of personhood—and unable, therefore, to distinguish a living being from a cadaver. The success of Synagogue 2000 followed from its insistence on reconceptualizing just what synagogues are.

We shall see later (chapter 5) that we ended up thinking of synagogues as models of sacred community. In one way, that is hardly news; it is just a translation of *K'hillah K'doshah* (usually shortened to K.K.), the designation that precedes many synagogue names. In another way, it proved radical in that most people do not even know their congregation's name begins with "K.K.", let alone what the initials denote. The connotation of "sacred community" allowed us to tap the wellsprings of Jewish values in modern ways.

More and more, we came to realize the chasm that separates the era now opening up before us from what we are used to. We are challenged by the dissipation of traditional religious and ethnic loyalties; radical religious freedom (even to be irreligious); the ubiquitous search for personal spirituality; a changeover from print to computer culture; adults with lives that begin all over again at forty; and a generational turnover from baby-boomers, who are aging, to their Gen-X children, who are beginning to attain positions of authority and power. In the pages that follow, we shall see why "sacred community" seemed an apt term for describing the spiritual niche that synagogues will need to occupy, and we shall see also just why and how that concept challenges us to rethink everything else about synagogue life: its governance, its mode of relationships, its spatial organization, its business ethics—everything.

RELIGIOUS, SPIRITUAL, SACRED

All three words recur regularly here, so I should be clear about what I mean by them. Religious is the opposite of secular, from the Latin *seculum,* used by the medieval church to denote "of the world." Originally, it was a positive term denoting clergy who lived and worked with the people, as opposed to those who chose monastic seclusion. Eventually, it took on negative tones, referring to people who denied religion. A great number of Jews define themselves that way. But what exactly is it that they deny?

If pushed, most secular Jews would say they deny the existence of God. When I ask them for a description of the God they deny, however, it usually turns out that I deny that kind of God also. Grown-up religion need not affirm the kindergarten concept of a deity who looks, acts, and thinks like a superhuman being. Belief in God need not in any way conflict with such scientific tenets as evolution, the "big bang," and entropy.

Jewish theology posits all sorts of definitions for God that might be attractive to people who think they are secular because they have outgrown simplistic notions of the divine. I find no single definition *totally* sufficient; I revert to bits and pieces of many to make sense of the complexity of life. Back in the twelfth century, philosopher Moses Maimonides insisted that no positive descriptions of God can do God justice. I find it easier to speak negatively, as he advised.

A religious person believes that life is not without meaning. It is not devoid of transcendent purpose. Ethics cannot be relative, as if to say, I am right for me, you are right for you, and Hitler was right for Hitler. Enslavement, torture, and mass murder are immoral, absolutely. It cannot be true that life demands nothing of us, leaving us free to search out pleasure at whatever cost to others.

By "religious," I mean to connote people who affirm purpose, meaning, morality, and duty—to name but some of the things that science does not investigate—and who, therefore, are willing to concede some transcendent force, being, entity, power—none of these words suffice—that stands behind those otherwise irrational affirmations. Statements about God in the Bible, Talmud, and other classic Jewish works can be taken as metaphoric descriptions that worked in their time, and that have a claim on us too, even though they need to be translated into idioms that work better nowadays.

When I say that we need to think religiously, I mean we need to take those claims seriously, believing that there is more to life than our meager lifetime; that we matter in some ultimate way; that our lives are invested with purpose; that our actions must accord with some absolute standards of right and wrong; that when we die, we can look back on a life meaningfully lived; and that purpose, rightness, and meaning are not mere fictions that we independently or communally invent.

As hard as it is to define "religious" in a mature and responsible way, it is harder still to say what I mean by "spiritual." Jews seem to be divided into seekers of spirituality, who think the organized Jewish world is dominated by closed-minded bureaucrats, and tough-nosed realists, who cannot fathom what spirituality is and suspect that those who seek it are slaves to mindless irrationality. As with "religious," the problem here is that "spiritual" is too narrowly defined.

The word has gone through many incarnations. Originally, it just meant the opposite of "immoral." By the Middle Ages, it denoted the sphere of the church as opposed to the monarchy. We shall see later that powerful figures in American history—Ralph Waldo Emerson, Walt Whitman, and William James—thought spirituality was the elemental experience of the sacred before churches tamed, institutionalized, and ruined it. By the 1960s and '70s, "spirituality" came to mean popularized forms of Eastern religious consciousness and practice. By the 1990s, spirituality had become an inchoate "something" that defied definition but was readily recognizable in a variety of venues. In 2001, *Fortune* magazine even ran a lead story entitled "God and Business: The Surprising Quest for Spiritual Renewal in the American Workplace."

For many, nowadays, specifically Jewish spirituality is largely the melding of 1960s and '70s ideas with Judaism. It features yoga, meditation, and withdrawing from the daily hustle-bustle to a state of interior mindfulness and quietude. Jews who are dubious about spirituality usually have a stereotyped notion of that in mind. I emphasize the word "stereotyped." It is not as if these critics have ever experienced the practices that they consider worthless.

In any event, that is only one form of spiritual practice. Spirituality can mean a whole lot else. It can, for example, be the studied consciousness of a kind of Jewish "being in the world," the way, that is, that Jewish texts suggest we live, with the greatest mindfulness of our selves, our world, and our cosmos. To name but one example, Judaism has the Land of Israel at its center in ways that Catholics do not have the Vatican. Catholics do not yearn to return and live in Rome; it is not their home. Jerusalem, by contrast, is our Jewish spiritual home and, for many, their real-life earthly one as well. Spirituality derives from the Jewish significance of "home," and the horror of its opposite, "wandering" or "exile."

The entire Bible contrasts home with exile. The Torah begins with Adam and Eve being exiled from Eden; it ends with the People of Israel, having been exiled to Egypt, finally going home to their Land. The rest of the historical books and the prophets who punctuate it are consumed with exile in Babylonia, then restoration under Ezra and Nehemiah. Until relatively recently, the rest of Jewish history has been an exercise in "living in exile" (the Yiddish word *golus*) and yearning for return.

What makes this deeply rooted Jewish consciousness spiritual is the way it obligates Jews to take "home" seriously. On the elementary level, our own homes matter metaphysically. Unlike Christianity, for instance, home ceremonial is as important as what transpires in synagogues. Home and synagogue are equally sacred places. But there are ethical consequences too. Homelessness becomes a specifically heinous social problem for Jews. We know what it is to be without a home, to be wandering in a desert of city streets all night, to go without food, but to be without manna also.

By spirituality, then, I include both examples given here: the Eastern model and the deeper message of Jewish texts. Spirituality may also be the sense of connectedness that comes from singing together in prayer, attending a healing service, experiencing nature at its finest, or knowing the reality of perfect strangers reaching out in a moment of need.

In general, all these instances become spiritual when they prompt the recognition that we are at one with something beyond ourselves; it may be the earth, our community, humankind, or the transcendent "something" we call God.

Finally, we come to the sacred. I will later have occasion to cite Jewish sources that identify the sacred as things, actions, and places that exist for their own sake, not for utilitarian ends, even though they may have consequences that flow from them. Here, all I need to say

is that Synagogue 2000 subsumed under the "sacred" both spirituality and morality. Since spirituality is part of the sacred, we can say
that the sacred, too, connects us beyond ourselves. The critical breakthrough for us was the determination that Jewish continuity demands
religion, spirituality, and the sacred.

RELIGION AND SECULARITY

The American synagogue arose in the first place because America is a
uniquely religious country. Colonial villages built churches at their
center, then fashioned life around the churches. As cities developed,
urban synagogues paralleled urban churches, slowly coalescing into
denominations. Pre– and post–World War II congregations, Jewish
and Christian, dominated urban skylines or laid down new roots in
suburbia. The primary question before us is whether either one (as we
now know it), church or synagogue, has any hope of succeeding in the
twenty-first century.

There are those who claim that secularity will inevitably win out
over religion, in which case Jews—who, as the saying goes, are just
like everyone else, but more so—are really prophets of religion's
demise. Jews, after all, lead the trend of advancing secularity at the
expense of religion. As religion necessarily recedes—goes the theory—
religious institutions (both churches and synagogues) are doomed.
The downward trend in membership, attendance, and engagement
that we now see in mainstream churches and synagogues alike is irre-
versible.

This topic will recur in chapter 7, but for now, I can say simply
that I am convinced of the opposite. There is equal evidence, especially in America (but elsewhere as well), that religion is strengthening
its hold on popular thought. It is just that many churches and synagogues have not kept pace with the population. Since Judaism as ethnic memory is dead, the synagogue as ethnic preserve is dead as well.
Yet that is exactly what synagogues here have been: ethnic enclaves.

After World War II, Jews built synagogues (as Christians did
churches) as the family places America valued in the Ozzie and
Harriet days. They suited the Eisenhower era's insistence on visible
signs of religious Americanism. Theologian Will Herberg attacked

that synagogue as merely a local Jewish address with little that was religiously trenchant. After the Six-Day War, ethnicity was repackaged as a national effort to guarantee the survival of Israel and, by extension, to save Jews abroad, especially those behind the iron curtain. It took powerful Federation-UJA coalitions to do that, and as these attracted more and more leaders of stature, the authority of the local synagogue languished, a shadow of what it had once been.

*E*specially in America (but elsewhere as well), religion is strengthening its hold on popular thought. It is just that many churches and synagogues have not kept pace with the population. Since Judaism as ethnic memory is dead, the synagogue as ethnic preserve is dead as well. Yet that is exactly what synagogues here have been: ethnic enclaves.

That all changed in the 1990s, when a new generation of rabbis began occupying positions of influence. All across America, a spiritual revolution was under way, as maturing baby-boomers reclaimed a word that had cropped up in the 1960s of their youth, when they had replaced synagogue loyalty with varieties of experience they called "spiritual." Recognizing the thinness of Judaism's ethnic patina, the best of these rabbis initiated a radical overhaul of synagogue existence. They still supported Israel, unstintingly, just as they worked to save Jews facing persecution in lands far away. But the American ethos that provided freedom of, but also freedom from, religion was taking its toll. Without a compelling religious rationale, synagogues were becoming increasingly marginal to Jewish life. Synagogue leaders worried also about the well-being of the American Jewish soul, hoping to save it from eclipse by making synagogues spiritually satisfying.

The new generation of rabbis, lay leaders, and the men and women who worked with them as cantors, educators, synagogue administrators, and their extended staffs were Synagogue 2000's target audience. We provided what they couldn't easily get alone: intellectual and social glue, which is to say, novel ideas and a chance to think them through in a network of people like themselves. We and they set as our joint mandate the spiritualization of synagogues for adults.

This book, then, challenges not just nostalgic ethnicity but Jewish secularism also by claiming that if people show signs of leaving Judaism as a religion, it is because synagogues have yet to foster a religion that adults can reasonably conclude they ought not to leave. In the end, I hope I will have made the case for religion and its promise, for synagogues as the religious backbone of Jewish continuity, and for a theoretical understanding of what synagogues are and what they can yet be.

I do not claim that everything I say fits all synagogues equally. My charges are both specific and general. As to the specific, I make many particular claims here: that synagogues lack good spiritual leadership; that they do not use volunteers well; that they squander their members' natural gifts because they never ask what they are; that synagogues do not rise to the level of excellence that the new generation expects; that their websites are poorly utilized; that their bulletins fill a congratulatory function (they reward the regulars who plan everything) but are inefficient as announcements; that tension is growing between rabbi and cantor; that, despite the claims of the regulars, synagogues are by and large neither welcoming nor warm; and so forth. To these and other similarly specific claims, some readers will retort, "Not *my* synagogue!" And they may be right. If so, I can only respond that I wish most other synagogues could honestly say the same thing. I do not know the specifics of every synagogue, but I believe I am correct regarding the majority.

In any event, more important than any of these *specific* claims is my *general* one: the need for an overall theory of synagogue life. The specifics are symptoms of a general malaise, an underlying synagogue culture that has been taken for granted over the years and that I now call into question. Among other things, I charge synagogues with being a market, not a sacred community; hewing to an ethnic and corporate model that was outmoded twenty years ago; and pursuing an atomistic existence (as if they need not collaborate with each other or with other Jewish organizations). It is this set of larger claims that really matters here. More than any specific manifestation of trouble, I hope to convince my reader of the need to change direction in general: to think theologically, not programmatically; to foster the synagogue as a spiritual and moral religious institution; to appreciate the increasing role of ritual, spirituality, and healing, not just formal and didactic education; to overcome the dominant fee-for-service mentality that haunts the way synagogues are perceived; and to take risks rather than settle for the safety of the status quo.

I take my own risks in what I say here, stretching hypotheses rather than containing them, so as to fuel public debate about synagogue life. I have not shirked from implicating all the systemic parts of our institutional "thinking" apparatus: clergy who get too busy to remember how spiritual is their calling; seminaries that still train graduates as if it were the 1950s and '60s, attending little to the kind of competence demanded in the 2000s and beyond; denominational bodies that deliver ever more programs, rather than devising ever deeper purpose; Federations that still relegate synagogues to the margins of Jewish continuity; and old-time leaders who delude themselves into thinking that healthy Jewish life here can continue by responding to anti-Semitism, threats to Israel's survival, and yesterday's ethnic memories. There are, however, no villains in my story, only victims who should be helping one another.

My first law of systems is "Most institutions are mostly efficient most of the time." It follows that "If an institution seems to be failing, you are probably not noticing what the institution is doing efficiently." My example is a toaster that burns toast. It may be failing as a toaster, but as a burner, it is an undeniable success. I will argue that most synagogues are similar unparalleled success stories at what they have drifted into doing: catering to children, providing bar/bat mitzvah and High Holy Day services, organizing committees that plan events like *mitzvah* days, and holding Shabbat services for those who like them. It is just that as admirable as these things are, synagogues cannot afford doing them alone anymore. All my examples, even Shabbat services, are examples of programs, because what most synagogues are truly successful at is programming. What they do not do well is think deeply about anything. A ship adrift on a soft and gentle tide can lull its passengers into thinking that because their daily programming remains pleasurably intact, the ship is still anchored close to shore, rather than being slowly swept out to sea.

But as I say, the synagogue is part of a system, and it is the system that has to rally if we are going to save the ship. Seminaries still train students how to program on board ship, without acknowledging the drift; denominational headquarters provide programs and reward the programmers. Federation leaders who are not internally tied to congregational life the way synagogue loyalists are have been watching the drift from afar and should know better than to think we can keep on drifting without leaving the majority of American Jews behind on shore. I fault Federations too, then, not for what they do well—support Israel, provide human services and a modicum of Jewish programming—but for what they avoid: recognizing that without the synagogue ship, Jews on shore are going to run out of what the ship alone carries in its hold—Judaism.

The synagogue has been our religious reservoir of record. More than any other institution, it has sustained American Jewry, nurturing and educating the individuals who compose it. I have only the highest regard for the dedicated men and women, professional and volunteer, who devote their lives to synagogue success. I write not just about them, but for them. What I have to say comes mostly from them, for I have logged hundreds of hours listening to my colleagues, lay and clergy, say privately what they would not admit publicly. These good people are allies, not enemies, in the task of synagogue transformation. This book should help them do what they want to do anyway. It is not their fault that their seminary education never trained them to do it, that their professional organizations do not encourage it, that the denominational bodies do not emphasize it, that Federations do not support it, and that, especially if they are rabbis, they are spread too thin to have time to think thoroughly through what "it" even is.

But I am far from trashing everything we have, a simple task, for there is hardly an institution in the world that is immune to yellow-press headlines of incompetence and looming failure. To say that synagogues should evolve to better serve the future is not at all to claim that they have been failures in the past. My critique is offered from within, with love, concern, and respect.

I have been guided by yet a further consideration: that this book report not only on the synagogues with whom we worked, but also on who "we" at Synagogue 2000 were. We sought to model what we preached. Believing that synagogues should be driven by Jewish principles, we practically obsessed over our own theological rationale, asking such questions as, Why are we doing this? Does this fulfill our spiritual mandate? Similarly, we insisted that synagogues become places where God's presence was patently present in the way people treat one another. So our own staff meetings began as we hoped synagogue board meetings would: with personal "check-ins," where people brought to the table not just their institutional business but their lives in progress. We prayed together, studied together, and ritualized life's surprises together, even as we worked very hard together to help others do the same. Everything about Synagogue 2000 as an organization was to reflect the Synagogue 2000 ethos. This book, then, must do the same. It will be judged a success by the extent to which it, too, models what we were in the years that it reports on.

This is no do-it-yourself manual of becoming a Synagogue 2000; it is a think-it-yourself challenge to change the way we conceptualize synagogue life. In order to prompt different thinking, it provides a new vocabulary with which to make new sentences about old problems. Joel Hoffman never fails to remind me, "If we always think the way we always thought, we will always get what we always got." And "what we always got" is just not good enough anymore.

Somewhere, someone—it may have been C. S. Lewis—said, "Christianity is an excellent idea yet to be tried." The same can be said of synagogues in our time. It is time we tried out synagogues as a new idea.

Concepts from This Chapter

Jewish culture: The totality of wisdom, practices, folkways, and so forth—the content of all our texts, songs, poems, artwork, stories, and axioms—that constitutes what we choose to remember of Jewish experience.

Jewish ethnicity: A nostalgic yearning for Jewish folkways that once sustained us as a people apart. Jewish ethnicity is what we *think* Jews have done, and what we may continue to do, but with no transcendent purpose.

Praxis: The combination of practice and theory—an idea that explains transformation and then proves successful in bringing it about.

Activities and Topics for Discussion

1. What about your synagogue appeals to Jewish culturalists? What opportunities exist to meet over Jewish texts, songs, poems, artwork, stories, and so on? How often does your community delve into the "cultural reservoir"?

2. What about your synagogue appeals to Jewish religionists? What kind of "God language" is employed, and in what contexts? How is religious experimentation supported for the congregation as a community and for individuals in their private practice?

3. What was the last "big idea" your congregation sprouted and nurtured? In what context did it emerge? What parts of Jewish tradition did it draw upon? What did it glean from modern thought? What kind of transformation did it bring about? Did people speak differently because of it?

2
Thinking Spiritually

What we learn about things depends, in part, on what we are looking for. I wrote my first draft of this chapter, for example, after glancing at the morning *Wall Street Journal* with the headline:

HOUSES OF WORSHIP ARE REACHING OUT TO A FLOCK OF PETS:
PURR BOX GOES TO COMMUNION AT ST. FRANCIS EPISCOPAL
A GROUP "BARK MITZVAH"

Among other things, it appears that a synagogue in California has instituted "an animal prayer sung to the tune of 'Fiddler on the Roof'"; a rabbi in Baltimore organized a service for pets in which "more than 100 animals and their owners showed up, including guinea pigs and a king snake"; and a rabbi in Florida has begun making "pastoral house calls on ailing animals." The reporter, Elizabeth Bernstein, has learned something about synagogues. But what exactly has she learned?

She has obviously learned enough for a front-page article in her newspaper, enough also, no doubt, to prompt discussions in synagogue board meetings around the country where, for all I know, rabbis are even now being urged to get on the animal bandwagon. But an equally insightful headline for the same story might have read:

CHURCHES AND SYNAGOGUES ADOPT COMMON STRATEGIES FOR COMMON
PROBLEMS AFTER CENTURIES OF DISTRUST; MODERN JEWS AND
CHRISTIANS COOPERATE IN THE FACE OF RELIGIOUS CHALLENGE

That article would discuss the evolution of something called "contemporary American religion" and contrast it with religion in Europe or in earlier eras of American history. We would learn the extent to which synagogues and churches are subject to common social trends, the impact of religious freedom in a country with separation of church and state, and the foreboding effect of secularity on Jews and Christians equally. The article would be onto something deeper than simply a parade of dogs and cats in *shul*. The strategy of bringing animals to prayer would be seen as a typical form of shared religious programming in America, like "generic" American religiosity of the 1950s, guitar music in the 1960s, and official greeters in the 1990s.

The point of this exercise in alternative headlines is to say up front that reporting on "what we learned" in Synagogue 2000 is no straightforward task. It requires a prior decision as to what counts as learning, what we consider most important to share, and what headlines we want to attach to the raw empirical data that is equivalent to the interesting but not necessarily intriguing news that some synagogues summon pets to prayer.

As I look back on the last ten years, what stands out for me, and what surprised people the most, was our insistence on integrating Jewish theology into what we did. We spoke incessantly about God—not in sermons, mind you (where it is expected), but in lectures, discussions, and workshops (where it is not). In many cases we drew lessons from rabbinic aphorisms that people had heard but never took seriously, like "We are made in the image of God," from which it follows that everyone who enters the synagogue should be treated with respect for who they are and with reverence for the divine spark within them. Similarly, we regularly consulted Rabbinic literature as a set of values to guide conversations in synagogues back home. Bet Hillel and Bet Shammai, for instance, were two rival schools of thought in the first century. A voice from heaven is said to have announced the selection of Bet Hillel as the opinion to be followed. But first the voice said, *Elu v'elu divrei elohim chayim*—literally, "these and these," that is, both sides "are the words of the living God." From this it followed for us that when synagogue members negotiate positions on difficult questions of change, they should argue their case as forcefully as Bet Hillel and Bet Shammai must have, knowing that in the end, one side will triumph. But throughout the debate, they should remember that the other side is not composed of stubborn lamebrains. They, too, speak the words of the living God.

Judaism holds words in high regard. In theory, it makes slander a capital offense, holding that the destruction of a reputation is tantamount to murder. Before reciting our most important daily prayer of petition, the *Amidah*, we say, "God, open my lips that my mouth may declare your glory," and when we finish, we add, "God, guard my tongue from evil, and my lips from speaking falsehood." God even *spoke* the world into being. It turns out that we, too, can speak worlds into being. Since this book is about speaking differently, we should look at the amazing power of words.

WORDS AND WORLDS

It is the way of the world that words get applied to objects and experiences and then continue to be used, even though the objects and experiences they once denoted change to the point of being hardly recognizable as what they were when the words first came to be used for them. The biggest mistake would be to insist that just because the word hasn't changed, the world continues also as it was, so that the object or experience that the word once described should remain changeless as well.

Take the English word "tradition," which goes back to the fourteenth century when John Wycliff, early religious reformer and the first person to render the Bible in English, contrasted our own "veyn tradiciouns" with "Goddis [com]maundementes." What he had in mind was traditions that get handed down as intellectual property from one generation to the next, what Tevya the Dairyman, in *Fiddler on the Roof*, celebrates also as "Tradition." Wycliff knew (though Tevya probably didn't) that the Latin root for "tradition," *tradere*, means "to hand over." Originally, the thing being handed over was actual property. "Tradition" applied to the legal transfer of a title to property. When you got the deed, you knew you owned it, and if you didn't own it, it wasn't yet "tradition." Wycliff, then, was using an old word in a new way to imply that what we believe and do is passed along to us like property. He was questioning whether what we pass along in the way of ideas still accords with the richness of what God wants us to believe. As it happens, the same process marks the meaning of *masoret*, the Hebrew word for tradition. It, too, comes from a root (*masar*) meaning "to hand over," as in property. Like Wycliff, serious Jews worry about what to pass along to the next generation.

Even as Wycliff defined "tradition," he challenged it, asking if what was being passed on was truly in keeping with what God wants. By contrast, the romanticized Tevya wants to pass along what we have "always" done, just because we have "always" done it. He is unable to level an external theological critique, because his ideas about God are part of the tradition he wants to pass along. What then do we mean if we say that our synagogue is "traditional"? Surely that claim implies that we have successfully passed along intellectual property to a new generation. But what intellectual property? Is it sufficient, as Tevya imagined, that people still do what their grandparents did just because they did it? Is it possible that the Rabbis—no less than Wycliff—would have insisted on a judicious judgment of what we are passing along?

Synagogue life is part of the tradition that we seek to pass along. But what exactly is a synagogue, if such judicious judgment is applied to it? Is it a specific institution best left in blissful isolation from the flux of future shock? Or is it a name applied to a variety of institutions that have changed over time? Originally, "synagogue"—from the Greek *synagoge*—meant just "a gathering," and not a religious one at that. Early synagogues were not Rabbinic bastions, and Rabbinic prayer (the origins of the worship service we use today) did not take place in it. Rabbis did not even lead it. The Hebrew word was *bet knesset*, which means *synagoge*, "gathering"—no more, no less. The first word, *bet*, from the Hebrew *bayit*, meaning "house," seems to imply that synagogues were at least permanent structures, but there, too, a change in meaning has occurred. *Bet Hillel* (literally, "the house of Hillel") does not mean the house where Hillel lived, and *bet hamidrash* was not a building where midrash got studied. "Synagogue" also was not a permanent structure; it was just the gathering. Only with time did the word come to denote a building.

But even after "synagogue" came to be a building, the buildings called synagogues varied from culture to culture. I do not mean the architecture only, though of course that changed too as Jews built their synagogues to accord with the religious aesthetics of the societies where they found themselves. The very *concept* of "synagogue" evolved as much as the structure did. Synagogues have always been places where people gathered; very early synagogues (from the first century CE) seem to have been places where study, too, occurred—Jesus and Paul go there to argue the meaning of scripture, and a first-century inscription by a synagogue donor named Theodotus promises (among other things) a place to study also. Prayer came to synagogues somewhat later, perhaps as late as the second or even the third century. Since that time, it has become commonplace to say that a synagogue is a *bet knesset* (house of gathering), *bet midrash* (house of study), and *bet t'fillah* (house of prayer).

But that truism does not do justice to the enormous variety of ways that synagogues have crystallized these three traditional activities. Nor does it even begin to capture the role synagogues played for Jews through the ages. Did women attend synagogues, for example? Sometimes yes, sometimes no. Did life-cycle events happen there? Hardly at all, at the beginning. A synagogue-based wedding ceremony is medieval, and the necessity for a standing communal *huppah* was still novel in the sixteenth century. Boys are usually circumcised in homes nowadays, but in the thirteenth century, their *brit milah* ceremonies occurred in community synagogues, on their mothers' laps (there was no *sandek* yet) just before the closing prayers. Renaissance Italians held court in synagogues—you went there to find out who was suing who—and a medieval Ashkenazi tradition allowed people feeling aggrieved to interrupt the Torah reading in order to seek justice. If Tevya had wanted to pass along as "traditional" just the synagogues that he attended, he would have done a grave injustice to the many other things that synagogues have been through the ages, and he would have missed entirely the obvious fact (for us) that American synagogues would have to be American—a reality Tevya could never have anticipated.

For our oldest synagogues (like the Sephardi Touro synagogue in Newport, Rhode Island, or the Ashkenazi Gemiluth Chassed in Port Gibson, Mississippi), that meant independent communal gatherings, no different than churches on a colonial village green. For us today, it means being touched by broad cultural currents like feminism, the computer era, the graying of the baby-boomers, and religious openness (carrying with it easy religious switching and rising rates of intermarriage). Given all of this, the American synagogue will again either change or atrophy.

The events that force us to think differently do not at first announce themselves in neon; they begin in infrared—potent, but unobservable. By the time they become visible, their effect is already far advanced; and when finally they get mounted in screaming headline circuitry, they are probably yesterday's news, not tomorrow's. Yet institutions cannot afford to invest their future in conditions that have already run their course. So farsighted leaders put aside their customary glasses that admit only neon to train their vision on the infrared signs of what is coming.

The tomorrows of our institutional lives are never easy to spot, of course—that is why successful businesses fail, why marriages stop working, and why people consult technology or even horoscopes. A sure sign that they will fail, however, is if they consult nothing because their attention is diverted elsewhere while their business or home goes on as usual.

Synagogue 2000 was an early call to don infrared glasses. It heralded the general field of synagogue transformation that many are pursuing now. But it did so in its own unique way—by putting theology first.

PUTTING THEOLOGY FIRST

General Douglas MacArthur famously said, "Old soldiers, never die; they just fade away." The same goes for institutions, which manage sometimes not even to fade. Down the road from where I live stands a stodgy old building that advertises itself as the local lodge of "The Benevolent and Protective Order of Elks," a remnant of Victorian and Edwardian days when men practiced manly virtues by participating in ritual hazings within secret societies. Eventually, they became lodges dedicated to charitable work and pleasant socializing. The Elks' national website advertises more than a million members in over twenty-one hundred local lodges. I assume my local lodge has members, and I mean them no injustice when I question their justifiable viability into the new century. Beside zero-base budgeting (justifying an institution's expenses each year), we need zero-base reasoning in general (justifying the institution's existence anew).

What goes for Elks goes for synagogues. That synagogues still exist is self-evident, but should they? Synagogue 2000 began its critique of synagogue life by invoking radical doubt as to whether the synagogue's time had come and gone. We tried, that is, to think with the mind of our worst critics. Why, exactly, do synagogues deserve attention? What exactly will synagogues do for the Jewish project?

The term "Jewish project" deserves its own scrutiny. Like all Jewish institutions, synagogues might be justified on any number of grounds, but the one that matters most is fealty to the Jewish project over time, begun, we say, at Sinai, and stretching until the end of history. How we define that project determines the kind of synagogue we choose to have.

I said before that synagogues are traditionally conceived as providing three basic activities: prayer, study, and gathering. Though admittedly a gross oversimplification (Italians, we saw, also held court there, and some synagogues nowadays offer soup kitchens), the traditional triad is nonetheless useful, if only because it parallels the three concepts generally regarded as the pillars of the Jewish project: God, Torah, and Israel. God corresponds to prayer, Torah to study, and Israel to gathering. Allowing for other activities also, and recognizing that they, too, can usually be subsumed under these three dimensions, we can imagine synagogues taking different shapes as a direct consequence of the way we weight the relative value of God, Torah, and Israel.

The founder of Reconstructionism, Mordecai Kaplan, for instance, thought them all equal and argued for synagogues that did them all in equal measure. He himself, I believe, would never have countenanced synagogues that skewed the emphasis on Israel to the point where Saturday morning basketball games or swim teams compete happily with Shabbat services, but he did lay the groundwork for synagogues that think they follow his advice when they do just that.

The Conservative Movement, where Kaplan taught so long and so successfully, implicitly rejected his evenhanded approach as contrary to its own emphasis, which was Torah. Not that Conservative ideology downplays peoplehood or ignores God, but Conservative Judaism was founded with a seminary at its center, where, for years, even the administrators were expected to produce scientific studies of Rabbinic texts.

Classical Reform Jews underscored God. True, as part of the general religious trend of the 1990s—called, by historians, the era of the "social gospel"—and again in the heady civil-rights days of the 1950s and '60s, they emphasized social justice, but overall, Reform temples have been known best for the majesty of their worship, the centrality of their sanctuaries, and even their scholarly forays into theology. The first American work in Jewish systematic theology was by Kaufman Kohler, the second president of the Hebrew Union College, and arguably, the very field of modern Jewish theology is the product of that college's distinguished professor, Eugene B. Borowitz.

Modern Orthodoxy has varied in its emphasis. For most of American Jewish history, Torah (as displayed in attention to *mitzvot*) was central. But small *shuls* established by eastern European Jews, which could afford only a single room, provided a visual demonstration of its twofold focus, God and Torah, when it arranged an ark on one wall and tables with opened Talmud folios for study at the wall opposite. Orthodox rhetoric has changed in the last several decades, moreover: the God-givenness of *mitzvot* has become an Orthodox hallmark, putting God firmly at the center.

Synagogue 2000 had, therefore, to decide for itself what the Jewish project centrally required, if not for every era, then at least for our own. We consciously reacted against the pervasive secularism that, in our view, had virtually ignored God. Jewish history, we believed, makes quantum leaps forward when Jews who live in freedom adopt appropriate societal trends and filter them through a Jewish prism. Medieval Jewish commentary, for instance, was part of a parallel Christian interest in scriptural exegesis; the Talmud was codified in the place and time when our host culture, Zoroastrianism, was compiling its own sacred writings. If, then (we reasoned), America was undergoing a spiritual renewal with God at the center, and if (in fact) God has always been at Judaism's core, it made absolutely no sense for synagogues to continue ignoring what was sure to be a pervasive Jewish search for the divine, not just a Christian one. It followed for us that synagogues of the future would have to be places where the presence of God was manifest.

Our work with synagogues regularly turned up insidious class distinctions that had crept into synagogue behavior. On the average, Jewish education now is better than it ever was, but those who have access to it make the Jewishly unschooled feel inferior rather than unfortunate; fearing intermarriage, we erect walls of opposition to non-Jews in relationships with Jews; and being mostly white and European by heritage, synagogue members have not readily welcomed minorities and people of color. So we emphasized the God-given equality of every single person the synagogue encounters, reminding people that anyone who crosses the synagogue threshold is "made in the image of God." We steadfastly denied the notion that Jewish gathering alone was sufficient reason for synagogues to exist; since other organizations quite successfully "bring in the Jews," there is no reason for synagogues to replicate them. To be sure, Torah is critical to Jewish life—it is the way we think—so synagogues without study were unthinkable. But study was to be rooted in the reality of the God who gave the Torah to us. I do not mean to say that we insisted, or even that we taught, a traditional image of God as a personalist deity who met Moses on Sinai or who meets us in prayer. We left theological niceties to individual interpretation. To the consternation of many synagogue stalwarts still in the throes of old-time ethnic culturalism, we spoke regularly and imploringly of the need to take God seriously.

Eventually, our ideas crystallized into the ideals of Synagogue as Sacred Community, by which we meant that relationships, agenda, activities, debate—everything—would be swept along by the recognition of God's reality. Like the desert sanctuary of Exodus, the *mishkan*, the entire purpose of synagogue life would be to fashion an institution where God quite evidently dwells.

That simple insight—that the synagogue be God-centered—had enormous consequences. The midrash, for instance, explains the human audacity to be healers by saying, "You shall heal because I [God] heal." The Talmud sees God's presence above every bedside. Surely, then, synagogues should be places of healing. We emphasized ritual at every step along the way—not just study of Torah, for example, but ritualized study where standard Jewish blessings accompany

learning, and where study is spiritual, not just cognitive. We worked
with teams of representatives from each synagogue, and we insisted
that whenever they met back home in their congregations, they not
only work toward synagogue transformation, but they study and pray
as well. Even during heated debates, they were to treat each other as
if patently created in the image of the Holy One.

This conscious theologizing of synagogue life was, I believe,
what truly marked our work. Unless things ultimately served theological ends, we didn't do them. But we worked very hard at presenting
theology in a sophisticated way. It was not enough to mouth talmudic truisms. Theology should not be confused with the platitudes of
relative know-nothings who get their views from simplistic summaries
not much better than religious comic books. We also took our stand
against new age religion that too often takes refuge in feel-good language that sounds nice but says nothing. Even elite restaurants, of
late, have begun serving the simple dishes of yesteryear as if they are
sophisticated fare—I mean meatloaf, and spaghetti and meatballs, the
things they bill as "comfort foods." There is nothing wrong with letting food comfort us, but it should provide nurture as well.
Theological pabulum doesn't do that. We knew we needed more than
comfort foods of the soul.

So we adopted a way of thinking that I call a "pincer approach."

PINCER THINKING

Our work presupposed a particular view of the way theological
thought proceeds. Of all the ways to describe it, the best, perhaps, is
through concepts borrowed from the philosophy of hermeneutics.

Hermeneutics is the philosophy of understanding. It began, in
part, with historians wanting to understand how history could be scientific, and, in equal part, with Protestant theologians trying to inter-
pret the Bible. Eventually, it was generalized into a science of
understanding how any text at all gets read and comprehended and
then was broadened further to ask how the world itself gets "read" by
us who are its innate human ponderers. We have discovered the exciting notion that texts (and, therefore, the world) don't get read without readers and that readers bring their own proclivity for

interpretation with them. Older theorists believed that texts have a single "true" meaning built into them: it is whatever the author intended it to be. Reading is the process of trying to arrive at this single authorial intent. Readers are scientific sieves who extract the single "true" meaning that the author intended. The model for the old view was nineteenth-century science, which sought perfect objectivity in deriving the rules of the universe. But the twentieth century threw doubt on whether that is even possible, especially in anything but the hard sciences, and maybe not even there. Inquiry nowadays is about the way the reader and the thing being read collude to establish meaning.

Philosophers sometimes use the word "horizon" to explain what they are after. Texts cannot mean just anything, obviously; there must be some limits that an author had in mind. But authors themselves may not know just what the limits are. Playwright Harold Pinter refused steadfastly to say just what his plays were "about." Shakespeare would probably not recognize the common claim that *Hamlet* is a study in the oedipal complex (a term he couldn't have known before Freud coined it). But readers are not altogether free to make just any claim about the things they read—it would probably be very hard to say with any cogency that *Hamlet* is a Marxist treatment about class exploitation.

Meaning comes about when our horizon of understanding meets the text's horizon of reasonable elasticity.

Both the text being interpreted and the reader doing the interpreting have horizons beyond which they cannot legitimately stretch. Meaning comes about when our horizon of understanding meets the text's horizon of reasonable elasticity.

Even people who claim absolute knowledge of what a text is saying are constrained by their own reader-imagination. The text alone does not speak *to* us so much as it speaks *with* us, just as we cannot help but speak with it, in an endless give and take between our life experience and a given text's words.

We shall see later, in some detail, how Synagogue 2000 adopted this view in our perspective on how Jewish sources should be used in synagogues. (They should never be preached as if they exist outside of the life of synagogue members listening to them. We sought, we said, to establish small groups called Jewish Journey Groups, "where text meets life.") For the time being, however, it is important to see how this theory of an interactive text tradition influenced Synagogue 2000's theologizing with synagogues.

First, we found the theory eminently consistent with Jewish tradition. Neither classical nor medieval Jewish sources spoke about horizons, but from the very outset, the Rabbis had established the written Torah as something that required an oral interpretation if it was to be sensibly understood. First midrash and then the tradition of biblical commentary responded by reading new meanings into older texts—or (better put), creating meanings in dialogue with them—but certainly not just extracting prior meanings from them (that would be the older theory of a single authorial intent being the only true meaning that a text has, regardless of what interpreters say). We always bring life to Torah. We never read it without life's circumstances and "horizons" of meaning in mind.

If, when we read, we actually manufacture meaning in conjunction with what the text presents to us, ideas turn out to be not just true or false. They are metaphors, analogies and comparisons, flashes of understanding, insightful anecdotes, and all the other means our mind employs to shape the way we think. Ideas function to promote understanding, get us further on our way, find harmony with what we already believe, and bestow new insights into old problems. Ideas have consequences because they let us see things we never saw before and then make sentences we never did before—that is, we produce our own texts, written or spoken, that challenge others to think in new and exciting ways with us.

Synagogues need to be critical of the taken-for-granted unreflective theories of congregational life, for it is never true that we act without any theory at all. We may just be unaware of what theory we implicitly hold.

In speaking differently, we asked synagogues to be critical of the taken-for-granted unreflective theories of congregational life, for it is never true that we act without any theory at all. We may just not be aware of what theory we implicitly hold. Nothing substantive will change unless we become actively reflective about the theory we are using (but may not believe) and equally purposive in substituting a theory we believe (but may not yet use). Theology allied to sophisticated novel conceptualization from philosophy and the human sciences was our way of speaking differently.

"It is not about programs," we announced incessantly. It is about doing synagogue differently. Thinking differently is what distinguishes transformational from mere additive change—the kind of change that synagogues generally thrive on. Synagogues operate as "default" institutions, doing business according to presupposed and unquestioned theories of operation. They provide programmatic "offerings": worship services, life-cycle ceremonies, hospital visits, supplementary religious school, adult education, and the like. As new congregant needs are intuited, synagogues just add to the offerings: a "Tot Shabbat," outreach to the intermarried, alternative *minyanim*, and so forth. The synagogue changes regularly, therefore, but only by adding new programs to old.

At stake (as we shall see further, in chapters 5 and 6) is an underlying *market* model of synagogue existence, accompanied by a *corporate* model of synagogue structure. Programs are the return for dues. Congregants "*shul* shop" to get the best bargain; corporate synagogues with CEO rabbis compete for members; boards meet regularly to oversee performance, measuring market share (members added or subtracted) and satisfaction level of current membership (the customer base). A division of labor sometimes reaches the point where the board meets for business but does not attend services.

*T*ransformative change starts with helping congregations surface implicit thinking, so as to question the assumptions that drive what they do.

As I say, I will return to this market model later, to revisit its negative consequences for synagogue life. In the meantime, I use it just to exemplify how underlying thinking affects the way synagogues operate, without their even recognizing that it does so. Transformative change starts with helping congregations surface implicit thinking, so as to question the assumptions that drive what they do. Otherwise, they will be doomed to making additive changes that keep busy people busier, without ever attending to the underlying mentality that is at the core of synagogue struggle.

INSTITUTIONS AND THEIR RULES

Pursuing the synagogue as if it is a corporate market-driven business can be called a *constitutive rule*. The term is derived from the philosophy of *institutional facts*[1] and represents an instance of thinking and talking differently. Marriage, for instance, is not a state of nature but a legal category; "friendship" is a social convention. We use uniforms (police), formulas (ethical wills), anthems ("Hail to the Chief"), jewelry (engagement ring), architecture (the corner office), diplomas (graduation), and just plain writing (signatures) to take lower-order actions with no inherent significance and give them higher institutional meaning. Institutions depend on such criteria—which then attract rules.

Now, some rules are just *regulative*, like "Do not steal." They regulate behavior by prohibiting some acts and allowing others. A higher class of rule, *constitutive*, not only regulates but actually constitutes the activity it directs, in the sense that if these rules did not exist, the entire activity would not exist either. The usual example given is a game of chess. Without the rules, you would still have a sixty-four-square board and some pieces, but there would be no game. Synagogues have both kinds of rules. The merely regulative variety is usually given by official documents: "Members shall pay dues annually" or "The Rabbi visits hospital patients weekly." These are the rules that accompany additive change. They are necessary. They come into being in response to newly felt needs to get the system working better, usually when some perceived wrong occurs because there isn't yet a generally assumed rule to govern the behavior that went wrong.

An office person loses a file, for instance, and a rule develops to the effect that membership data should be backed up every other day; or newcomers complain about not knowing the staff, so a rule is adopted calling for a new-members' Shabbat when teachers and office staff are expected to be on hand.

Authorities are the people who become expert at regulative rules. Problems are invariably linked to rules that do not work, rules that are unclear, or vacuums of behavior where "we don't have rules yet, but need them to tell people what to do." But as often as not, the rules are not the real issue. They are just regulative, not constitutive. They record the obligation to pay dues annually (not every six months) or inform congregants that the rabbi visits the hospital every Tuesday (but not Thursday). They do not address such deeper constitutive issues as what it means to have an organization built upon dues in the first place or to have clergy who are perceived as therapeutic workers. Thinking changes from regulative to constitutive when, instead of wondering whether dues should be paid once or twice annually, we address the deeper constitutive rule, "Synagogue is made of members who pay dues at given intervals and have rights of clergy visits in return"; or when, rather than establish days when clergy visits occur, people consider the underlying assumption that visiting the sick is the professional responsibility of clergy who are hired to do it as a religious service to dues-paying members.

Another example comes from synagogue committees. Committees receive regulative oversight from boards, but they should undergo constitutive oversight as well. When boards (or "management"—the executive director, in large congregations) control committee programming by preventing calendrical overlap or by setting boundaries to a given committee's fiefdom, they are applying regulative oversight. Few synagogues discuss the constitutive question of what a committee is supposed to do, or whether committees should continue existing at all. In most synagogues, for example, a ritual committee determines how congregational members are honored during services. Since the committee may be composed of people who know nothing whatever about the *halakhah* and principles of communal worship, rabbis and cantors hold the committee at arm's length from the actual prayer service, which the two clergy partners see as their own domain. An alternative constitutive rule might establish a ritual committee whose members are obliged to study worship before joining the committee, and who then advise and help the clergy. The synagogue might even decide that the job of *every* committee is to constitute encouraging and supportive networks for the professionals. In some churches, we saw committees chosen by the pastor to work on important sermons together! Its members supply him with illustrative stories or honest feedback on the evolving sermon's clarity and relevance. It remains the pastor's work of sermonic art, but when it is delivered, it bears the stamp of many contributors, all of whom attend the sermon, silently cheering the preacher on, and then go out to celebrate.

Not knowing how to discriminate one kind of rule from another, synagogues too easily go to the mat on something relatively unimportant. What would happen if synagogues truly questioned their constitutive rules? By analogy, go back to the game of chess and imagine the following scenario.

A blind girl carrying a board game meets a friend, who promptly comments, "I see you have a game; let's play. Since you do not see, I will place the pieces on the board and move your pieces according to your instructions." She agrees. The friend arranges the board and announces, "You go first."

"I'll take a standard opening," says the girl.

"Standard opening?" asks the friend. "What's that?"

"Move the piece in front of the king two squares forward," she explains.

"But pieces move diagonally, not forward or sideways," the friend objects. "Besides, you don't have any kings. You get them only at the end of the game."

Clearly, this is a disagreement not on regulative rules but on constitutive ones. The girl is playing chess; the friend is playing checkers. They disagree because they do share something: a board with sixty-four squares, some pieces, and the common notion of a game that has rules and implies taking turns. So they have enough rules in common that they can easily misunderstand each other. (It is not as if the friend said to the girl, "Deal the cards!" That would have occasioned no ambiguity with chess.)

There are actually three levels of rules: *underlying understandings* ("This is a game played by two players on a sixty-four-square board"), *constitutive rules* ("The rules that constitute chess as opposed to checkers"); and *regulative rules* ("Let's play chess but allow players to take back moves if they see how bad they are"). Let's now see how this applies to synagogues.

Despite their differences through history, synagogues through time are like a game board. Their recognizable "squares" are a collection of underlying understandings: people pray, study, and gather; they find God's presence; justice is meted out; Jewish peoplehood is primary. We could probably list others too, the idea being that in all times and places, however synagogues differ, they must have some commonly shared underlying understandings of what makes them synagogues. You can alter the emphasis of some of these items, but without any (or even most) of them, you have no "game board" left at all. They are the underlying understandings, the truly necessary things without which there is no such institution that we can properly call a synagogue and mean by it a reasonable extension of what has counted as a synagogue in the Jewish past. We know, for example, of a Hellenistic Jewish institution from Egypt in the second century BCE, and referred to in Christian scripture as well (e.g., Acts 16:13), called a *proseuche* and meaning some sort of praying place. Does it count as the earliest synagogue? Probably not. It lacks too many of the necessary underlying understandings on which synagogue identity depends.

These underlying understandings need to be kept firmly in mind. Synagogues, by now, just are the places where people expect to be able

> There are actually three levels of rules: *underlying understandings* ("This is a game played by two players on a sixty-four-square board"), *constitutive rules* ("The rules that constitute chess as opposed to checkers"), and *regulative rules* ("Let's play chess but allow players to take back moves if they see how bad they are").

to study, pray, find God's presence, and so forth. These are nonnegotiables. By contrast, their regulative rules come and go all the time. Like an ad hoc chess decision to allow players to take back moves, synagogues could decide to let members take back dues if they are not satisfied after a month of membership. If synagogues cannot afford to question the underlying understandings of their existence, they ought to also go deeper than the relatively insignificant regulative rules. The true battleground for a synagogue's soul lies in the constitutive rules, the ways in which synagogues remain true to their historic mission but open to altogether creative ways of doing so. Regulative rules are additive; constitutive rules are transformative.

It is useful to recall the analogy of games. All games have a point: in chess you checkmate the opponent's king; in Monopoly, you bankrupt the other player. What is the point, then, of synagogue? Without establishing that, you cannot know what questions to ask of the constitutive rules. I will argue here that the *point* of synagogue in our time is to constitute sacred community, by which I mean a spiritual and moral center in the context of twenty-first century problems and challenges.

Synagogue 2000 retained continuity with the underlying understandings that make synagogues of any era synagogues, but we asked questions about our own synagogues' constitutive rules that might impair our efforts to become a sacred community. We did that by

Synagogues change the conversation when they go from program (what we do) to ideas (why we do it); from pragmatics (what works) to theology (what counts); from regulative rules (tinkering with the surface) to constitutive rules (building a deep foundation); and from additive change (program change that reacts to the newest perceived need) to transformative change (structural change that responds to the deepest theological considerations).

applying pincer thinking, finding the place, that is, where the horizon of meaning from Jewish texts meets the horizon of meaning from the best of contemporary creativity.

This book questions our constitutive assumptions by introducing a new vocabulary into the conversation. How often are we in committee meetings where we can classify the whole discussion and even predict its outcome? Synagogue boards complain regularly that they are having the same conversation over and over again, and to no end. "We discussed this already, didn't we?" goes the familiar objection. If we cannot make new sentences, we cannot think anew. Synagogue 2000 sought to change the conversation by going:

- from program (what we do) to ideas (why we do it);
- from pragmatics (what works) to theology (what counts);
- from regulative rules (tinkering with the surface) to constitutive rules (building a deep foundation);
- from additive change (program change that reacts to the newest perceived need) to transformative change (structural change that responds to the deepest theological considerations).

This last-named initiative, abandoning the notion of responding to expressed needs of member-consumers, was especially critical.

CLIENTS, CUSTOMERS, CONSUMERS, AND NEEDS

Synagogue 2000 agonized regularly over large issues of "client needs." We found ourselves embroiled with colleagues in the field over the subject, our own position being critiqued, on occasion, for being "top-down"—meaning that we were improperly determining synagogue needs, rather than allowing synagogues to decide them on their own, so that we might be properly responsive to them. On the macro level, this need-orientation reflects the dominant consultant model of synagogue intervention (which, we shall see, we largely rejected); on the micro level it mirrored the prevailing assumption that synagogues are places that members join to have their individual needs met.

As we built relationships with synagogues, a kind of "equation" suggested itself:

members : synagogues :: synagogues : Synagogue 2000

Members are to their synagogues what those synagogues are to Synagogue 2000. As synagogues serve members' needs, Synagogue 2000 should serve the needs of member synagogues. On the face of it, that seems obvious enough; if not the synagogues' needs, then whose? But the answer presupposes a consumerist model of relationships. That very model is a constitutive rule that we questioned.

Why are we overwhelmed by the impulse to respond to needs? The obvious answer is that in these psychologically sophisticated days, everyone knows that perceived need governs motivation. If we do not appeal to people's needs, they will be unmotivated to join us, patronize us, or consult us.

But servicing people's needs is not necessarily high-minded. Need-orientation comes on a spectrum, from Mother Theresa to Niccolo Machiavelli. At one extreme we have utter selflessness in delivering help to people who need it. At the other, we find pure manipulation. How, for that matter, do we even know what people's needs are? Do people even know for sure themselves? People say they need a house, but they may really mean security for themselves and their family. Madison Avenue marketing actually creates needs that never existed before.

If synagogues openly subscribe to the policy of meeting their members' needs, what needs are they supposed to meet? Where, for that matter, did the whole idea come from? It is hardly the traditional synagogue rhetoric of two thousand years. In the early days of synagogue formation, when synagogues were not yet religious, perhaps people did choose to attend for their own selfish interests. But once synagogues became Rabbinic ideals of study and prayer, they became places of obligation. You were supposed to attend whether you liked them or not. Expecting synagogues to respond to needs is revolutionary. Where indeed did the revolution arise?

The focus on individual needs came here philosophically with the founding fathers, enshrined by Jefferson as the individual's right to life, liberty, and the pursuit of happiness, a patent critique of the New England Protestant mainstream of the time, which preached the utter depravity of human beings, who deserve nothing, least of all being happy. American churches, therefore, had traditionally said little about member needs. For churches, and synagogues too, religion was a responsibility, not a right.

All that changed with the baby-boomers, raised on Dr. Spock, whose bombshell book on parenting was first published in 1946. It had been common for nineteenth- and early-twentieth-century parents in central Europe to raise children by purposely ignoring their wishes, making them delay gratification, refusing to intervene when they cried, and inculcating humble patience in the face of even hunger, let alone less elemental needs. That punitive attitude continued in America. Puritan pediatrician L. Emmett Holt, for instance, warned against contrary infants who might cry for hours to get mother's attention. They should be left to cry it out. Babies under six months old should never be played with, and certainly not kissed![2] Holt's book went through dozens of editions between the years 1894 and 1934.

This cold-hearted, religiously based approach morphed into equally distant (albeit secular) behaviorist psychology. It was codified by John B. Watson, whose writings were treated as gospel at many hospitals. Watson regarded human behavior as reducible to stimulus and response. Accordingly, he abhorred any stimulus that might "indulge" and spoil children. Parents must teach patience and fortitude, lest children cry needlessly at "small difficulties in the environment." These "good children" unquestioningly eat what is placed before them and sleep when put to bed. Watson cautioned parents, "Never hug or kiss [your children], never let them sit in your lap.... If you must, kiss them once on the forehead when they say good night. Shake hands with them in the morning."[3]

To all of this, Spock countered that cuddling babies and showing affection to older children would only make them happier and more secure. Parents should enjoy their children without fear that coddling causes harm. Instead of the judgmentalism typical of early Protestant preachers, Spock spoke in a friendly and reassuring fashion, an attitude that parents emulated as they applied Spock's insights to their children.

Parents who now doted on children were matched by the educational theory of John Dewey.[4] The Watson-Holt approach to children was laced with puritanical distrust of human nature. The purpose of education was to correct the essential depravity into which individuals necessarily were born, by filling them with morally uplifting discipline and doctrine. Their native needs were of no account whatever. Dewey decried this notion. The needs of individuals and the needs of society coalesce in the potential for civilization. Dewey thus championed human needs as altogether proper and healthy. By the time baby-boomers came upon the scene, schools that had integrated Dewey's educational philosophy were prepared to welcome a new generation of children who had been raised by Dr. Spock to expect no less.

Finally, as the boomers went to college, they discovered Abraham Maslow's psychology of self-actualization. Maslow posited an entire hierarchy of needs that people have the right to satisfy. Once basic needs like hunger are met, and once material possessions become commonplace, it is psychological satisfaction that next gets massaged. Soon, almost everything got marketed with the promise of making us feel better. By the 1990s even the United States Army pitched recruitment as the way to "be all that you can be." Is it any wonder that baby-boomers saw synagogues as just another place to satisfy needs?

> Armed with a Dr. Spock infancy and a John Dewey childhood, baby-boomer children entered college to find an Abraham Maslow expectation of self-actualization.

The new psychologism was announced for synagogues in 1946 by Reform rabbi Joshua Loth Liebman's bestseller *Peace of Mind*. Except for Betty MacDonald's *The Egg and I*, which had come out in late 1945—a humorous account of living on a rundown chicken farm, which inspired the Ma and Pa Kettle movies—it sold more copies that year than any other nonfictional offering.[5] Liebman died just two years later, only forty-one years old. But his *Peace of Mind* announced a new role for rabbis: a counselor who combined psychological know-how with religious wisdom.

The great American rabbis until then had been preachers, scholars, and activists. Stephen S. Wise (1874–1949) died a year after Liebman, but at age seventy-five, not forty-one. Wise is representative of the rabbinate that Liebman implicitly challenged. He is rightly lionized to this day for his early support of unions, his passionate

Zionism, his synagogue oratory, and his institution building (the Jewish Institute of Religion, now merged with Hebrew Union College, and the World Jewish Congress). He had met Herzl at the second Zionist Congress in Basle, was an intermediary to Woodrow Wilson, helped write the Balfour Declaration, attended the 1918–1919 peace conference in Versailles, cofounded the NAACP and ACLU, and represented Zionism to Franklin D. Roosevelt. But he had neither the time nor the inclination to visit congregants. He didn't, as the saying goes, make house calls. Individual needs meant little to rabbis like Wise. But Liebman foresaw a time when American middle-class Jews would increasingly either be therapists or in therapy, and synagogues would more and more become the first line of inquiry for congregants troubled by life's perplexities.

Need-orientation was now complete. Dr. Spock convinced parents that synagogues should serve their children's happiness. John Dewey made over synagogue schools into places that serve the child's best interests. Abraham Maslow assured parents that their higher-order needs would be met as well. This psychologization of religious life has successfully combined with child-centeredness and the implicit theory of synagogues as service institutions to make us think the needs of members are everything. These are our operative constitutive rules. Congregants expect synagogues to keep them and their children happy.

This expectation is not altogether wrong. Synagogues should certainly not add to people's misery, and some needs really do matter. The only question is whether they matter just because people think they do. People want to educate their children Jewishly, and so they should, but in theory, synagogues would properly pursue quality education whether or not people say they want it. It is a need of the Jewish People, part of its covenant with God. Then, too, there are accepted needs with efficient but unacceptable ways of meeting them. Synagogues need to meet their budget, but most of them balk at bingo. Needs drive us, but so do other considerations, we hope.

The strategy of Synagogue 2000 was to integrate need-thinking into a broader perspective. To start with, we pointed out that synagogues sometimes do a relatively poor job of providing for even those needs that they acknowledge people properly have. Supplemental schools are not the overwhelming success we should like, religious services go unattended, and most synagogues have a long way to go to provide a healing environment, if by healing one means healing as the Rabbinic tradition defines it. "Permission is given to heal," says the Talmud, but Nachmanides ups the ante when he says, "This permission to heal is really a *mitzvah*." The Tosafot explain, "Where humans cause damage, humans should repair what they caused. But for illness that comes from heaven [that is, as if from God], cure is like opening up a divine decree that has been hidden away."[6] A sacred community has this broader concept of healing at its core. More than people need healing, they need to be healers, but the latter need is not like the former. We "need" healing in the sense that we are hurt and want relief. We "need" to be healers in the sense of being obliged to heal whether we like it or not.

Maslow once framed his hierarchy of needs in terms of "grumbles." Everyone grumbles about something, but there are lower-order, higher-order, and even meta-order grumbles. The health of a society or institution is measurable by the kind of grumbles people have. In truly backward societies, people complain about life-threatening problems: lack of food or hygiene. Advanced societies supply such things as a matter of course but may miss feelings of respect and self-worth. Eventually, a relatively satisfied population focuses its grumbling on the way others—the poor, say, or illegal immigrants—get mistreated.

We therefore conceptualized a hierarchy of *Jewish* needs and (at least in theory) imagined we could rate a synagogue's success by the level of Jewish grumbling that went on. On the lowest rung stand basic needs for which people ostensibly join synagogues: a bar or bat mitzvah, High Holy Day tickets, and clergy on call for illnesses or life-cycle ceremonies. Synagogues thus become *limited liability communities*, organizations established specifically to satisfy a limited list of payoffs for which members hold the synagogue responsible.

Synagogues market other services too, usually in what are called programs, hoping people will add them to their list of expectations: a book club, a Sunday morning *minyan*, and the like. These are higher-order needs, needs people may not have thought of when they joined. But adding them to the synagogue's offerings represents just additive change. Another way to conceptualize transformative change, then, is to see it as the synagogue's ability to shift its thinking to higher-order needs that may be expressed in programs but are themselves not programmatically capturable. We bundled these under the rubric of "sacred community," believing that at the very highest level, human beings innately seek the sacred and

At the very highest level, human beings innately seek the sacred and each other. Just by virtue of our humanity, we ultimately are drawn to curiosity about God, connection with the sacred, a sense of life's purpose, and a place to build a life narrative alongside others who are doing the same thing. Morally speaking, proper synagogue grumbling would be of the meta-order: worrying about issues of social justice and the synagogue's role in promoting it.

each other, but may never have experienced the synagogue as a place where either one is found. Our question became how we might awaken the dormant sense of sacred community and make synagogues more than programming places where busy people can be coaxed or cajoled into keeping busier. Regardless of the lower-level needs that had prompted membership originally, it should (we reasoned) be possible to shift attention to the highest-order needs that are implicit in all of us, just by virtue of our humanity: curiosity about God, connection with the sacred, a sense of life's purpose, and a place to build a life narrative alongside others who are doing the same thing. Morally speaking, proper synagogue grumbling would be of the meta-order: worrying about issues of social justice and the synagogue's role in promoting it.

Is this being driven by theological purpose (as I proposed above) or by appeal to need, albeit a deeper need than merely dropping children off at religious school? It is both. Wherever did we get the idea that theology, obligation, responsibility, and spiritual growth are not innately satisfying? Jewish sources insist, regarding Torah, "It is a tree of life to those who hold it fast; all who rely on it are happy." Maimonides' pedagogy assumes that people begin Torah study for extrinsic rewards (candy for kids, esteem for adults) but someday find ultimate joy in study for its own sake. Recognizing higher-order needs puts lower-order needs in perspective. Synagogue 2000 sought, therefore, to reprioritize needs. Rather than expend all their effort on immediacies, we asked people to conceptualize the lasting benefits of a synagogue with a genuinely sacred community at its core. Theology and need-satisfaction go together.

COMING TO TERMS WITH A NEW SET OF TERMS

Believing that we make progress by speaking differently, Synagogue 2000 provided new categories with which to think. The categories were spiritual through and through. They were suffused with talk of God and lessons from Torah, but also with the other side of pincer thinking, ideas gleaned from secular thought that may not be Jewish but that leave their mark on how we think.

That meant reducing dependence on programs and pragmatics. And it meant looking deeply at the constitutive rules that make synagogues what they are. We defined transformative change against its opposite, additive change, holding that transformation requires coming to grips with the hidden assumptions about what synagogues are. It also entails going beyond the immediate needs that synagogues think their members have and emphasizing instead the highest-order need of living in sacred community.

Not everything I say here was neatly packaged into a systematically worked-out theory before Synagogue 2000 began. Much of it is evident to me only now, as I go back over my own inchoate thoughts at the time. Sometimes we never actually used the language that I use. But the principles were there, whether explicitly named or not. Synagogues 2000 will recognize the trends of thought I mention as saturating everything we said and did together.

But books go further than the experiences they report. They provide overviews that are available only in retrospect. This is such a book, my own coming to terms with what we did and why we did it. I tell it by modeling what we asked of every Synagogue 2000 participant: a first-person-singular narrative, the only thing we ever know for sure, after all. We called it "telling one's story." Lives get sorted out after the fact—ultimately, in a eulogy. We trust that those who knew the deceased will hear us give the eulogy and trust its insights. "Yes, that really was old So-and-So," they say. "You caught the essence of him. I understand him better now, even though I thought I knew him well while he was alive." We trust also that eulogies, properly given, will inspire another generation to live as the deceased did.

This book is hardly a eulogy. It is my own recollection of the principles that made Synagogue 2000 the exciting experiment it was. It is in that sense, if not a eulogy, then at least a sacred bequest passed along from the first ten years of Synagogue 2000 to people who follow.

Concepts from This Chapter

Pincer thinking: The combination of the best of Jewish tradition with the best of modern thought to come up with big ideas with which to think and speak differently.

Limited liability communities: Organizations established specifically to satisfy a limited list of needs. People join synagogues as limited liability communities, expecting a good religious school, a bar/bat mitzvah, guaranteed High Holy Day tickets, and clergy on call for illnesses and life-cycle ceremonies.

Sacred community: A place where relationships, agenda, activities, debate—everything—are swept along by the recognition of God's reality.

Regulative rules: Rules that regulate behavior by prohibiting some acts and allowing others in order to get the system working better. Regulative rules accompany *additive* change, a program change that reacts to the newest perceived need as expressed by consumers.

Constitutive rules: Rules that not only regulate behavior, but actually constitute the activity they direct. Constitutive rules accompany *transformative* change.

Transformative change: Infrastructural change that responds to questions about constitutive rules. It necessitates coming to grips with hidden assumptions about what synagogues are and replacing them with goals that go beyond the immediate needs that synagogues think they have.

Underlying understandings: Nonnegotiable, truly necessary things without which there is no such institution that we can properly call a synagogue and mean a reasonable extension of what has counted as a synagogue in the Jewish past.

Activities and Topics for Discussion

1. Look over the minutes from recent board meetings. If you are a synagogue professional, look at notes from staff meetings as well. How many new rules/policies were discussed and implemented? How many of those came about in response to a particular situation or issue that arose?

2. Allow yourself the opportunity to envision new policy that would emerge, not from occasions in the past, but new possibilities for the future. Choose an "arm" of the synagogue (e.g., worship, education, youth) and brainstorm new rules that would *not only regulate behavior, but reconstitute the activity* as well.

3. Collect synagogue documents such as the congregation's mission statement, summary of the congregation's history (often posted on the website), general information included in new-member packets, religious school handbooks, and so on. Identify those *underlying understandings* without which there would be no institution that could properly be called your congregation.

3
Telling the Story

"We dream in narrative, daydream in narrative, remember, anticipate, hope, despair, believe, doubt, plan, revise, criticize, construct, gossip, learn, hate, and love by narrative. In order really to live, we make up stories about ourselves and others.... Life stories express our sense of self: who we are and how we got that way."[1]

Our Torah, too, begins with stories: Genesis. Comparing law with narrative, author Philip Pullman insists, "'Thou shalt not' might reach the head, but it takes 'Once upon a time' to reach the heart."[2] Appropriately, then, a large part of Synagogue 2000 involved people telling stories—about their synagogues and about themselves. As we have seen, congregations participating in Synagogue 2000 sent representative teams to conferences. To set the tone, we asked them to huddle for an evening of shared spiritual autobiographies. They learned also how to start meetings back home with personal check-ins to find out what had happened to each member since the meeting before. Sharing of lives changes lives.

Transformation is a four-step process that begins with individuals, not their institutions. Individual change is a necessary precursor for deep institutional change to occur. Sharing of lives changes lives.

We were led to envision transformation in four stages, beginning with individuals.

1. *The individual: Experiencing first-hand the Synagogue 2000 team where people share life honestly in an ambience of the sacred, individuals begin reassessing who they are.* A doctor, for example, reflecting on the way he made hospital rounds, decided to greet roommates of his patients as a form of *bikkur cholim* (the *mitzvah* of visiting the sick). A rabbi, jaded with thirty years "on the job," saw Synagogue 2000 as his way to find new Jewish meaning in his old Jewish calling. A mother began blessing her children on Shabbat. A synagogue board member started attending services.

2. *The team: Individuals realize the importance of their Synagogue 2000 team, without which their own personal transformation would never have occurred. They see their team as a microcosmic example of what the entire synagogue can become.* Team members began coming to meetings as much to be with one another as to solve the synagogue's problems. Were they to need help in their own lives, they knew their team members would "be there" for them. When one team member's mother died, the team canceled a meeting that fell during the week of mourning (*shivah*) and, instead, came as a group to the mourner.

3. *The synagogue as a whole: The Synagogue 2000 team replicates its experience throughout the synagogue's standing committees, the board, and the office staff, until eventually, the entire institution is transformed in a similarly sacred way.*

4. *Other individual members: The synagogue as sacred community touches individual lives throughout the entire institution.*

To the extent that we accomplished these ends, we owe our success in no small part to our insistence on telling sacred stories of the self: nothing earth-shattering or arcane (we distinctly urged people not to "overshare," as one of our Fellows, Rabbi Elaine Zecher, dubbed it), but simply saying how we are in the presence of others who listen sincerely to the everyday (and sometimes not so everyday) life happenings that people inevitably carry into meetings but never get to talk about. We called these *check-ins*; every meeting of Synagogue 2000 teams began with it.

We preached individual narratives because they are the real truths of our lives, the "low-tech, high-touch"[3] absolutes on which we can rely. Animals, too, live from event to event, but only humans come home at night to ask each other, "How was your day?"

When we lived in small towns, we shared stories all the time. It was unthinkable simply to run into a store and not share a few words with the proprietor behind the counter, whose daughter was a high-school classmate with your son, and whose elderly cousin (someone told you) had recently undergone surgery. While mowing the lawn or hanging out clothes to dry, neighbors even in larger towns gathered across fences to share gossip—a lifestyle recognizable in Thornton Wilder's *Our Town*, where the narrator knows all the characters, who also know each other and go through life's joys and tragedies together. By contrast, our corporate economy occasions constant mobility and the disappearance of neighbors whose names we hardly bother learning; urban malls and sprawls have replaced compact downtowns that everyone visits; women are no longer home all day to nurture neighborhood relationships. In the previous chapter, I introduced the concept of limited liability communities, the institutional affiliations we maintain simply to satisfy a list of "must-dos" and "must-gets." With them come also *limited liability encounters*, where we "do" or "get" what we contract for, but have no story to tell or hear while "doing" and "getting" it

Historians tell us that from time to time, America undergoes a "religious awakening," a time of intense religious fervor that shapes our destiny. We are living through such a moment now, much of it evident in what are called megachurches, whose success is in large part related to their recovery of storytelling—not just in services, where worshipers explain how they have been saved from alcohol, bad marriages, or obsessive concern with a job, but in small groups that meet regularly around a common focus like Bible study or being a single parent.

Synagogues, however, have remained relatively untouched by the move toward personalization. In most synagogues today, stories do not get told because there is no ritualized way to tell them, and without ritualization, people are loathe to interrupt proceedings to blurt out news of a miserable day in a doctor's office or the happy discovery that a daughter-in-law is pregnant. Through check-ins, Synagogue 2000 embedded ritualized opportunities to share such stories before turning to synagogue business, which would then, by virtue of the personal touch, no longer just be business as usual.

Through check-ins, Synagogue 2000 embedded ritualized opportunities to share stories before turning to synagogue business, which would then, by virtue of the personal touch, no longer just be business as usual.

As an organization, Synagogue 2000 modeled what we preached to others. In this chapter and the next, therefore, I illustrate the value of storytelling by giving a first-person narrative of how Synagogue 2000 began and how it unfolded thereafter.

FROM ETHNIC TO SPIRITUAL; PEDIATRIC TO ADULT

Think back to the dying Concord Hotel, a symbol of dying ethnic nostalgia. Sometimes that nostalgia was conditioned by anti-Semitism, a deeply felt sense of being alone in history, fatally different from everyone else. I have already noted (chapter 1) how writer Philip Roth, who made Jewish literary history with a series of short stories about eastern European ethnic religion here, recalled in an interview that he was a Jew only insofar as he knew that the world was divided into "them" and "us." Historian Yosef Yerushalmi calls Jews like Roth "psychological Jews"—Jews who "evince no special need to ... embrace any particular form of Jewish commitment, but feel themselves to be somehow irreducibly Jewish nonetheless."[4]

Central European Jews who had arrived as part of the nineteenth-century immigration were quite different. Growing up in the Enlightened West, they had yearned to be proper Prussians or Viennese; they appreciated European music, arts, and letters—indeed, in Vienna, they very much created it. Theodor Herzl edited the equivalent of the *New York Times Book Review*. Sigmund Freud lived there until 1938; Arnold Schoenberg until 1933. Gustav Mahler was also born Jewish. So central European immigrants brought a love of German language and culture with them, in ways that Polish Jews did not import anything Polish. Both groups came as ethnics. But German Jews were ethnically Jewish and German, while Russian or Polish Jews were just ethnically Jewish.

The Concord Hotel institutionalized eastern European ethnicity, serving ethnic food that was inedible (rather than incredible), and making up for the taste by delivering extra-large portions. Piling on more and more platters of dead ethnicity does not produce resurrection.

By 1994, when Ron and I met, only the people hopelessly nostalgic for nostalgia could still believe that it would take us anywhere but backwards out of history altogether. The 1990 population study had made that painfully clear. Baby-boomers may have gloried in Israel's exhilarating Six-Day War, but their children were raised with the Lebanese debacle and the Arab intifada. Intermarriage was approaching 50 percent, and huge numbers of Jews were Jews by choice, whose ethnic memories, if they had any, were not Jewish.

Of special interest is the fate of Yiddish, the folk language of central and eastern European Jews. The baby-boomers' grandparents spoke it, their parents at least understood it, and they themselves appreciated it. Their own children, however, a fourth generation, classified Yiddish with Latin (equally dead) and Chinese (equally foreign, but more trendy). Significantly enough, Yiddish turns up as an index of identity among Messianic Jews, who affirm the divinity of Christ but still want some attachment to the Jewish People. They pepper their remarks with Yiddishisms like *mishpochoh* (family) as a symbolic indication that they are still part of the ethnic Jewish family, even if they have denounced that family's religion.[5]

Historian Marcus Lee Hanson traced the vicissitudes of ethnicity on immigrant culture. The first generation speaks the old language and misses the comfort of the old country. Ashamed of their greenhorn parents, their children (born here) cringe at old-time ethnic ways. Grandchildren, however, dote on the very fond memories of ethnicity that their parents purposefully (and, to them, stupidly) trashed. To Hanson's three generations, I added a fourth—"Hanson plus one." Given freedom of acculturation, meaningful ethnicity (anything beyond an annual parade or so) lasts only three generations, during which you either love your people's jokes, food, and petty rivalries or you hate them. The fourth generation does neither; it just doesn't care. By the 1990s, ethnicity was failing miserably.

> Given freedom of acculturation, meaningful ethnicity (anything beyond an annual parade or so) lasts only three generations, during which you either love your people's jokes, food, and petty rivalries or you hate them. The fourth generation does neither; it just doesn't care.

By contrast, spirituality was in, taking root in new age religion, Jewish forays into Eastern mysticism, and more instances of conversion to Christianity than are generally recognized. *Girl Meets God* is an aptly named autobiography by Lauren Winner, tracing her journey into Christianity to find the life of the spirit. Her Judaism "broke," she recounts, not because she was Jewishly unlearned (on the contrary, she had become a studying Orthodox Jew) and not because she suffered loneliness or craved care (she enjoyed a thriving Orthodox community). At one point, however, the rationale for Judaism dropped from sight; lacking spirituality, its practices seemed empty. "I couldn't recall why I was keeping Shabbat, why I was praying in Hebrew, why I was spending Friday nights and Saturday afternoons at long Sabbath meals, full of singing and wine, with people I love." Winner missed the ultimate purpose behind the whole thing, as she discovered when she accidentally picked up a novel about "ordinary Christians working out ordinary faith," quoting the Bible not for ethnic history but for spiritual promise.[6] And the ironic thing, as she describes it, is that no one in the synagogue world even noticed her drifting away.[7] Had anyone done so, she might have met God as a Jew.

Another convert to Christianity, Beverly Rose, explains, "Despite my adherence to Jewish rituals and practices, I just couldn't feel the presence of a caring God.... Lost in a spiritual wilderness, I came upon an invitation from the rabbi of Nazareth to first century Jews to follow him."[8] Sociologist Robert Wuthnow underscores the extent to which spiritual promise and the presence of God are absent in a market-driven congregational culture, where clergy maximize emphasis on managerial know-how to the extent that "it becomes better to run a smoothly operating congregation than to head one with a deep sense of mission."[9]

Mission is what Rabbi Sidney Schwarz misses in his 2000 influential search for spiritual congregations: "Few synagogues," he says, "spend much time articulating their mission," but his success stories do, and they do it in such a way that the members "develop a much higher level of ownership."[10] Ownership, we saw above, is exactly what tradition demands, if it is to be passed along successfully. Over our shared cup of coffee, Ron and I began articulating our own mission to be passed along to synagogues: we would move synagogues "from ethnic to spiritual."

In the congregational environment of our time, the accent on a market-driven culture plus clergy who maximize emphasis on managerial know-how means that "for the clergy, it becomes better to run a smoothly operating congregation than to head one with a deep sense of mission."

Along with "ethnic to spiritual," we floated a second idea. American Judaism had become pediatric, catering to children and youth but saying little of substance to adults. Noting that Moses had not sent children up the mountain to get Torah, we urged synagogues to recapture Judaism as an adult way of life.

"Kiddy Judaism" came of age after World War II, but it had been building for some time. Part of nineteenth-century industrialization and urbanization entailed having fewer children but investing more in them. To complicate matters, central European Jews here depended on a steady stream of immigrants to reinforce their ethnic identity as Germans. When that migration slowed, the combination of smaller families and the cutoff of new blood threatened their continuity. An obvious response, though doomed to failure, was redoubled efforts to keep children in the fold, not just religiously, but ethnically.

Something else was going on as well: a change in immigration and education trends.

Before the mass migrations from eastern and southern Europe, children here rarely finished high school. But by 1890, the number of high school graduates began to rise, the result being that childhood dependency now extended all the way through the teenage years. With more and more teenagers still in school, congregations began appealing to youth. Simultaneously, the influx of eastern European immigrants was multiplying children of all ages at enormous rates, making every religious group anxious to keep kids off the streets.

In Christian circles, the YMCA had come into being to fill the youth gap. Having no such institution of their own—the Y was clearly Christian back then—German synagogues that could afford it became community centers, with gymnasia, pools, and even sewing circles. The same approach would be used in the 1920s and '30s by Mordecai Kaplan. In both cases, the pattern is clear: rather than establish Judaism as a religion in the modern American sense of a "faith," we relied on ethnicity for our identity. Churches had done the same, but when the German part of German Lutheranism, say, or the Italian part of Italian Catholicism flagged through acculturation to Americanism, Christian churches reasserted the religious half of the equation. Jews did not.

We did, however, worry about the next generation, especially in what became the height of child-centeredness, the suburban era of the 1950s and '60s. As the baby-boomers grew into the largest American cohort of children ever, churches and synagogues began marketing to families with an eye on parental concerns. It may be that synagogues even outdid churches in that regard. We had lost a whole generation of children in the Shoah, and Professor Emil Fackenheim's plea for a 614th *mitzvah* (not to award Hitler a posthumous victory) was readily received. In the 1960s, suburban synagogues were built with tiny sanctuaries but massive school wings and ample driveway space for carpoolers to drop kids off and pick them up.

Ron and I both knew that despite the many millions of dollars poured into Jewish education as the panacea for our problems, synagogue schools were not substantially better than the ones that had so ineptly educated us; and day schools, for all their virtues, have their faults and, in any event, will never attract enough Jewish children to make synagogue schools marginal, much less irrelevant. It is important to see how our answer differed from the standard Jewish response: another committee or commission to study educational policy. We treated the crisis in childhood education as an adult problem, the underlying absence of spiritual vision and, consequently, the paucity of adult role models for children to aspire to.

The crisis in childhood education is really an adult problem, the underlying absence of spiritual vision and, consequently, the paucity of adult role models for children to aspire to.

In our later thinking, we developed a "hand-off" model of Jewish survival. Imagine all Jewish children becoming learned in masterful day schools and then attending successful Hillels while in college. Then what? What would they graduate into as adults? In America, where churches are the norm, spiritualized synagogues would be the only likely next step. Without such synagogues, regardless of how much Judaism we fed a child, the time would come when Jewish adults would wonder, as Lauren Winner did, why in the world they were learning Hebrew or keeping Shabbat anyway.

And that was the best scenario. The real world had been opened up for me ten years earlier while I was giving a set of weekend lectures to a mostly Federation crowd at an upscale Jewish camp in

California. At the Saturday night question and answer period, I awaited comments from the very thoughtful people who had listened to three lectures on matters related to prayer, liturgy, and spirituality. To my surprise, most questions had nothing to do with anything I had said. People asked me instead about Israel, Jews in the Soviet Union, and the like. That was their intellectual comfort zone, obviously, and they expected any "real" Jewish scholar to want to discuss it as much as they did. I pled ignorance of expertise in such things, but still the questions came, sometimes not as questions, but as statements of opinion meant to elicit my agreement. The participants could discuss peoplehood, politics, and funding, not prayer, ritual, and God.

A couple at the back of the room stood out. As the only people under forty, they had sat quietly for all of Shabbat, somewhat ignored by the others, who were regular attendees at such weekends, many of them on the camp board of governors. It wasn't even clear how this young couple had found their way to what must have been a formidable environment for them. Hesitantly, one of them raised a hand. "I do not understand any of the questions so far," the woman said. "We came here not knowing what we would find, so maybe we just lack the background, but it seems to me that none of the questions asked so far has any relevance. The only question that counts for us is 'Why be Jewish?' That is what we came to find out."

After a momentary hush, the room erupted in one denunciation after another—all quietly delivered, as if the crowd of older attendees were disciplining their children. How could these young Jews be so callous as to be unconcerned about Israel? Didn't they give to Federation? The reason for being Jewish is self-evident, isn't it? How dare they even question that, after what had happened in Europe?

As we adjourned for evening coffee, I waited behind to thank the couple for their courage. More conversation revealed the fact that they were in twelve-step programs, searching for spiritual experience. Unable to find it in the several synagogues they had visited, they were trying a camp setting as a possible solution.

For several years, I stayed in touch with the two people. To the best of my knowledge, they eventually joined a synagogue for their child, remained unmoved personally themselves, and found spirituality outside of Judaism.

Their story epitomized a more likely scenario than the ideal one I painted above. Here were people without a day-school education and untouched by Hillel. On their own spiritual journey, they had gone from synagogue to synagogue but found nothing that spoke to them as adults. A few years later, when they had children, they decided to join, but only for their kids. They sought their own spiritual meaning elsewhere—not in Lauren Winner's Christianity, but in Buddhism. At camp, meanwhile, they encountered the worst of what well-meaning leaders in synagogues (not just Federation) sometimes offer. They were never made to feel welcome, even though they represented the very Jewish continuity that the older people present purported to care endlessly about and work tirelessly for. Their honesty was rebuffed as self-centered ingratitude.

> We seek synagogues that are welcoming and respectful of whoever walks through the door, synagogues that ask spiritual questions and are not judgmental of people who lack Jewish learning.

Their story became part of the expanding Synagogue 2000 vision. We sought synagogues that are welcoming and respectful of whoever walks through the door, synagogues that ask spiritual questions and are not judgmental of people who lack Jewish learning.

As my coffee time with Ron at the Concord ended, we settled on a next step: market testing our vision.

MARKET TESTING SPIRITUALITY

I use the business term "market testing" purposely here to indicate that even synagogues intent on overcoming the default congregational model of "fee for services" should not on that account ignore good business practices. Business itself is not the problem; business is a tool, and a good one. I simply do not understand why people in business sometimes "confess" to me that the helping professions (including my own) are somehow on a higher moral level than what they do—they just make money, they say. That is hardly a Jewish position. Rabbinic literature is saturated with a high regard for the marketplace. Business can be a sacred enterprise in its own right, a means to move the world's population from abject poverty to advanced economic development. Religion has neither ethical nor spiritual reason to avoid

Business can be a sacred enterprise in its own right, a means to move the world's population from abject poverty to advanced economic development. Religion has neither ethical nor spiritual reason to avoid it. Synagogue 2000's only objection is when synagogues compete for people's time (as they must) without remembering or putting into practice the spiritual reason why.

business. On the contrary, it has a moral imperative to include it. Besides, speaking practically as well, religion today competes for people's time, money, and commitment, and business is all about the fine art of successful competition. Synagogue 2000's only objection is when synagogues compete (as they must) without remembering or putting into practice the spiritual reason why.

Indeed, one of the most striking characteristics of successful churches is precisely the care in marketing that goes into planning them. This is particularly the case with the megachurches I mentioned above. The first and still the largest of these, the Willow Creek Community Church, launched officially in 1975, northwest of Chicago, enjoyed such spectacular growth that the Harvard Business School wrote it up as a case study of business success.[11] As of 2004, the Willow Creek Association counted ten thousand member churches from ninety denominations and thirty-five countries.[12] Another instance of entrepreneurial religion is Saddleback Church in Irvine, California, a business initiative remarkable enough for *Forbes Magazine* to say, "Were it a business, Saddleback Church would be compared with Dell, Google and Starbucks."[13] In 1984, church historian Martin Marty reminded us that writing an account of American religion without highlighting evangelicals would be like drawing a map of the United States without including the Rockies.[14] His wisdom should be updated to specify the megachurch phenomenon as the most influential evangelical movement in our time. So even as we chastised synagogues for their corporate and aspiritual "feel," we recognized how poorly they are run and marketed. Alongside other poor business practices (there is usually little accountability for personnel; synagogues rarely develop endowments) is their shoddy attention to such things as marketing, image, and attention to their constituencies.

True, we took it as axiomatic that the perceived needs of potential congregants alone should not drive us; we should be mission driven. But we can hardly proceed without really knowing what the situation is out there. An advertising executive once told me, "Hoffman, you think you know what people think, but it doesn't matter what you think they think; it only matters what they think."

We envisioned synagogues that would substitute spirituality for ethnicity and transcend pediatrics for an adult-oriented message that children would not immediately understand but into which they would grow.

So following the Concord coffee, we embarked on a campaign to find out if what we think people think is really what they think. For a solid year, we traversed the country speaking to focus groups of synagogue leaders to see what they were thinking about synagogue life.

To call them focus groups is to stretch the scientific understanding of the term. Still, we invited a broad range of people active in synagogue life or in Jewish communal affairs, generally, to attend open meetings to voice their concerns. After five such meetings around the country, we began getting redundant information, which, we felt, justified our moving on to the next stage of implementation, an invitation to people on the cutting edge of synagogue life to attend a weekend think tank at Camp Ojai (a Conservative Movement retreat center outside

Los Angeles). The information that informed our retreat was the redundant data of the focus groups, set beside our initial vision of synagogues that would substitute spirituality for ethnicity and transcend pediatrics for an adult-oriented message that children would not immediately understand but into which they would grow.

Early on, we faced the question of our relationship to Jewish denominations. Denominationalism took root in America in the mid-nineteenth century as a way to export religion to the steadily receding frontier. It peaked after World War II, when churches and synagogues could not be founded fast enough to satisfy people moving to the suburbs. But by the time Synagogue 2000 was born, denominations seemed threatened. At issue are actually two tendencies, non-denominationalism and post-denominationalism. They should not be conflated.[15] Non-denominationalism refers to a growing number of people who respond to surveys by saying they are Jewish but claiming no movement identity. The number rose from 20 percent to 27 percent from 1990 to 2000. But hardly any of these people belong to synagogues. More significant is post-denominationalism, a growing number of synagogues that refuse to affiliate with any denomination. Most of them are Orthodox or Conservative in practice. It is hard to give precise numbers, since by their very nature there is no central body keeping track of them. Nonetheless, post-denomination synagogues are growing in number. The question is whether they spell the end of denominations. Ron and I were convinced that they do not. Denominations still play a vital role, we held, albeit a changing one, a matter I will return to in chapter 7.

Given our commitment to denominations (suitably transformed), we were shocked to find how little our focus groups thought their national organizations did for them, especially among Conservative Jews, for whom the United Synagogue is seen as relatively inconsequential (only about five hundred people attend its national conferences). But Reform Jews, too, thought their organization was deficient. The Union for Reform Judaism (URJ)—formerly Union of American Hebrew Congregations (UAHC)—regularly attracts upward of five thousand delegates to its biennial conferences. Its many departments disseminate programming packets to all member synagogues. But most people in our focus groups had not even the vaguest idea what the URJ offers and had little desire even to avail themselves of it. Reform congregations may receive these mailings, but it is not clear that anyone reads them or, if they do, how well their contents find their way into board meetings, temple policy, and synagogue programming. Focus groups were unanimous in asking for the establishment of Synagogue 2000 as a transdenominational institute to help synagogues and their movements.

When we asked what that would look like, people replied with less certainty. But we left those meetings determined to establish some kind of research and development organization that would remain abreast of current trends in the sociology of religion, work directly with synagogues in some capacity, and function alongside the denominations to help but not compete with them. We most assiduously stayed clear of becoming or even presenting the semblance of yet one more denominational movement, which would then have to take ideological stands to carve out our own market niche and justify our existence to member synagogues.

One prevailing metaphor stood out in what the focus groups told us. It was an image of cataclysmic disaster projected as the consequence of continuing with no clear spiritual direction to guide us. We asked, "When you wake up in a cold sweat in the middle of the night, what is it that disturbs you?" Reform rabbis responded with the fear that their congregants would all marry out; they would go down in history as having presided over the demise of the Jewish People. Conservative rabbis had a parallel fear: their congregants might stop keeping kosher. I heard both responses as amounting to the same thing: "marrying out" and "eating out"—twin images that betray the underlying fear of a widening gap between a shrinking

> Synagogue 2000 was created as a research and development organization that would remain abreast of current trends in the sociology of religion, work directly with synagogues in some capacity, and function alongside the denominations to help but not compete with them.

population of serious Jews (symbolized by the rabbi) and the growing number of everyday people for whom Judaism is peripheral.

This issue of peripheral versus loyal Jews is evident also in the Jewish population study of 2000.

We have population surveys from 1970, 1990, and 2000. The 2000 study differed from the earlier ones in that initial phone calls differentiated a core Jewish population who had some genuine connection to Judaism from nominal Jews for whom Judaism is peripheral (I call them marginals). It then interviewed just the core population as its study of Jewish life in America. The marginals, that is, did not officially count. "Core" Jews in the year 2000 number 5.2 million. By standards of the two prior surveys, which included everyone, the total would be somewhere between 5.7 million and 6.5 million. If we take a figure in the middle (6 million), we would have eight hundred thousand marginals. Not having interviewed them, of course, it is hard to say how marginal they are, or even in what ways their marginality is revealed. Even within the core population, we find a large spectrum of attitudes and practice. To what extent should people low on their "Jewish" scores be considered marginal?

Here is an example of the way "meaning" is a function not just of what we observe, but of the horizon of possibilities with which we observe it. Synagogue leaders often rank Jews as "good" or "bad" depending on the number of *mitzvot* they do and the Jewish institutions they support—such things as keeping kosher, visiting Israel, observing Shabbat, attending synagogue services, and giving to Jewish charities. The lower your score, the less the leaders think of you, and the less attention you get from them. Now imagine someone who knows his mother was Jewish (so is halakhically Jewish himself), but attends church, not synagogue. He is truly a marginal Jew (if he is a Jew at all) and will require no attention, since he will never come within the synagogue's orbit. But consider a Jew who does not light Shabbat candles, keep kosher, or belong to the synagogue, but who identifies with Israel and has something of a seder. Here is a marginal who really might show up at synagogue someday. The question is how he will be greeted.

Quite regularly I encounter people who hear I am a rabbi working with synagogues, and who then apologize for being a bad Jew, saying something like, "I am afraid I don't go to services, Rabbi; I know I should." The fact is, were such a "marginal" to choose to attend, she might never be noticed and receive no help whatever in negotiating the service. We asked regulars to simulate what they do when they go to services. They look around the parking lot for people they know and walk in together. If they are alone, they look for friends in the hall or foyer. By the time they are in the sanctuary, they have

> We should shift from envisioning a hierarchy of Jewishness to validating different ways for people to be Jewish. All Jews should be pictured on progressive stages of their own personal journeys.

probably begun several conversations. Inside, they know where to sit, how to open the prayer book, what songs to sing, and so forth. Newcomers know none of this. They walk through the hall with no one talking to them, then worry about where to sit, how to open the prayer book, and how to follow the service. They will likely not be greeted at the *Oneg Shabbat* either. Their marginality is only enhanced.

We would do better to shift from envisioning a hierarchy of Jewishness to validating different ways for people to be Jewish. For many years researchers have been doing just that.

A recent example, by Bethamie Horowitz, for example, proposes three separate indices of Jewish identity: (1) the usual *mitzvah* index, as I have called it (things like keeping Shabbat, keeping kosher, and fasting on Yom Kippur); (2) a "cultural-communal activity" scale (reading Jewish magazines and attending synagogue); and (3) a measure of "subjective Jewish centrality" (having Jewish friends, caring for the Jewish People). She finds *intensively engaged* Jews, who score high on all three scales; Jews with *mixed engagement*, who score high on at least one of the three scales but not on *all* of them; and finally, the *otherwise engaged*, who are just not interested, let alone involved, in an active Jewish life, and who score low on all three scales.[16]

Horowitz's conclusions reinforced Synagogue 2000's emphasis on treating Jews nonjudgmentally and denying the simplistic metaphor of a tightrope with synagogue professionals pulling Jews in and Jews trying to pull themselves out. All Jews should be pictured on progressive stages of their own personal journeys. For some, the journey is rather stable, their engagement with Judaism steadily low or steadily high. Others lapse increasingly farther away from Jewish involvement or equally steadily toward it. Most interesting is what Horowitz calls an *interior* journey, where a person's subjective commitment to Judaism intensifies, while religious and communal practice remain low or decrease. Fully one-third of Horowitz's sample experienced this *interior* journey, suggesting that "there are critical periods and moments in people's lives that offer potential opportunities for Jewish institutions to play a role, if only these institutions can be open and available to individuals in a way that meets their changing needs and concerns."

The operative words for us should be "if only these institutions can be open and available to individuals in a way that meets their changing needs and concerns." Thinking about other studies on religious life, Horowitz adds, "Compared to the spectrum of feeling that seems to have characterized earlier generations of American Jews, the range of emotion about being Jewish has shifted, from acceptance versus rejection to meaningfulness versus indifference."[17] It followed, for us, that when marginals fail to join synagogues, it may say as much about the synagogues as it does about the marginals, who may not be marginal at all, but simply on an interior journey, while synagogues as places where programs happen are not destinations for meaningful encounters.

More recently, sociologist Steven M. Cohen has suggested dividing Jews into three categories according to patterns of marriage: the in-married, whom studies show to be more open to Jewish engagement; the out-married, whose level of engagement is generally much less; and the not-yet-married, for whom standard institutions of Jewish involvement (including synagogues) are not yet relevant to their lives, but will probably become relevant later, if they marry other Jews.[18]

Cohen's finding came out too late for Synagogue 2000 to integrate into our work with synagogues. But retrospectively, it parallels Horowitz's patterns (and, therefore, Synagogue 2000 principles) in that Cohen advocates separate strategies for each of his categories, not judging them on their Jewish engagement by condemning those who are less actively seeking institutionalized Jewish lives. The young couple who asked, "Why be Jewish?" was written off as marginals who should feel guilty. Synagogue 2000 firmly established the policy of welcoming everyone at whatever stage of whatever Jewish journey they proclaimed, and reminding synagogues to do the same.

I do worry that the synagogue is slowly having less and less impact on people's lives. Anecdotal evidence, for instance, shows a general falloff in attendance at such things as the annual "scholar-in-residence" weekend and a noticeable graying in the population that still attends. Cohen may be right in predicting a return to the synagogue by the in-married. But for how long and to what ends? Will they join synagogues just for their children? Will they themselves even come to High Holy Day services? In many places Yom Kippur attendance booms as much as ever for the introductory evening *Kol Nidre* service but, compared to a decade ago, falls off badly on Yom Kippur day. We saw as our mission enhancing the synagogue's ability to engage not just regulars, but marginals also—and without making them feel guilty. Synagogues would become compelling places of the spirit for adults on interior journeys.

Synagogues would welcome marginals without making them feel guilty. They would become compelling places of the spirit for adults on interior journeys.

FUNDING

What we were discovering about synagogues was matched by lessons learned in building our own organization to help them. The parallelism was not perfect. Most synagogues have lengthy histories; we were a small start-up organization. Synagogues operate locally; Synagogue 2000 was decentralized, with offices in Los Angeles and New York, and individuals working out of San Francisco and Washington, D.C. But as we went about structuring our professional team and gathering a board, we were continually struck by institutional similarities that

helped us appreciate what synagogues face. First among them was the
need for financing.

Both synagogues and Synagogue 2000 epitomize what sociologists call the *third sector*. The first sector is the state, which operates
by implicit coercion (you have to pay your taxes), raising money by
fiat for the public good. The second sector is the marketplace, where
the whole point is making money, and not for the public but for the
private ends of owners and management. The third sector is the middle ground, organizations that people join by choice, without inbuilt
funding capacity—neither the power to levy taxes nor the market
structure to make money by design. We can call the three sectors
"government," "markets," and "voluntary organizations." Religion
is a voluntary organization. As a third-sector enterprise, Synagogue
2000 (like synagogues themselves) had to raise money regularly by
convincing people to invest in our work.

Not every society operates as America does. Fully Communist
countries eradicate free markets (sector two), or try to, but discover
that government is unable to replicate the benefits that free markets
provide. As official markets fail, black markets thrive. Voluntary
organizations (sector three) are suspect as potential breeding grounds
for opposition, so they are infiltrated, spied upon, or even banned.
Another model is represented by countries like Israel and Sweden,
which mesh together government and voluntary groups by supporting
religion and its social-service arms with public funds. By stark contrast, America gives enormous freedom to markets and voluntary
organizations, protecting both from an overreaching government and
altogether separating church from state. Religion is expected to operate in a free market environment, raising money independently. Like
synagogues, then, Synagogue 2000 began as a sector three organization, dependent on voluntary funding.

We see even further the dilemma of synagogues (and Synagogue
2000) if we transpose the three-sector model of civic life onto the
Jewish community alone. If we look back historically, we can see that
as tolerated minorities in medieval Europe, Jews were generally given
their own corporate status, so that, among other things, authorities
could have a single Jewish entity with which to deal in such matters
as collecting taxes. Jewish community was a given. The only way to

leave it was to convert out. With full emancipation, however, that corporate accountability ceased, leaving Jews, like other citizens, responsible personally for their civic duties. Now Jews could decide what kind of Jew to be, choose a sub-community to join (Reform, say, but not Orthodox), or simply practice Judaism a lot or a little, yet affiliate with no one. Especially in America, with the separation of church and state, the government cannot compel Jews to constitute their own community. Still, there remain internal pressures that force Jews to constitute a quasi form of self-government, the problem being that the traditional means of claiming authority disappeared with the medieval conditions that spawned them.

Over the years, American Jews have managed to build a loosely knit but effective system of self-government—a first sector.[19] It began with an 1887 abortive effort by immigrant Orthodox Jews to establish a *k'hillah* (the traditional name for a communal government system) in New York City. The *k'hillah* was to be directed by a chief rabbi, Rabbi Jacob Joseph, a recognized Talmudist and former rabbi of Vilna, who was invited to fill the post. But European conditions could not be imported with him, and when wholesalers refused to be bound by the *k'hillah*'s attempt to regulate *kashrut,* the experiment died aborning. In 1902, Jacob Joseph died, penniless.

A second effort was launched by Reform rabbi Judah Magnes in 1909, not just for Orthodox congregations, and with no chief rabbi, but organized instead in an acceptable American manner of a federation of local organizations that ceded some of their power to professionalized bureaus, like the Bureau of Jewish Education (still operating), or the Bureau of Social Morals (now defunct), established to eradicate Jewish crime. This *kehillah,* too, failed, when it proved unable to centralize *kashrut*, and in 1916 its bureaus were set free to seek independent funding and, with it, actual independence.

Meanwhile, other organizations were taking root, including a variety of welfare federations, which eventually began reaching out to include educational agencies as well, and by the 1950s these were being merged with parallel communal funds established in the 1930s for Jewish relief overseas. The stage was being set for the establishment of a Federation of federations as a sector one de facto government for American Jews.[20]

When Synagogue 2000 began, Federation had gone through four stages of growth (by the time we finished, it had entered yet a fifth): (1) It began as a voluntary *league* of agencies, working together to boost their total campaign, but allocating monies received according to a percentage plan that paralleled what would have happened had the agencies acted separately. (2) It then became a *confederation* with a governing operating body that determined a system of allocations. (3) It graduated to becoming a true *federation* whereby that operating body undertakes community planning and resultant expenditures, not just community fundraising. (4) With the 1980s, a fourth stage set in: federations no longer just *represented* their agencies in concert; they now *controlled* them. (5) In 1999, independently operating federations were merged into a national entity called the United Jewish Community (UJC), and with that move, Federation as government was complete. It effectively holds the funding key to most of Jewish life and is to that extent the de facto government of America's Jews, funding much of the voluntary sector (sector three)—cultural organizations, especially. In 2003, for instance, the National Foundation for Jewish Culture had a total income of $1,372,474. Fifty-one percent ($701,099) came from the Federation system.

Private donors and foundations provide a second avenue for funding, and of late, that source has burgeoned. First, several particularly wealthy philanthropists, widely nicknamed "the megafunders," meet informally to discuss collaboration on major Jewish projects; they thus constitute something of an alternative "government in (voluntary) exile," operating their own programs, sometimes in outright defiance of Federation-based efforts to do the same thing. Second, in

1991, the Jewish Funders Network came into being as a loose amalgam of independent members wishing to learn about Jewish causes so as to maximize their giving potential. By the turn of the millennium, then, sector three efforts had the following options for funding:

1. Self-funding, through their own fee-for-service organization
2. Federation funding
3. Appeal to megafunders
4. Build a base of smaller independent donors and family foundations, usually through the time-honored methods of developing a fiduciary board and a variety of fundraising activities.

When Synagogue 2000 began, I knew nothing of any of this, a sign, by the way, of an enormous deficit in seminary education. Ron and I had become exceptionally lucky, however, in that funders who believed deeply in our vision came to us. I have already mentioned Rachel Cowan, who encouraged and then funded an entire network of creative initiatives that have changed the Jewish landscape. Shortly after Ron and I met, a second Rachel, Rachel Levin, along with a colleague, Marge Tabankin, arrived at my office, representing the recently formed Righteous Persons Foundation. They were interviewing people to determine their approach to funding a Jewish future. Not long after, Righteous Persons joined Cummings as our funders. Meanwhile, Ron had long enjoyed a close relationship with Bruce Whizin, who had founded the Whizin Institute for the Jewish Future. The Whizin Foundation became a third funding partner as part of Bruce's far-seeing effort to reshape American Jewry.

In 1995, our funders, some rabbinic advisors, Ron, and I met at a hotel outside the airport in San Francisco. By the end of the day, an institute to help synagogues had been born. With prescience that I did not yet appreciate, one of the participants warned that we were embarking on at least a twenty-year venture. Looking ahead to the new millennium, someone suggested the name "Synagogue 21," and that is what we were for a short period of time. When people thought we sounded like Century 21, the franchised realtor firm, we altered the name somewhat, and Synagogue 2000 was born. Despite the "twenty-year" warning, we did not realize that we would still be doing our work more than a decade later, with an emended name, "Synagogue 3000."

EARLY LESSONS LEARNED

We left our San Francisco meeting with a mission, a name, and a principle, namely: we will learn from anyone, but not work with everyone. As the first part of our principle, we set about learning from anyone who might have figured out what it was that we should know.

There was, first of all, the megachurches that have successfully responded to some deep current in the American psyche. Among other things, the megachurches taught us that:

- "Big" need not be "impersonal."
- If services demonstrate the reality of God, and if they highlight the personal issues that everyone inevitably faces in life, people will come without our dreaming up some external motivation.
- In worship, excellence matters; megachurch worship is planned in detail and executed with technological brilliance.
- Sermons and prayers can be intertwined so that they reinforce a common message.
- Synagogues are woefully understaffed. Megachurches employ entire teams to effect what synagogues assign to no one.
- Megachurches are welcoming; synagogues are not.

We also learned about "small groups." I had encountered these a few years back, as part of an advisory committee for an initiative headed up by sociologist Robert Wuthnow and George Gallup Jr.[21] They were begun in the 1950s with traditional Sunday school adult study. They grew through the 1960s and '70s, as part of a psychological turn inward and a parallel quest for "community." By the 1980s, most were self-help groups, especially having to do with addictions, but by the 1990s, they had branched out beyond the original therapeutic model. In 1994, some 18–20 million people were still in Sunday school groups, 8–10 million went to self-help groups, and 15–20 million went to groups that, one way or another, featured Bible study.[22] By then, 40 percent of American

Synagogue 2000's work was guided by the principle: we will learn from anyone, but not work with everyone.

adults claimed to be involved "in a small group that meets regularly and provides caring and support for those who participate in it." Thirty-eight percent of those so involved actually belong to more than one group, and of those not involved, one-quarter say they would like to find and join one. Fifty-seven percent of the groups meet weekly, and 41 percent have meetings that last two hours or more. Perhaps the most remarkable statistic is that 78 percent of all group members attend all the time; barring illness or unusual circumstances that prevent their attendance, they never miss meetings. These groups are hardly peripheral to people's attention![23]

People who say they belong to small groups do not have in mind a weekly bowling league or bridge game. Sixty-three percent are in groups that "focus on religious or spiritual matters," 65 percent say their "interest in spiritual matters has increased in the past five years," and 61 percent say their "faith or spirituality" has been positively influenced by their groups. All of this accords with the fact that 79 percent of the American public reported thinking about their relation to God "a lot" or "a fair amount" of the time.[24] There are no available statistics specifically for Jews, but with few exceptions, we knew of no synagogues anywhere that feature this kind of small group, certainly not groups that assemble to discuss God and build spirituality. The exceptions occur primarily in Orthodox environments, where a Talmud study group may assemble regularly, or (in all movements) where alternative Shabbat morning gatherings meet for prayer, study, or both. But even synagogues that feature such groups rarely manage to have more than one, and these rarely function as small groups anyway; even people who come regularly may hardly know each other. It could be, of course, that Jews do not look for small groups the way the rest of the American population does. But it would be odd indeed if Jews were not somehow touched by the contemporary search for spirituality, community, and even God.

I have had occasion already to mention Saddleback Church. Rick Warren, Saddleback's founder, maintains that mainline churches (and synagogues) go about building community all wrong.[25] They start with a tiny group of key supporters, who ultimately become the board; then slowly, they bring in their friends and neighbors, until eventually the church gets a good reputation and attracts strangers.

The inevitable result is that commitment varies inversely with size, with the most recent recruits usually uncommitted to the church's message altogether (they may not even know what it is). They join for personal reasons having little to do with the church mission and contribute nothing back.[26] So Warren reversed the process, first reaching out to the entire community, then providing worship that speaks deeply and spiritually to people who come to try it out. As he puts it, he begins with "community" (everyone in a targeted vicinity), of which a "crowd" may show up on any given Sunday. Some of the crowd will be so moved by the experience that they will inquire about becoming a member, but they are allowed to join only if they subscribe to the church's message. Members constitute the next step: "congregation"; some members become further engaged to become "committed," and of those, a tiny few graduate to become lay ministers themselves—a stated goal of a church that boasts an evangelical calling. Warren's church, then, moves successively ever inwardly in concentric circles: first "community," then "crowd," then "congregation," and finally, "committed."

People who join the congregation are immediately expected to join a small group that meets for a short period of time to acquaint its members with the core Christian message, the uniqueness of the church they are joining, and their covenantal responsibility as members, part of which encourages membership in other small groups, to be selected according to what Horowitz would have called a person's own "interior" spiritual journey. When we visited Saddleback, we were impressed by the sheer number of people involved—some three thousand attendees at each of two Sunday morning services. Between the two services, people line up in droves at various booths. Some buy cassettes of the day's sermon or reading matter relevant to a spiritual quest; others sign petitions on such matters as abortion (against it) and prayer in the public schools (for it); but many just investigate small groups, like "Single Parents with Teenagers," or "Looking for God in My Life."

We shall see that small-group formation became an important part of Synagogue 2000. Jewish text study is in vogue today, but it is rarely related to the lives of those doing the studying. So we conceptualized a new kind of study: study of Jewish texts, but in affinity groups whose members share some underlying concern on which they hope Jewish texts will shed light. Our own formulation became "Jewish Journey Groups: Where Text Meets Life."

At the other end of the religious-secular spectrum is Disney University in Tampa, where we studied customer service. We were struck by how Disney trains even the people who clean the streets to believe they are performing a sacred mission: making people happy. "They think *they* have a sacred mission?" I remember thinking. Then and there, we began reminding Jews of the sacred mission we have carried from Sinai onward: "To be a kingdom of priests and a holy people" (Exodus 19:6), committed to a partnership with God in the ongoing work of creation.

> *J*ewish Journey Groups are small groups, organized according to people's gifts and passions, where "text meets life" as members engage in Jewish learning to shed light upon a shared underlying concern.

Then, too, we were struck by the rules that Disney provides for workers who dress in Disney character costumes and wander the streets of Disney World shaking children's hands. They are instructed to remain in costume unless they see someone in danger or (for any other reason) in distress. They learn to watch for signs of how people are doing around them. By contrast, we were struck by how little synagogue regulars (professionals and volunteers) keep a watchful eye on how people feel. I have already mentioned the horror tales we heard of marginals attending synagogue for the first time and never being greeted or helped. Surely their nervousness counted as psychological distress, we reasoned, and we began raising the sensitivity of synagogue members to their plight. Sometimes we asked them to attend a church service, to experience the unease that comes with being completely out of one's element. We asked them whenever they are at synagogue to watch others around them and leave what they were doing if they saw people feeling awkwardly uncertain.

Another major lesson came from some sociologists whom we assembled at that year's Federation General Assembly. Sociologist Barry Kosmin spoke at some length about the peculiar difficulty we would face in changing synagogues. There is, he said, no inbuilt motivation for synagogues to want to be any different. We were to have that truth driven home endlessly. I later dubbed synagogues *default institutions*, because failing a dying neighborhood, they can quite successfully continue doing what they have always done, without anyone even asking what it is that they do. If the neighborhood disappears, they build a branch in the new area of Jewish settlement and then eventually relocate, where they set up shop as usual. One way of explaining that phenomenon is to say that the perceived needs of people at the new building are identical to those the former generation brought to the old one. It is more likely, however, that synagogues specialize in a particular set of services that they export to their new place, thereby self-selecting the kind of people who join and the kind of expectations that those people bring. Members accord with what the synagogue offers; it does not work the other way around, with the synagogue intuiting the spiritual needs of a new generation and responding accordingly.

By analogy, take community libraries. "In successful change efforts," says John Kotter, "the first step is making sure that sufficient people act with sufficient urgency."[27] But the library system feels little urgency to change. With no profit motive, libraries easily default to their old mandate and practices. To be sure, they adapt somewhat to new times: they feature books on tape and even DVDs nowadays, a mode of entertainment that pristine librarians of the past would have abhorred. But changes are modest. People who like libraries go there; most people in town do not. It is not that the library is not doing a fine job at what it does. But what it does has minimal attraction to most people. If the library represented a religion, we might see it as ineffective, except for a tiny swath of people who believe in it. From time to time, commissions might be established to investigate library continuity, but in the end, libraries and their clientele would remain relatively stable. Library frequenters would boast about the nice library they have: and they would be right—for library goers. Synagogues are very much like libraries. They are both third-sector default organizations.

A true third-sector institution, however, is, by definition, nonmonopolistic. People who don't like borrowing library books can buy them. People who don't like synagogues cannot so easily arrange life-cycle events elsewhere. In that way, synagogues maintain a monopoly on what they do. But that is changing. In the San Francisco Bay area, only 22 percent of all Jews belong to a synagogue. Outside the synagogues, however, in just the east Bay area alone, there are "more than one hundred rabbis, cantors, Jewish educators and other ritual facilitators ... conducting traditional rituals as well as creating a whole host of new ones."[28] In another city, an independent philanthropist disagreed with the synagogue monopoly and hired a communal rabbi willing to do life-cycle events independently. Synagogues that lose their monopoly on life-cycle events will find themselves faced with the frightening fact that there is one less item on the limited liability list that people carry with them. If they can "purchase" a bar mitzvah at a country club and buy High Holy Day seats separately, why will they affiliate with synagogues that do not address the spiritual and moral dilemmas of our time?

Like the library, then, synagogues may move to new quarters, but they are unlikely to overhaul their offerings very radically. They do a splendid job at what they do. When we began, I must confess, we tended to have a far too dismal view of how most synagogues serve their constituency. What we found was just the reverse. Like libraries, synagogues by and large are hardly failing institutions, run by inept or unscrupulous clergy. Synagogue 2000's argument was simply that:

- what synagogues do by default is insufficient for our time; Jewish continuity demands more;
- clergy are not trained to design synagogue alternatives and are so overworked they have no time even to think about them; and
- lay leaders are in no position to think differently, first because they achieve their position precisely because they thrive in the system that is in question, and second because their lay denominational organizations regularly reward the default thinking that they represent.

The Jewish community is a vast interlocking system. We found we were unable to deal with synagogues without simultaneously taking into account connecting links to seminaries especially, where clergy education stood out as requiring change. There, too, insufficient people act with urgency. Seminaries, no less than synagogues, are third-sector default organizations. Professionals get trained for synagogues of the past, not the future, since their teachers know best the synagogues in which they grew up. Laypeople look to rabbis for a spiritual vision. But seminaries do not train their students for spiritual visioning. In all our seminaries, there are few courses that challenge standard definitions of what synagogues should be.

Ask the faculty where they pray and where they send their children for Jewish education. There are no figures here, but anecdotal evidence is very powerful. Where possible, seminary faculty largely avoid synagogues, send their children to day schools, and pray in specialized private *minyanim* that attract other Jewishly learned people like themselves: the Library *Minyan* in Los Angeles, for example, or the *Minyan M'at* at Anshei Chesed in New York. These people are neither evil nor ingenuous; they are part of a system that accepts the synagogue for what it is—something quite excellent, but nonetheless limited by the default definition of what it should do.

The list of people from whom we learned that year is extensive. Knowing the well-deserved reputation of the Alban Institute's congregational consultants, for example, we dedicated research time to being graciously hosted by Jim Wind and his outstanding Alban team. We investigated other change programs that had preceded us: a local effort headed up by Sandy Dashefsky in Hartford, Connecticut, and the ECE (Experiment in Congregational Education), founded by Sara Lee and Isa Aron, at the Rhea Hirsch School of Education, part of the Hebrew Union College in Los Angeles. We paid researchers to scour sociological literature for recent articles on congregational life. We recruited Richard Vosko, a Roman Catholic priest with a reputation for knowing more about sacred space than anyone else in the country; and choreographer/dancer Liz Lerman (later honored as a MacArthur Scholar), who had been alienated from synagogues for most of her life but had recently begun experimenting with movement in a Reform congregation (Temple Micah) in Washington, D.C. And we interviewed anyone we heard of who had a reputation for pushing the envelope in synagogue life. We were especially interested in hearing from the disaffected, who would tell us the unvarnished truth about why they were disaffected in the first place. We genuinely did try to learn from everyone.

But we chose to work only with some. We put our team and our board together with insistence that they share our values. As I described above, we invited a large and diverse group of people to a weekend visioning retreat at Ojai, a camp outside Los Angeles. Of those present, some remained closely connected to us and became known as our *Fellows*. They helped us hone our vision, became presenters at our conferences, and brought our message of synagogue transformation to their own circles of people back home.

We regularly added other talented and spiritually motivated people, but only if they shared our core values. Sometimes our "clients"— members of the congregations we were serving—crossed over and became Fellows as well. Our organization remained porous, then, with people regularly coming in and out of the circle of influence. But in the end, we owe our entire vision to a collaborative effort by all the wonderful people we consulted. Their names are included in the acknowledgments, not just pro forma, but with genuine gratitude for all they did and still continue to do.

The vision became crystallized as *PISGAH*, the topic we turn to next, in chapter 4.

Concepts from This Chapter

Four-step process of transformation: Transformation that progresses from the individual, to the team, to other synagogue committees and the synagogue as a whole, and finally to other individual members.

Limited liability community: The institutional affiliations we maintain simply to satisfy a list of "must-dos" and "must-gets." With them comes also *limited liability encounters*, where we "do" or "get" what we contracted for, but have no story to tell or hear while "doing" and "getting" it.

Jewish Journey Groups: Small groups organized according to people's gifts and passions, where text meets life as members engage in Jewish learning to shed light upon a shared underlying concern.

The third sector: The set of voluntary organizations that people join by choice, but which have no inbuilt funding capacity—neither the governmental power to levy taxes (the first sector) nor the market structure to make money by design (the second sector).

Marginals: Jews for whom Judaism is largely peripheral to their life, but who might visit a synagogue and must be especially welcomed there.

Activities and Topics for Discussion

1. What opportunities exist in the course of a day or week in your life to "check in" with others and share your own "everyday and not so everyday life happenings"? What would you answer right now if someone were to ask, "How are you?" and really mean it?

2. Share with each other something of the story about what brought you to the synagogue in the first place and what keeps you there now.

3. When you wake up in a cold sweat in the middle of the night, what is it that disturbs you?

4. Map your relationship with Judaism using Horowitz's descriptors of personal journeys: steadily high, steadily low, moving away from personal involvement, moving steadily toward it, interior journey. What stand out as pivotal moments on your journey?

4
Crafting the Vision

It will be easier to understand what follows if we first identify the various components of the Synagogue 2000 system and only then elaborate on what each one was. Our work with synagogues depended on eight variables:

1. Funding partners
2. Cohorts
3. Synagogue 2000 teams
4. Conferences
5. Curricula
6. Fellows
7. Team meetings
8. Consulting

By *funding partners* (1) I mean local institutional funding, not donors on the national level. The sophistications of Synagogue 2000 were such that no single synagogue would be likely to afford it, so we worked with many synagogues at a time, each group of which we called a *cohort* (2). Cohorts were usually regional (ranging from five to eighteen congregations), but on two occasions cohort synagogues were spread out nationally. When we began, we thought we could do our work with each cohort in a two-year span; we eventually raised it to three.

   Details of our system changed with time, but in its final iteration, each synagogue designated some twenty to twenty-five members as its *Synagogue 2000 team* (3), whom they sent to *conferences* (4), where they were given take-home *curricula* (5). Our conferences, highly experiential simulations of "doing synagogue differently," were dominated by presentations made by *Fellows* (6).

For three years thereafter, back home, monthly *team meeting*s (7) were dedicated to going through the curriculum, the agenda of each meeting having been developed by a small internal planning group of five to eight team members. Curricular study was to be actualized in synagogue change. There were several curricula, each one handling a discrete area of synagogue life; "Prayer," for instance, allowed teams to learn about, evaluate, and determine afresh their synagogues' ritual life. Curricula contained readings and exercises and were interactive, demanding discussion and experimentation. They were deliberately thick in pages and deep in concepts, their goal being to educate laypeople, clergy, and synagogue professionals as partners in an exciting synagogue venture. Teams were helped step by step in the process by *consultants* (8).

When I say "we" worked with cohorts, it is important to know who the "we" were. In many Jewish not-for-profits, "staff" are contrasted with lay volunteers, who constitute committees and *are* the organization. The committee chairs inherit professional "staffers," who execute what their lay committees decide. We found that with some frequency, the chief professionals, the de facto ongoing civil service of the Jewish People, considered their lay constituency more of a hindrance than a help. We were warned at times that laypeople should be coddled and cuddled for their money and their time but be held at arm's length in practice, lest too much involvement hamper the professionals, who really know best. In one instance, a top-level Federation executive warned me never ever to talk directly to "his" laypeople unless so instructed or cleared by him to do so. Laypeople are not totally unaware of this background static—they may even buy into it as the proper way to behave. But it creates enormous distrust and squanders the benefit that genuinely collaborative work might accomplish.

High-level professionals who have worked their way up the system at least mix, eat, and talk with the powerful laity. But further down the organizational ladder, lower-level staff are cordoned off as the nameless "my people," as in the expression "My people will talk to your people." At public dinners, these staff members are sequestered off to their own corner table, like a separate servant class.

This de facto class discrimination evoked for me the talmudic adage, "I work in the city, others work in the country; I get up early for work, others get up late. They do not presume to do my work, and I do not presume to do theirs. Can you say that I do a lot, and they do a little? We have learned, it is all one as long as we direct our hearts to heaven." Wishing to exemplify a sacred community, the national Synagogue 2000 organization eschewed a multilayered hierarchy for an interdependent team. Each person was expected to do his or her job as if no one else in the world could do it better. But we willingly helped each other when we could. Prior to conferences, for instance, Ron and I frequently stuffed delegate packets late into the night. We took pride in each other, regardless of the roles we played.

In our synagogue cohorts, too, we aimed at empowering lay-clergy teams to work together in creative and nonthreatening ways. Like Abraham and Sarah, they would leave their familiar terrain and head off to an as yet unknown land that God would show them. At our best, we built a lasting bond of trust between rabbis who were used to going it alone (and were frequently burning out, as a result) and lay leaders who were newly educated through curricular study. As one rabbi put it, "For twenty-five years I have dreamed for my people, and this year I discovered we can dream together." Another rabbi remarked, "You gave us permission to take the risks that we were afraid to try on our own." In many cases, the lay members of the Synagogue 2000 team eventually became synagogue leaders overall, sharing a trusting relationship with their clergy, born of studying and working together.

Synagogues that failed usually lacked that trusting relationship. Sometimes rabbis or cantors proved unable to overcome suspicions that went back to seminary training, where well-meaning faculty had once warned them against getting too close to laypeople—or to each other. But sometimes the problem was intrinsic to not-for-profits, where "pathological" laypeople, once empowered, abuse their power but cannot be "fired." One rabbi described a member of her team trying to ride roughshod over the rest of the group. "As a rabbi," she explained, "I have a global view of the synagogue that most laypeople cannot achieve. I know people's personal stories, after all. This man is impervious to the potential damage of ramming through change without due regard for the feelings of others." Other causes of failure were synagogues hopelessly mired in politics or suffering from tentative rabbis afraid of experimentation and resistant to collaboration with laity.

But when we succeeded, we were able to create magnificent teams who met regularly and successfully back home. Each team had a *content director*, who oversaw curricular progress, designating appropriate team members to lead discussions or facilitate exercises. Since the curricula were high in Jewish content, it often fell naturally to the rabbi, cantor, or educator to do the teaching, but on other occasions, lay members of the team with appropriate expertise filled that role (an architect, say, for the discussion on sacred space). In addition, a *process facilitator*—someone trained in group process, a social worker perhaps—was charged with advancing conversations when progress broke down or when interpersonal roadblocks got in the way. The process facilitators of every cohort had regular meetings with Linda Klonsky, our national expert in organizational development, who sometimes oversaw a local expert charged with staying in personal touch with each team on the ground.

> Movements develop separate networks, where members talk repeatedly with the same subset of people, sacrificing enrichment that derives from conversing cross-denominationally.

Our first step along the way was the planning retreat in Ojai, where we arrived with our funders and two separate circles of contacts whom we sometimes called Ron's friends (largely Conservative) and Larry's friends (largely Reform). It was a shock to see how little the two sets of friends had intersected. Movements develop separate networks, where members talk repeatedly with the same subset of people, sacrificing the enrichment that derives from conversing cross-denominationally.

ENCOUNTERING SADDLEBACK

Even before we settled in at camp, we visited the Saddleback megachurch for a Sunday service. Saddleback is clearly evangelical, its entire purpose mission-driven, to "bring glory to God by presenting Jesus Christ with as many Christlike disciples as we possibly can before he returns."[1] It is marked by a belief in biblical inerrancy and sees itself locked in a militant battle with liberals for the soul of America. It is probable, therefore, that not a single member of our party agreed with much that Saddleback stood for.

We were amazed, therefore, to find how comfortable we all felt and the respect we developed for what we saw. Here was a culture that lives its faith and proselytizes by example, welcoming rather than rebuffing and appreciating rather than ignoring all who come as seekers. We Jewish visitors, uncertain and suspicious about being dropped into an evangelical service for the Lord's Day, were made to feel at home.

We couldn't help contrasting that environment with most synagogues, where guests arrive and leave with patent anonymity and without much help. At one synagogue I had to walk around the entire perimeter in driving rain, trying each door in turn, until I found the one that was open. Signage is frequently confusing, unhelpful, and sometimes hilariously misleading—like the synagogue that labeled its car lanes one-way, so that the first sign you see as you turn into the synagogue area is "Do not enter!" You walk from car to sanctuary unsure of yourself, with no one to talk to. An usher hands you a couple of books without indicating what they are or what to do with them. Worship goes unexplained, leaving you uncertain about what to do and afraid you will be summoned for a task that will demonstrate your ignorance.

In one particularly telling example, a woman attending a bar mitzvah was surprised to find herself summoned for *g'lilah*, a Hebrew word she had never encountered. (It denotes "rolling" up the Torah scroll after it is read, and "redressing" it in order to return it to the ark.) Shepherded up the aisle, she arrived at the front to find someone else holding aloft the Torah scroll, then sitting down with the scroll on his knees, expecting something or other of the poor woman.

"Roll the two sides of the Torah together," someone whispered; so she did.

"Put the covering over the top," was the next piece of advice, so she did.

"Put on the breastplate," she was finally told.

"The what?"

"The breastplate. Put on the breastplate."

So she did that too, but on herself. Congregants looked up to find the woman, not the Torah, bedecked with a breastplate. I wager the victimized woman never came back to synagogue again.

We were impressed by the large corps of volunteers that is commonplace at megachurches. At Willow Creek, I talked to a woman who volunteers every Sunday to serve hot food to the three thousand (or so) people who stay for lunch around large tables where families meet and discuss the pastor's sermon.

"Why do you do this?"

"It is my gift," she replied, "given by God for me to offer back to the church."

The language of gifts is central to the churches we visited. So, too, is conversation about passions. When potential members are interviewed, they are asked to share their *gifts* and *passions*, which then form the basis of affinity "small groups" that we looked at in chapter 3. We contrasted membership initiation in the church with what passes for the same thing in most synagogues by sending a "mystery shopper" to several synagogues to report how he was treated. No synagogue discussed any responsibility other than dues. No one expected him to be anything other than a "customer" balancing synagogue offerings against other demands on his time. No one engaged him in discussions of religious commitment, spiritual search, the gifts he had, or the passions that move him.

Whenever I discuss the Saddleback model of member engagement, I use my own life as an example. My wife and I are blessed with three children, now grown up. One of them suffers from intractable epilepsy, a horrible disease that most people know little or nothing about. Unlike victims of cancer, strokes, and heart attacks, the 2.5 million Americans who suffer from epilepsy go largely unnoticed; the half a million of them like my daughter, whose seizures are uncontrolled, feel the pain of their disease, the further pain of being unable to pursue a normal life, and more pain still when people avoid them on the street, fire them from jobs, and mistake their seizures for drug addiction or psychosis. Every synagogue has members who at least know someone with epilepsy, and others who actually deal with the disease, as we do, on a day-to-day basis.

Suppose a synagogue membership committee actually inquired about my life and discovered (as they would) the story of my daughter and her illness. Suppose further that someone suggested that I meet regularly with others like myself, perhaps only for several months a year, but regularly enough to get to know one another and organize an annual way to educate the community about epilepsy. As busy as my wife and I are, we would volunteer eagerly for such an opportunity; we would find time somehow to do it; and we would benefit from meeting others like ourselves while studying Jewish wisdom that might give our lives direction. Like it or not, erasing epilepsy has become our *passion*. We would happily organize a program on it. And by studying and praying together, we would find that our epilepsy *Jewish Journey Group* nurtures us as much as we nurture others.

As to *gifts*, Willow Creek pastor Bill Hybels describes an automobile mechanic who apologized for not having any. He was an ordinary unlettered mechanic. Hybels identified his expertise with cars as his gift and suggested that he form a ministry with other mechanics, fixing the cars of poor people for free. The ministry burgeoned. After some time, the mechanic approached Hybels with a request. People were returning week after week with the same broken-down cars. As soon as one thing was fixed, something else would break. But the owners couldn't afford to buy another car. So perhaps Hybels would ask people to donate their old cars to the automobile ministry; the mechanics would overhaul them and exchange them for the unreliable heaps that were obviously beyond repair.

Recognizing the inherent Jewish concept of "gifts," we can reconceptualize synagogue membership as a sacred contract with a community, where our gifts and passions are recognized, nourished, and directed toward the enrichment of others.

Why have we abandoned the language of gifts? True, it is traditional Christian terminology, as is so much of religious rhetoric in general. But surely the idea is not alien to Judaism. Beyond the monetary donations that the Israelites contributed for the desert sanctuary, Nachman of Breslav taught that they brought also the uniqueness that was within them. Bezalel, the chief architect for the project, was selected because he had within him "the spirit of God, as well as wisdom, understanding, and skill in all manner of work" (Exodus 31:3). Aren't these gifts? Recognizing the inherent Jewish concept of "gifts," we reconceptualized synagogue membership as a sacred contract with a community, where our gifts and passions are recognized, nourished, and directed toward the enrichment of others.

PISGAH: MORE THAN JUST A LOGO

The planning meeting at Ojai was our first indication that synagogue transformation operates best if the personal lives of the people doing the transforming are themselves already transformed in the process. For three days, we ate, sang, prayed, thought, and dreamed together. We left Ojai convinced that whatever we did would have to be Jewish and spiritual to its core; we would think and speak theologically; and we would attend to six discrete areas of synagogue life and culture, all of which would have to be spiritualized. We adopted an acronym for the six areas: PISGAH, a word drawn from the account of Moses's death (Deuteronomy 34:1–4):

PISGAH spells out a promised land for synagogues; its letters define the six congregational tasks that it entails:

P   Prayer
I   Institutional change
S   Study
G   Good deeds
A   Ambience of the sacred
H   Healing

From the steppes of Moab, Moses ascended Mount Nebo, to the summit of Pisgah, opposite Jericho, from which God showed him the entire Land.... God said, "This is the Land of which I swore to Abraham, Isaac, and Jacob, 'I will assign it to your offspring.'"

Synagogue transformation is an intergenerational project, and we were like Moses, beginning the task, but passing it on to others to continue after us. PISGAH spells out a promised land for synagogues; its letters define the six congregational tasks that it entails:

P   Prayer
I   Institutional change
S   Study
G   Good deeds
A   Ambience of the sacred
H   Healing

SYSTEMS AND HOLISM: WHEN "THE WHOLE IS GREATER THAN THE SUM OF ITS PARTS"

We thought holistically, seeing the various parts of the synagogue as mutually interdependent. By contrast, most synagogues think atomistically, as if individual parts are not systemically related. They assign discrete functions to separate committees that may never talk to one another. Committees produce programs in their assigned area: the education committee, for instance, oversees a school wing; the social action committee organizes a *mitzvah* day. But committees are mentally zoned off into separate cognitive regions. Like the fabled Chinese menu, congregants feel free to choose (as their monthly offering) a service this Friday and a lecture next Wednesday, while passing up a social action project on Sunday—or vice versa. As we shall see later (chapter 6), the unconscious model is "synagogue as retailer in a free market." It competes for people's time and money by accessing program ideas from various wholesalers, particularly their movements, who showcase programmatic wares at biennials. Within the synagogue, rivalry for attendance occurs. We saw some synagogues where committees even strategized about how to draw off people from each other's competitive offerings.

Synagogues should engage in an ongoing institutional *cheshbon hanefesh* (examination of the soul) and, if necessary, institutional *t'shuvah* (repentance) to redirect the congregational path toward becoming a *k'hillah k'doshah* overall. A *k'hillah k'doshah* (sacred community) is a synagogue of honor, welcome, acceptance, and trust—the characteristics that promote healing as wholeness.

In Synagogue 2000's holistic model, the six areas of PISGAH do not represent discrete programming areas; they are parallel pathways to becoming a sacred community. The four consonants in the acronym (PSGH) refer to content: prayer, study, good deeds, and healing. The vowels (IA)—institutional change and ambience of the sacred—represent general attitudes that should suffuse everything the synagogue does, not only programming, but how people answer the telephone, for example, or how the clergy treat each other.

In everything it does, then, a Synagogue 2000 congregation would reflect the following two considerations:

- Inculcate *Institutional* change as a welcome and ongoing reality
- Develop an *Ambience* that reflects a culture of welcome rooted in a view of human relationships that manifest the sacred

Over the course of years, a Synagogue 2000 congregation would look at the following:

- *Prayer*—examine critically its *t'fillah*
- *Study*—develop opportunities for lifelong learning of Torah
- *Good deeds*—practice social justice
- *Healing*—promote practices that bring healing of mind, body, and spirit

Synagogue transformation should not be mistaken for a retooling of any single area of activity. It denotes the application of theologically based principles to everything a synagogue does. Which of the four "content" areas synagogues choose first is arbitrary. Though it might start with study, it would eventually have to look at prayer, healing, and social justice too. Successful synagogues would engage in an ongoing institutional *cheshbon hanefesh* (examination of the soul) and, if necessary, institutional *t'shuvah* (repentance) to redirect the congregational path toward becoming a *k'hillah k'doshah* overall. A *k'hillah k'doshah* (sacred community) is a synagogue of honor, welcome, acceptance, and trust—the characteristics that promote healing as wholeness.

Unable to prepare curricula for all four program areas (PSGH) simultaneously, we began with prayer, healing, institutional change, and ambience. That is, congregations could address their ritual (or prayer) life (P) or make themselves over into healing centers (H). In either case, they would inculcate a culture that welcomes institutional change (I) and construct an ambience (A) that marks the synagogue as a sacred community.

DIDACTIC VERSUS CONSULTATIVE

Adrienne Bank, who advised us in our early years, notes that interventions come in two modes, the *didactic* and the *consultative*. They are polar opposites, sitting at either end of a spectrum. Work in the real world takes place somewhere on the spectrum, but even when the two poles are mixed together, as they usually are, one or the other approach usually predominates.

The didactic mode is best pictured as a university lecture. The lecturer intervenes in the lives of students by feeding them the information she thinks they need. This model assumes a giver and a receiver, with the giver knowing everything and the receiver knowing nothing, so passively taking it all in, on faith that whatever the teacher says is true. Knowledge is passed along on a one-way street, entirely top-down.

At the opposite pole stands the classical intervention stance of consultants, whose job is to facilitate deeper insight and decision making by the client. In this model, the client, not the consultant, stipulates what will count for success. The client has all the knowledge necessary for a decision but lacks the process by which the knowledge can be accessed. The consultant recognizes patterns of institutional interaction and surfaces them to help the client reach clarity. Consultancy is dialogic, even therapeutic. If didactics are top-down, consultancy is bottom-up, in that the consultant helps the answer bubble up from the midst of the client. The client organization learns to recognize its own institutional patterns and dysfunctions, and it solves the designated problem through insight facilitated by the consultant.

When we entered the synagogue world, the consultancy model was well established as "the obvious way to go." But I was ambivalent about it. The support for its centrality came primarily from crisis situations, when the need for change is so clear and urgent that a synagogue cannot help but try to do something to move forward, knowing that it cannot do it alone. The best example is conflict resolution. A rabbi and synagogue board are fighting to the point where the board wants to fire the rabbi and the rabbi threatens to sue the synagogue. When a congregation is ready to dial 911, consultancy intervention is needed, welcomed, and likely to be the only road to success.

Another example is transition planning, where, again, the parties have an important stake in solving a discrete and readily identifiable problem. After forty years of service to a single congregation, the rabbi has announced his retirement. He is so beloved that the board fears his successor will not succeed unless the congregation plans for the transition. Here, too, is a problem tailor-made for consultancy.

In organizational literature, cases like these have been labeled "adaptive" as opposed to "technical."[2] With purely technical problems, an expert diagnoses the difficulty and prescribes a solution. In adaptive cases, no one knows the solution in advance. Consultancy here means enabling the client to frame the problem in such a way that a solution emerges. Whether (in the first instance) the rabbi stays or leaves is of no intrinsic concern to the consultant, who takes no principled stand on the matter one way or the other—not officially, anyway, even though she may have an opinion. Similarly (in the second example), how the older rabbi retires only the synagogue and rabbi can decide.

Psychologists differentiate negative from positive motivation. *Negative motivation* is like emergency surgery that we would rather avoid but are forced to undergo against our will. We face up to problems for fear of what will happen if we do not. *Positive motivation* is like elective plastic surgery. We could live with the way we look, but it occurs to us that it might be worth trying to look better. In Jewish terms, negative motivation is *yirat shamayim,* "fear of heaven." Positive motivation is *lishmah,* pursuing a course of action "for its own sake." Both are appropriate, but for different ends. There is nothing wrong with trying to do the right thing because of *yirat shamayim.* But Maimonides tells us that pursuing the good life *lishmah* is a higher level of behavior. Crisis intervention and transition planning are the result of *yirat shamayim* (negative motivation). Synagogue transformation follows from the desire to act *lishmah* (positive motivation). Some synagogues never move from *yirat shamayim* to *lishmah.*

Synagogues in crisis who try to undertake transformation fail because crisis generates negative motivation. The crisis itself becomes an institutional black hole that sucks all the energy away from the rest of the system. Faced with an emergency, the threatened synagogue remains in the mode of *yirat shamayim,* not *lishmah.* Everything it does is motivated by fear. Until the crisis is solved, synagogue leaders are unlikely to have the luxury of generating the positive motivation necessary to dream boldly of a new vision.

By the time Synagogue 2000 began, independent consultants were already at work in many congregations solving urgent and discrete problems marked by *yirat shamayim.* But consultancy alone was not as successful, we judged, in long-term transformational work, where the urgency of change is

> Negative motivation is *yirat shamayim,* "fear of heaven." Positive motivation is *lishmah,* pursuing a course of action "for its own sake." Both are appropriate, but for different ends. Transformation requires *lishmah.* Synagogues in crisis fail at transformation because they remain in the emergency mode of *yirat shamayim.*

never absolutely clear and motivation *lishmah* is required. This is not
to say that good consultants cannot help congregations who want to
change. But they must truly want the consultant's intervention, there
must be a good match between consultant and congregation, significant funds must be available to pay the consultant, and the consultant must understand how synagogues differ from other organizations.
Frequently, we found at least one of these conditions lacking. In one
case, a well-known consulting firm agreed to help synagogues develop
a mission statement and then put it into operation. In large part the
experiment failed. Synagogues did not have the patience to engage in
the lengthy and onerous process of arguing though their mission. As
governing representatives of a default organization, boards saw no
striking need to rethink the synagogue's purpose. In a nutshell, they
could generate no positive motivation.

In the end we mixed both approaches, the didactic and the consultative, but we differed from other approaches to synagogue transformation in that we were not afraid to emphasize the didactic. We
came to our task convinced in advance of certain truths: the inevitable
demise of ethnic nostalgia, the bankruptcy of pediatric Judaism, the
need to think theologically, synagogue as sacred community, and PIS-
GAH. As much as we provided process, then, we also insisted on content. Synagogues that preferred to remain ethnic, wanted only new
and better programming, liked being child-centered, or had goals
incompatible with our own were told that Synagogue 2000 was not
for them. But in the end, all we could do was advise. Federations paying for synagogue change represented the entire community and were
forced to insist that we admit every synagogue that applied, even if we
thought it a mistake for a given synagogue to do so.

I have already said that the main body of our work involved
working with entire cohorts of synagogues over a two- or three-year
period. But in addition, we were often asked to consult with individual synagogues on one thing or another. We agonized over which invitations to accept and which to reject, deciding (1) we would not be the
911 of synagogues—that kind of work was being done successfully
elsewhere; and (2) we would engage in long-term transformative work
alone. Emphasizing our commitment to spirituality, we advertised our
availability as consultants, but only for "consulting in a spiritual

vein." We would accept invitations if, and only if, the client congregation saw its presenting problem as part of a long-term effort to reevaluate what it was doing from the viewpoint of Jewish values and an eye toward becoming purpose-driven rather than programmatic.

In some cases, I came to doubt the necessity of consultants altogether. Where congregations lacked good leadership, consultation was imperative (poor leadership is a flaw that generates negative motivation); but in systemically healthy congregations with good leaders, having the right internal process facilitator was just as effective. I cannot overstate the role of rabbinic leadership especially. Some rabbis wanted change so much and were so effective in their leadership that having an outside consultant proved virtually irrelevant. In well-governed systems where rabbi and lay leadership work well together, other aspects of Synagogue 2000—the curriculum, for instance, which provided a Jewish road map to change, or the meeting regimen, which created spiritual small groups out of the participants—were all that were required. I have come to believe that consultants are necessary for some institutions but not for others. And I have come more and more to appreciate the wisdom of tapping local volunteer talent in the congregations (the process facilitators), who adapted the curricula and lessons learned at conferences in ways we would never have imagined.

WHY PRAYER?

The decision to first address prayer instead of study and good deeds came relatively easily. I had been studying prayer for thirty years. We could just as easily have turned to study, which Ron, as an educator, could have put together with similar ease. But we deliberately decided to leave study for last. Therein lies a lesson from past experience and a theory of Jewish continuity that deserve discussion.

It is "common knowledge" that the way to fight assimilation and apathy is through quality Jewish education. But we found no data to demonstrate the singular importance of education compared to other variables that haven't been tried yet. Prayer is one of them. The ethnic Judaism of our past virtually guaranteed that no one took prayer seriously. Until relatively recently, no one has even imagined what it would be like to have a full and rich ritual life in congregations. Services are assumed to be what you go to out of obligation, something you sit through because you must. But it doesn't have to be that way. Anthropological literature suggests that ritual is the very thing that binds people to tradition, connects them with the transcendent, and bonds them to each other.

We see that occur in summer camps, and not just for teenagers. When adult retreats feature moving ritual, Shabbat services, not individual classes, become the highlight of the experience. We live in an era of worship ferment anyway, we reasoned, so why not see if prayer might be a better starting point than study? Similar reasoning lay behind healing. The synagogue is the place people go as they move through their life cycle. If we think of those transitional moments as nodal points in personal identity, it follows that synagogues that celebrate or mourn them in proper fashion would guarantee a strong synagogue identity for the people who go through them. So we began where others hadn't: in-depth efforts to make prayer a vital part of synagogues.

Ritual binds people to tradition, connects them with the transcendent, and bonds them to each other.

By "prayer" I mean more than the liturgy, the prayer-book content that gets prayed. Far more significant is the way the prayers get said: to what melodies and with what accompanying gestures, where and how the Torah is lifted and carried, whether people stand or sit, and who gets seated where. These things, the choreography of the service, the "how" as opposed to the "what," constitute worship, not liturgy.

Worshipers rarely argue about liturgy. The handed-down wording of prayer may be boring, but as long as it is not outright offensive, people will probably read the stuff just because it is there, especially if it is in Hebrew, which they do not understand. The choreography of worship, on the other hand, the activity everyone sees, packs worlds of symbolic meaning. Prayer choreography is the religious version of such customs as bowing before royalty and seating banquet guests at a head table. When Mordecai refuses to bow to Haman, he sends a message beyond anything words might say. Weddings are often held with no head table, so that no one will be offended if they are not placed there.

Prayer choreography has always received attention. Living in a Muslim world, Maimonides urged Jews to take their shoes off before entering a synagogue and tried to eliminate the silent *Amidah* because he found its cacophony embarrassing. Nineteenth-century Reform Jews in Germany outlawed running through the sanctuary and spitting on the floor, common occurrences that were alienating a modern constituency. Everyone notices who gets an *aliyah* or is seated on the *bimah*.

There are two watershed events in all of this. The first was a Jewish Reformation in the nineteenth century. The Christian Reformation of the sixteenth century had not impacted Europe's Jews, because they were still ghettoized. By the nineteenth century, however, as Jews were freed from ghettos and acculturated to the modern world, they were affected by the same winds of change that had created the Christian Reformation four hundred years earlier. Anglicanism and modern Orthodoxy represent minor changes from medieval ritual. Protestantism and Reform Judaism are more revolutionary overhauls. The Christian Reformation brought about a counter-Reformation, when the medieval church hardened its stand against any liturgical alteration whatever. Similarly, in what is a Jewish counter-Reformation, some nineteenth-century rabbis became ultra-Orthodox, opposing all change. The Jewish Reformation was helped along by the Industrial Revolution, part of which made it possible to create and distribute new prayer books inexpensively. By the twentieth century, however, liturgical ferment had largely run its course.

A more recent reformation (the second watershed event) followed the heady days of the 1960s, capitalizing on the exuberance of baby-boomers, who were coming of age. At first it showed itself in mass-mimeographed services that people called "creative liturgy." But it matured into new denominational prayer books. Even Orthodox Jews, the sector of the community that had most resisted liturgical innovation, developed the *ArtScroll* series, which replaced *siddurim* that had been used for decades.

Liturgical renewal was accompanied by a rising interest in the scholarly study of ritual, and by the 1980s, ideas about how ritual works began influencing how prayers were said. The influence was gradual, but as ritual began to matter more and more and as people seemed to be attending services less and less, even though they had spanking new prayer books to pray with, worship innovation became a central concern.

Synagogue 2000 was formed at the very height of that concern, the 1990s, when the population study showed a decline in Jewish numbers relative to the American population as a whole, and everyone started fearing for Jewish continuity. Our focus groups had emphasized the tug of war between rabbis drawing people in and laypeople taking themselves out. Attendance at services was perceived as a symbolic gesture of the desire to remain in.

It is not true that Jews have always attended services in droves. In post–World War II Wilkes Barre, Pennsylvania, for instance, out of 250 families, only 6 single souls showed up for Shabbat morning worship. Jewish men mostly owned stores that opened for business on Saturdays, the week's busiest shopping day (blue laws prohibited opening on Sundays). To solve the problem, Reform, Conservative, and even Orthodox Jews experimented with Friday night prayer, and that worked for a time. In 1953, Conservative synagogue Mishkan Tefila in Boston boasted one thousand worshipers every Friday.

But that was before the 1960s. Those were not the baby-boomers, but their parents, who were experiencing the McCarthy era, which implicitly defined worship attendance as a patriotic statement against godless Communism. After that, with two-career families and with more and more demands competing for less and less time, attendance diminished. Not the least of the problems was the fact that the boomers (unlike their parents) felt no obligation to attend, neither as a matter of *mitzvah* nor as civic Jewish duty—the sense that going to synagogue is just the right thing to do. Given the pediatric Judaism of the time, large congregations turned Shabbat into a "bar/bat mitzvah service" focused on the celebrant and his/her family.

Conservative *shuls* demanded a Torah reading that seemed eternal to the average congregant, who knew no trope and could not follow the Hebrew; that was followed by an equally endless *Musaf* service, not for halakhic reasons, but for cantorial ones. Given the length of the service, people delayed arriving until the actual moment of the bar/bat mitzvah reading; cantors relegated *Shacharit*, the earlier portion of the service (the part most favored by tradition), to lesser voices, saving their own artistry for *Musaf*, the part guaranteed to have a captive "audience" who had arrived to hear the bar/bat mitzvah and then to "party," so could hardly leave before services ended. For many, Conservative worship—now featuring cantor and choir— was experienced as long and boring.

Even more than Conservative Judaism, Shabbat morning in Reform temples was given over to bar/bat mitzvah families. The only communal service was Friday night, but it was saddled with its own baggage: still hampered by classical Reform practice that had eliminated congregational participation, *erev Shabbat* worship was (by standards of the 1960s and '70s) distant, cold, and unengaging. It is in that environment that ritual (not just liturgical) reform began. By the 1990s, it was in full swing, led by a generation of baby- boomers coming of age as senior rabbis, many of them with memories of camp-style prayer, and a few with professional training also in ritual studies.

When Synagogue 2000 began, interest in renovating tired prayer services was at an all-time high and increasing, particularly in Reform and Reconstructionist synagogues, but in forward-looking Conservative and Orthodox congregations also. The promise of prayer transformation via Synagogue 2000 provided positive motivation for many synagogues.

WHY HEALING?

Healing had also come into its own by 1994. The first Jewish healing center was established in San Francisco in 1991; several more across the country followed, and in 1995 they were networked under an umbrella organization called "The National Center for Jewish Healing." So when Synagogue 2000 began, Jewish healing was still in its infancy. We knew much less about it than we did about worship. We were not even sure what Jewish healing was.

Definitions vary. A broad understanding comes from the San Francisco website, where (among other things) healing is seen as "a personal journey toward wholeness." A more constricted view, from the New York Center website, is the mission "that no Jew be alone during the difficult transitions of illness and loss." Either way, "healing" is not the same thing as "cure" and not intended only for the sick. Insofar as we all strive for wholeness and all go through transitions of illness and loss, it seemed self-evident that synagogues should become adept at being places where people feel "healed."

The ideal synagogue of healing evokes what the prophet Ezekiel foresaw for the spiritual shape of a rebuilt Temple. He prophesied from exile after the destruction of the First Temple in 587 BCE. Had he lived to see the Second Temple finally take shape, I suspect he would have disapproved of its architecture, not necessarily because of discrepancies in its physical details, but because space limits function, and the Second Temple, like the First, was built with atonement at its core, whereas Ezekiel seems also to have had healing in mind.

The most sacred part of the Temple was the Holy of Holies, which only the High Priest entered, and only on Yom Kippur. Ezekiel begins with a common sentiment regarding sacrificial places: the earth's axis passes through the Holy of Holies and continues on to heaven, linking heaven to earth. Not so common is Ezekiel's belief that below the Holy of Holies is the river of life emanating from the Garden of Eden. Divine forgiveness would descend from the uppermost end of the heaven-earth axis; but in addition, the primeval subterranean river would split into tributaries, watering verdant trees along their banks, to nurture all humanity.

We, too, imagine an axis joining heaven to earth, but it extends through the ark where we keep our Torah scrolls—as our equivalent to the ancient Holy of Holies. So blessing for us descends through Torah. We bestow a blessing for healing (*Mi Sheberakh*) on those called to the Torah, and following Ezekiel's river metaphor, we can say that when they leave the synagogue, they are to carry the blessing with them to nurture others.

Synagogue 2000 therefore devoted enormous energy to identifying the metaphysical purpose of synagogues as healing. I say metaphysical because we had in mind far more than the physical "cure" that positivist medical science associates with the term. To be sure, the *Mi Sheberakh* does request physical healing, but alongside *r'fu'at haguf* (healing of body), the prayer specifies *r'fu'at hanefesh* (healing of soul). The healing that synagogues provide is the knowledge of being connected to God, during diseases of body and mind for sure, but also when afflicted with hidden forms of suffering that rarely get spoken—like miscarriage and infertility, disaffection with life, lack of purpose, and loneliness. Like Ezekiel's Temple, synagogues, we said, must be places whence healing flows, not because synagogues are for people who are sick, but because healing entails wholeness, the will to live, and engagement in relationships that are not toxic.

This notion of synagogues as places for healing ran so deep in our vision that we soon abandoned seeing it as a separate content spoke on the PISGAH wheel. We began viewing it like ambience and institutional change—the very essence of what synagogues are about. Rabbi Jonathan Rosenblatt best captured the concept when he described the normative Jewish community as a culture of blame, not a culture of honor. We now saw healing as embedded in a culture that honors the humanity of others; that looks for the best, not the worst in everyone; that helps people succeed, not fail; and that eliminates the cultural aggravations that drive up blood pressure, cause embarrassment, promote guilt, and chase people away.

Eventually, we combined healing and ambience to create an entire curriculum on developing a synagogue of honor, welcome, acceptance, and trust—the characteristics that promote healing as wholeness. Thinking theologically, we called it *k'hillah k'doshah* and set as our task the transforming of synagogue from a fee-for-service enterprise to a community of the sacred (chapters 5 and 6).[3]

> The healing that synagogues provide is the knowledge of being connected to God. At their best, synagogues are places whence healing flows, not because synagogues are for people who are sick, but because healing entails wholeness, the will to live, and engagement in relationships that are not toxic.

CONFERENCES, CURRICULA, AND CONSULTATION: MOTIVATION, EDUCATION, AND HELP

Ideas do have consequences, but only under certain circumstances. The first step is motivating people. As a public relations person once told me, "Getting the word out is not the same as getting the message through." Once they get the message, synagogues need to adopt it by adapting it to their own circumstances. Our method of delivery, if you like, spoke to each of these processes: *Conferences* got the word out by simulating how one might do synagogue differently. *Curricula* enabled congregations to deepen their understanding of what they had experienced at the conferences. *Consultants* helped teams adapt the general message to their own congregational culture. In sum, conferences motivated, curricula educated, and consultants advised.

Most conferences feature talking heads. They are far at the end of the didactic side of the spectrum. Chairs are lined up "theater style" in front of a dais or table, from which experts impart wisdom to passive listeners. Important speakers get plenum sessions; lesser lights sit on panels or give workshops. Meals and evenings are usually "free time"—"time out" from hearing someone talk. The only regular exception is the more or less compulsory banquet that features yet another speaker.

Jewish conferences borrow this meeting model, with, however, an added religious component: morning worship, perhaps; or prayer at mealtimes. But unless the conference represents a specifically religious constituency (the Union for Reform Judaism or the Cantors Assembly, for example), the religious overlay is treated as optional. People come for business, not prayer. Those who want may squeeze in early morning prayer or engage in their own private *Birkat Hamazon* after eating. A good example is the Jewish Funders Network, which features an optional *shabbaton* prior to the formal beginning of the meeting.

Asking after the fact, "How was the conference?" usually means, "How were the didactic sessions? What information got fed to you?" We would not expect the respondent to comment on religious ritual, which is not seen as what the conference is all about.

Lately, however, it has been the ritual, not the speeches, that have held most promise for conferences to get the word out, because all across America, a sea change is occurring with regard to our perspective on ritual. My case in point is drawn from the Wexner Heritage Foundation, a pioneer attempt to provide adult Jewish education to people slated to become communal Jewish leaders. That program is being morphed into a new stage, but for twenty years (1985–2005), it was without doubt the most impactful programmatic initiative in Jewish life.

The program offered annual conferences at executive retreat centers, where participants were promised the best and brightest speakers from around the world. For three days, they went from one talking head to another, interspersed with workshops, taking time out to eat and sometimes attending an evening cultural program. Since many of the participants were religious, and since the conferences were held on weekends, Wexner offered Shabbat services, one for the Orthodox, and one or two alternatives for the bulk of the participants who were Conservative, Reform, or Reconstructionist, or had no preference. At the beginning, the religious component was insignificant relative to the real business of the meeting: hearing lecturers. The Orthodox service was usually well attended; Orthodox Jews attend prayer as a matter of religious obligation. But the liberal alternatives sometimes had trouble attracting a *minyan*. Participants slept late Saturday morning or wandered the grounds rather than attend.

That began to change by the middle and late 1990s, when even Wexner, the paradigm of didactic learning, began featuring worship alongside lectures—to a constituency, moreover, that was heavily invested in cultural Judaism, but barely synagogued at all, and hardly demanding better worship, which most of them rarely attended at home. Unknowingly, Wexner was signing on to a "ritual revolution" in Jewish consciousness: prayer was no longer marginalized.

Harbingers of the revolution were several new models of prayer just being invented. New York's B'nai Jeshurun was attracting overflow crowds, week after week. In Los Angeles, Craig Taubman had invented "Friday Night Live," a service that was attracting a full house of young adults who otherwise never set foot in a sanctuary; and "One Shabbat Morning," a service that combined traditional chant with modern composition. In New York, Merri Arian had for years been leading worship at a small *chavurah,* with extraordinary engagement around music. Debbie Friedman's healing service was in demand everywhere. Cantors here and there were experimenting with new musical forms, not just the organ or the guitar, but entire bands. In New York, Eli Kranzler was attracting masses to an Orthodox service featuring congregational chanting of upbeat music by the late Shlomo Carlebach. In Temple Micah of Washington, D.C., choreographer Liz Lerman introduced movement into what had until then been the usual staid Reform service with little involvement of the congregation. In the national Reform Movement, Rabbi Danny Freelander, whose chief interest is worship, became the director of the biennial, allowing him to experiment with new musical forms on a majestic scale. Everywhere, moving, engaging, and deeply satisfying ritual was "in." At the very beginning, Synagogue 2000 established a corps of such worship entrepreneurs, all the people mentioned here and more, with the hope that our conferences would highlight the best in Jewish prayer and thereby become a place for the spirit as well as the mind.

To understand how central ritual has become, we can survey Sydney Schwarz's influential study of breakthrough synagogues.

The first is Temple Beth El of Sudbury, Massachusetts, where Shabbat services are "the central communal experience." It allows people to feel "the power of the moment, a sense of everyday miracle." Those who attend regularly "recount how often they have that feeling. It is a place where there is a lot of laughing and a lot of crying." Beth El is Reform, so as counterpoint, Schwarz gives us the Hebrew Institute of Riverdale, New York, where the melodies are "enticingly singable. Kranzler's energetic drumbeat on the reader's table is the cue for worshipers to clap hands and, on occasion, to link arms and join in a circular dance." For a Reconstructionist synagogue, Schwarz cites his own Adat Shalom Congregation in Bethesda, Maryland. A congregant recalls "the intense level of participation" in Shabbat morning services, which "have represented the essence of Adat Shalom." The important thing, says Schwarz, "was to design a service in which many voices might be heard." Instead of a frontal sermon, Schwarz leads a "Torah dialogue" and encourages people to "feel comfortable sharing their most personal stories with the community." His Conservative synagogue is New York's B'nai Jeshurun (BJ), which we have already met. There, too, on Shabbat morning, the rabbis introduce a Torah dialogue rather than a formal sermon. But most outstanding, perhaps, is its Friday evening service, now grown to the point where it has to provide two parallel services to accommodate people who line up around the block to be included. "Many things attracted people to BJ, but none was so compelling as the conduct of religious services."[4]

The accent on expressive and engaging religious ritual is not just Schwarz's personal predilection. A study of contemporary American religion in general cites a rebellion against the old-style version of religion in churches.

> We really distrust truth, the systematic study of theology and God's Word. We feel like it is going to be heartless and fake. We very much have an aversion to rebuke and exhortation.... We are very worshipful in the sense we appreciate worshipful experiences like singing. Our music is very expressive and it focuses a lot on the experience of God.[5]

What matters to this respondent's generation—he is twenty-five—is "an individual's own experience and journey [which] are privileged as a spiritual trajectory over rigid structures and expectations."[6] The "rigid structures and expectations" are the standard churches, which he associates with theological certainty and "rebuke and exhortation." Yet despite their distrust of "theological certainty," this generation is in quest of God—they just don't think the theological platitudes will get them there. Jews would say much the same thing. Recent studies show Jews have lost patience with the traditional rhetoric of *mitzvah*.[7] We, too, distrust authoritarian certainty. We want ritual that affirms our personal story as an authentic search after spirit, without crunching that search into a procrustean bed of dead liturgical forms.

Ritual is at the heart of today's synagogue transformation. Synagogues that regularly provide ritual with active engagement, personal expression, and authenticity will become forward places of the spirit. Music is crucial.

*R*itual is at the heart of today's synagogue transformation. Synagogues that regularly provide ritual with active engagement, personal expression, and authenticity will become forward places of the spirit. Music is crucial.

Every day of our conferences began and ended with ritual. In addition, we sang every day, not just at services but after lunch and dinner, and then again before bedtime. We drew on the most creative worship facilitators from across the country to show congregational representatives what was possible, telling them not to adopt but to adapt, to grasp the principles that make spiritual worship possible, and then to go home and think through how a similar experience might be authentically produced in their own synagogue with their own professional personnel.

We never held conferences on Shabbat, since clergy are busy then, and we wanted them in attendance alongside their lay leaders. Lacking Shabbat, however, we decided to declare Monday morning "Shabbat," or Tuesday evening "*Havdalah*." We brought entire teams of clergy and backup personnel from far and wide to replicate the service that they were doing successfully back home: Shabbat at New York's B'nai Jeshurun, for example; Debbie Friedman's healing service; "Friday Night Live" from Los Angeles; a worship model from Boston's venerable Temple Israel, which had dumped its old prayer formality and was handing out percussion instruments to growing crowds of worshipers.

The level of spiritual energy in which the hundreds of participants felt engaged is best described through an anecdote. Needing to leave one of our conferences early, B'nai Jeshurun's Rabbi Roly Matelon had summoned a car to take him to the airport. When the driver arrived, dutifully dressed in formal chauffeur garb, conference participants had begun spontaneously dancing around the room. Roly went to get his coat, only to return unable to find his driver—who had decided to join hands with everyone else and dance his way around the perimeter before returning to work.

Change managers are unanimous in saying that change begins only when people are sufficiently motivated to want to dare it. As default organizations that generally see themselves as successful, synagogues rarely have internal motivation based on how poorly they are doing. The burden of motivation falls on showing them a vision of what they might become—not *arguing for* something so much as *pointing to it* as they *engage in it*. Conferences became the Emerald Kingdom for us, a visible sign of what might be if people dared to take the long and difficult yellow brick road of change.

On a few occasions, in keeping with the received wisdom about the need for consultation, we decided to forego flashy speakers and tons of singing, and to spend our time instead in hands-on work with consultants assisting teams with the nuts and bolts of change management. These were inevitably a disaster. The evaluation forms regularly and summarily trashed our efforts to make spirituality second place on our list. The worst example was a one-day conference for a national team of eighteen Reform synagogues at the Reform Movement's biennial, held that year in Boston, to which we tacked on an extra day in advance and invited any team members present to put in time with our consultants. They hated it. One man had driven four hundred miles, all the way from Rochester, New York, just for the day (he wasn't even attending the biennial) so as to be exposed to the Emerald Kingdom once again. And he didn't get it.

Why did our conferences work so well? Five considerations were at work.

First, we brought only the very best. The people leading singing had national reputations as consummate professionals. Our choreographer, Liz Lerman, was later named as a MacArthur Fellow. There is nothing like genius, and when people are brought together for the purpose of developing sacred community, they deserve no less.

Second, we were funded sufficiently to bring those people. The Jewish community often treats its speakers and performers shabbily. We paid people well.

Third, we were true to our values and therefore able to build a system people wanted to be part of. There was first our theological thinking, so different from the usual institutional ambience that marks Jewish life. We believed we were indeed doing God's work reconstituting synagogue life. We remained true to our first principle also: to learn from anyone but not to work with everyone. From time to time genuine geniuses crossed our path asking to be invited into our "fellowship." But we took them on only if they shared our basic values. The conferences were filled, therefore, with people of character.

Fourth, we worked in mutual support of one another. Actor/singer composer Danny Maseng had written and acted a thoroughly professional one-man show entitled "Wasting Time with Harry Davidowitz." He regularly presented it to cohort conventions, to the point where we who had seen it several times already could practically predict the music and the lines. But no one ever left the room. Everyone stayed to show support. Regularly, observers commented on the ambience that permeated our interchanges. Instead of differentiating "professionals" from "staff," we treated and introduced each other always as colleagues. We modeled the culture of honor that we preached.

Fifth, our team of planners left absolutely nothing to chance. Harriet Lewis, in charge of our conference planning, prepared every detail brilliantly.

These five factors allowed us to design conferences where people connected with one another in a deep and powerful way—an experience that synagogues rarely permit. It happened every day in services, then in small groups, around singing at meals, and upon feeling free to tell each other the stories of their lives. On the final day of one conference, a somewhat elderly gentleman from a classical Reform synagogue stopped me to say, "The first day was so wild, I thought I'd never come back. But having done so, I want to tell you that I thank God for allowing me to live to have this experience."

TEAMS AND MEETINGS: BEING AN "UNCOMMITTEE"

It took some time to master the art of putting teams together: enough new voices to get honesty from the congregation's periphery, enough board members to prevent the team from being seen as a fifth column plotting against everything the congregation holds dear; a mix of ages; men and women; above all, people who will listen to each other and at least be open to thinking spiritually and differently.

We also learned to train the teams well. We brought the core planning people from each team together for a pre-conference conference, letting them know what their team would be asked to do and giving them a sneak preview of what the conference would entail. Once we got the idea of designating process facilitators for the teams, we started networking them separately and having them meet together before and during conferences.

We wanted team meetings to be totally unlike any other synagogue get-together to solve problems. Citing an old advertisement for Seven Up that urged its audience to drink an "uncola," we told teams to be an "uncommittee." Committees are part and parcel of the corporate synagogue structure, the normal way into the synagogue's hierarchy. The regulars use them as a social network, moving from one committee to another, then the board, and from there to regional and national committees, boards, and offices, where they extend their social reach to people like themselves in other cities. Committee work is enormously time-consuming, but enormously rewarding, not only for the work, which is valuable in itself, but for the social connections that one makes.

Synagogue 2000 never intended to displace committees. It did, however, recognize the problems with committees as they are currently constituted. Synagogue regulars invariably complain of how synagogue meetings drain them. Committee members are not always professionally trained for the tasks on the agenda. Depending on the chair, meetings may be anything but efficiently operated. Meetings occur when people are tired from work or in conflict over family responsibilities that the meetings displace. Unlike parallel structures in the corporate workplace, synagogue committees rarely have support staff, incentive for follow-through, and enough funding to encourage excellence of output. Moreover, since the committee cannot simply fire the "troublemakers," who are also dues-paying members, pathological personalities are often present. Synagogue committees are often a study in patent pettiness. There are many exceptions, of course, but quite often people wrangle, wear each other out, and rarely see the results of their labor carried out quickly, efficiently, with excellence, and to everyone's satisfaction.

We sought therefore to help committee members meet in an ambience of the sacred, to see their work as a calling, not a task, and to be respectful of one another. But tampering with a social system that delivers such personal payoffs is no easy matter. Indeed, when (on occasion) people suspected we were out to dismantle the system, we were ostracized from the entire synagogue power structure. How, we wondered, could we alter the committee process without destroying the system?

According to our theory of change, individuals transformed at our conferences would want to replicate transformative experiences with one another in their teams. So we began packing the teams with committee and board members, hoping that transformative team behavior could then be carried back to committees by individuals influential enough to introduce the changes without threatening other board members. Instituting successful meeting models at the team level was therefore crucial.

We expended considerable energy teaching teams how to meet differently. They could decide on their own schedule, but every meeting included five components:

1. *Prayer.* A few teams included whatever standard service their meeting times called for—*Minchah* if it was afternoon, *Ma'ariv* for the evening. Others simply sang one of the prayer melodies we had used at our conference. Some improvised prayers or constructed closing rituals. But meetings became sacred because people prayed at them.

2. *Eating.* There is something bonding about sharing food together. Some teams brought potluck lunches or dinners, one had them catered, most supplied cheese and crackers or dessert and coffee, but every meeting featured food of some sort.

3. *Study.* Judaism is inconceivable without study, so we built our meetings around the curricula. It was fascinating to see team members from different congregations sometimes running into each other in grocery stores or carpool lines and talking about music in worship or dysfunctional synagogue signage. Having curricula was the most controversial part of the Synagogue 2000 regimen. But I, at least, remain convinced that it was at the core of our success. People became excited at new ideas,

were thrilled to become Jewishly literate, and took ownership of their synagogue's problems from a new perspective: sacred stewardship rather than secular caretaking.

4. *Action*. Our study was always directed toward activity, to the point where people were often overly anxious to make changes. Team members were constantly asking us how far into the curriculum the other teams had advanced, assuming their own team was the only slow one. We developed the concept of "low-hanging fruit," relatively small changes that could be effected quickly and easily, so as to keep up with the teams' hunger for change, but generally speaking, the most dissatisfying part of our whole system was the pace and extent of change. Everyone knows change is painstakingly difficult, but I was constantly amazed at just how difficult it is. There is no shortcut to systemic, transformative change. Rethinking regulative rules is easy; revisiting constitutive rules is not, especially if it involves knowledge from both parts of the pincer, Jewish and secular wisdom.

> *P*eople became excited at new ideas, were thrilled to become Jewishly literate, and took ownership of their synagogue's problems from a new perspective: sacred stewardship rather than secular caretaking.

5. *Check-in*. Nothing proved as important to the meeting ambience as our insistence that no business be done until everyone in the group briefly responded to the question, "How are you?" We thereby created a healing environment from the outset. People often had little to report, but on one occasion, a woman said, "My mother was just diagnosed with breast cancer." In another instance, a man shouted joyfully, "I got a job!" In ordinary committee meetings, the woman would have sat quietly, hardly daring to interrupt and announce her bad news. And men feel famously guilty when they are fired and

out of work. But we ritualized the possibility of saying what normally goes unsaid, except in the hallways and behind closed doors. In the first instance, the rabbi reached across to the woman to put his hand on her arm while the cantor led the group in a prayer for healing. In the second, the group had been following the job hunt for several months, offering encouragement, and now celebrated with a resounding cry of congratulations.

It is a patent truth that people who share each other's joys and sorrows are reluctant to cause each other pain. Discussions of synagogue business take on a sacred quality when you appreciate the life of even your worst critic. People shout less, take pride together more. I am not surprised, then, that of all our meeting innovations, check-in has been the one most replicated within other synagogue structures. In some congregations, committees and boards customarily do it. One congregation even does it in the synagogue school.

When I was a rabbinic student in the 1960s, one of my professors reported on a board retreat at a well-known synagogue where a fishbowl exercise was featured. Two board members sat in the middle of a circle pretending they were alone one night chatting about life while everyone else looked on from the margins "listening in." They were shocked to hear the first speaker discuss what his life had been like when he was released from Hitler's camps barely alive. The second speaker echoed their surprise when he said, "You and I have attended the same monthly board meetings for fifteen years; I never knew you were even in the Holocaust. How could you not have told me?" The first speaker replied, "Well, I guess you never asked."

At the center of Synagogue 2000 is a different way of being with each other. We met not just to do business, but to share food, study, pray, and stay in touch with each other's lives.

I will not forget the reaction of the taxi driver who drove team representatives in shifts to the Los Angeles airport. When he returned for his second set of passengers, he remarked, "I don't know what you did here, but I have never seen anyone so anxious to stay rather than return home." We did much very well, but most of all, we built sacred community, a culture of honor, not of blame.

Concepts from This Chapter

Gifts: Our individuality and artistry that can be recognized, nourished, and directed toward the enrichment of others, all in service to a transcendent cause far beyond any of our individual selves.

Didactic intervention: Intervention that passes knowledge along on a one-way street. It is entirely top-down and assumes a giver and a receiver, with the giver knowing everything and the receiver passively taking it all in.

Consultative intervention: Intervention that uses observations and questions to elicit clarifying answers. Consultancy is bottom-up and treats the client-institution as if it has the necessary knowledge within itself.

Negative and positive motivation: With negative motivation, we face up to problems (often against our will) for fear of what will happen if we do not. With positive motivation, it occurs to us that it might be worth trying a new approach. In Jewish terms, negative motivation is *yirat shamayim*, "for fear of heaven"; positive motivation is *lishmah*, pursuing a course of action "for its own sake."

Activities and Topics for Discussion

1. At a board retreat, Sisterhood/Brotherhood weekend away, or other synagogue gathering, scatter card-stock sheets on the floor, each one containing an adjective or phrase indicative of a personal gift (e.g., artistic, politically active, caring for a loved one), with several copies of each. Instruct people to pick up a word/phrase they feel describes them. Form affinity groups by word/phrase and ask members of each group to share with one another a story about themselves that relates to the personal gift they identified.

2. Review the checklist of Synagogue 2000 meeting practices, and evaluate the practices of a particular committee with which you are involved. Did the last meeting include prayer? Food? Study? Action? Check-in? At upcoming meetings of the committee, gradually introduce those components that had

been missing. At the end of each meeting, conduct a brief evaluation to reflect upon how the new practices change the atmosphere of the meeting and relationships among committee members.

5
Sacred Community

Synagogue members can be divided into *marginals* or *watchers,* and *regulars* or *loyalists*. Marginals rarely attend anything, and when they do attend, they watch from the margins because they know so little about what is going on. Regulars are people who sit on committees and come to everything. They are fiercely loyal to the synagogue that would not exist without them.

Ask marginals why they join a synagogue, and you get the laundry list of limited liability expectations. Ask regulars, however, and a higher order of need gets mentioned: community. They do not mean "Jewish community" in the descriptive sense that merely denotes the Jews in town as opposed to the Protestants and Catholics. They use it normatively, almost mythically, to point proudly to a particular kind of relationship that characterizes their synagogue.

But what kind of community are they talking about? There are many kinds of community.

KINDS OF COMMUNITY

"Once upon a time," when we enjoyed uncomplicated village life with closely knit extended families determining our identity, we took community for granted. I say "once upon a time" because fairy tales start that way, and the halcyon days of village community, though real, were not as glorious as we imagine. Family historian Stephanie Coontz remarks:

Whenever people propose that we go back to the traditional family, I always suggest that they go back to a ballpark date for the family they have in mind. Once pinned down, they are invariably unwilling to accept the package deal that comes with their chosen model. Some people, for example, admire the discipline of colonial families which were certainly not much troubled by divorce or fragmenting individualism. But colonial families were hardly stable: High mortality rates meant that the average length of marriage was less than a dozen years. One-third to one-half of all children lost at least one parent before the age of twenty-one; in the South, more than half of all children aged thirteen or under had lost at least one parent.[1]

So, too, "uncomplicated village life" was constraining: roles were fixed; "misfits" could not escape reproach; closely knit extended families were wonderful, but only if you liked your family. Still, my contrast between the "once upon a time" and the way things are today is accurate enough to help us see how the mystical sense of community represents an attempt to recover the lost sense of belonging that did indeed come with *natural* communities.

"Once upon a time," then, in the villages that made up America, pretty much everyone was part of *natural* community of not more than a few hundred souls, organized around a central church (for Jews, a synagogue). They could easily walk there, and it seemed unthinkable not to conduct one's life according to its precepts and rituals. That changed with the great migration that swelled our urban populations—between 1880 and 1910, New York's population went from 1,200,000 to 4,766,000, and Chicago's from 503,000 to 2,285,000. But on the eve of that migration (1880), farmers still made up 43 percent of the labor force, and even at the dawn of World War I, most Americans still lived in small towns or farming villages, into which they had been born and where they eventually died. A convenient image that captures this kind of community is the general store, where people gathered to get the news, exchange gossip, and leave messages.

Without television, people saw little of the outside world; without airplanes, they rarely traveled far. Newspapers reported local affairs. As late as the battle for civil rights in the 1950s, southerners objected to northern "meddlers," not just because they threatened the southern way of life, but because citizens of Selma, Alabama, or Meridian, Mississippi, thought that people from up north had no right interfering in local southern affairs.

From the day they arrived in North America, Jews were urbanized more than the population at large. As a benchmark date, take 1846, the year Isaac Mayer Wise, the founder of American Reform Judaism, arrived. Fifty-five percent of Americans were farmers. But neither Wise nor the vast majority of Jews arriving with him went into farming. Instead, they followed the railroads west (the transcontinental railroad was not finished until 1869, but railroads linking east and midwest were being constructed as early as the 1830s). Other Jews followed canal and river systems, moving south, joining those who had landed there directly via the port of Galveston. In either case, they settled in small-town communities as merchants and participated in the sense of local permanence. West coast Jewry is largely the product of the gold rush of 1849–1850, when Jews arrived as peddlers and merchants.

What the general store was for farmers, the synagogue was for Jews—the taken-for-granted social centerpiece of their lives. Everyone joined, and at least on occasion, everyone showed up. The scene evokes the old Jewish joke: Schwartz says, "I don't go to *shul* to talk to God. But my friend Klein goes there to talk to God, and I go there to talk to Klein." As a distinctive minority, the Jewish community was to some extent natural. You could theoretically leave it by converting out, but it wasn't easy and most people didn't do it.

In large cities, where it was impossible for all Jews to know each other and feel part of a single community, ethnicity and immigrant memories established natural community. When my wife's family moved to Toronto from their *shtetl* in Poland, they took up residence near each other, often living in the same house. They loaned each other money, socialized together, and marked Jewish holidays at each other's tables. They came here along with individuals from other families, *landsleit* (as they were called), who were not actually blood relatives, but who had been part of the same community back home and who enjoyed "as-if" family status here too. I never could get straight just who was related to whom and how, but it didn't matter. They were all likely to be present at any given time to celebrate a wedding, make a *shivah* call, or just hang out for afternoon tea. Their children, however, moved farther away from each other and chose to be identified with friends and fellow workers. The immigrant natural community has no staying power.

To the extent that they took their American citizenship seriously, the immigrants were also part of a *civic* community, the town or city where they lived. It was the larger address where you did business, made acquaintances (if not good friends), and did your civic duty. You were more or less expected to participate in local ritual events. Many older Americans can still remember Memorial Day parades to local cemeteries. Everyone went to honor the dead and, while they were at it, to communicate a common set of beliefs that bound the entire town together in what has been called "civil religion."[2]

If they owned shops on Main Street, Jews were likely also to become part of a *market* community of merchants who banded together for business purposes. They established codes of fairness and honored the civic community's notions of right and wrong—closing on Sundays, for example. Sometimes they established a chamber of commerce to attract new business and market shopping opportunities. Market communities, however, are tenuous things, since they last only as long as individual members agree to curtail their entrepreneurial passion. The two shoe stores in town would theoretically want to put each other out of business, if they could. But out of common interest, they agree to coexist rather than engage in a price war that would ultimately hurt them both. Like civic communities, the old-fashioned market communities that depended on personal shopkeeper relations are mostly gone now. Among other things, chain stores make owners into managers, who just implement decisions made far away, and malls locate stores in impersonal settings, where community cannot even be imagined. But not too long ago, a Jew was likely to belong to a natural community, a civic community, and a market community, all at the same time.

The *limited liability* community to which I have referred is a kind of market community. The original market community was a social contract among sellers. The limited liability community establishes a relationship between sellers and buyers. If I have children in the public schools, I am likely to be active in the parent-teacher organization. The PTO serves many purposes: it is where young parents meet each other, and in some cases, it is also the first organizational foray into local politics. But it owes its existence to the primary purpose of providing quality education in town. If I attend meetings regularly, I hold it responsible for issues of schooling—not for other needs I might have. If I want to work out, I join the Y or a health club, which I hold responsible for having workout equipment, but not my children's blackboards and chalk. Most of us belong to many such limited liability organizations. We divide our life among them, deciding how much time and effort to put into any single one. For each, we have a theoretical list of expectations in mind. On busy days, we shuttle back and forth among them all, going from a meeting here to an appointment there, checking our satisfaction quotient to decide if it is still worth "paying dues"—both the money and the time that it takes to belong.

There are other specialized communities as well. *Academic* communities support scholarship. Members demonstrate their right to belong by reading or publishing professional papers. *Therapeutic* communities bring together people with common problems—Alcoholics Anonymous, for example. Professors giving papers argue with each other, unconcerned for how opponents feel when the debate is over. AA members never argue with each other and care deeply about how everyone feels.

Sociologist Robert Wuthnow differentiates communities from assemblies. People *assemble* for concerts, political debates, and marches—anything with a common end in mind. But the assembled crowd comes and goes; it has no sense of permanence. We do not actually *belong* to an assembly. But we do belong to a community, which presupposes "a supportive set of interpersonal relations."[3] Community type is determined by the quality of those relationships. Natural and civic communities, once the norm, are gone now. In their place, we create *communities of choice*, which differ precisely in the "supportive set of interpersonal relations" they offer.

We can now look specifically at synagogues and ask what kind of community the synagogue has been and what kind of community we want it to become.

For much of American history, at least in small towns where Jews were a tiny self-conscious minority, synagogues were *natural* communities. When I was a child, growing up in such a town in southern Ontario, pretty much everyone belonged to the synagogue. People who didn't join attracted negative gossip, until eventually they stopped identifying as Jews. In part, therefore, the synagogue was also a Jewish *civic* community: where Jews were just expected to do their Jewish civic duty, attending rallies for Israel, raising money for Jews abroad, and educating the next generation. As a natural and civic community for Jews, the synagogue also offered entertainment, visiting speakers, a social life, and a variety of other things that had nothing specifically to do with religion.

In big cities, synagogues were not nearly as popular. In 1919, less than a quarter of Jewish families in America belonged to synagogue. A 1926 census counted only one synagogue for every 1,309 Jews.[4] The immigrant population, still largely ghettoed off in significant Jewish areas of settlement, didn't much need what synagogues offered.

The boom years for synagogues came only with the post-war move to the suburbs, as part of the good-citizen religion preached by Eisenhower. Besides, as newcomers to American suburbs that were not always anxious to have them, Jews needed a safe place "to be Jewish." These are the synagogues that became oriented to "needs" and devolved into limited liability service communities. Rather than being integral to a Jew's existence, they occupied only a little corner of the larger lives that its members were leading at home, at work, and in the community.

As we saw, the suburban 1950s and '60s created synagogues that catered to baby-boomer children and their parents. To provide Jewish schooling for kids and advice for parents, rabbis were becoming religious educators and counselors. But the synagogue did not on that account become suffused with anything deeper than education and counseling as services in return for dues. Just dabbling in continuing education, it stopped short of being an academic community. And it never fully became a therapeutic community either. For significant problems, Jews found professional therapists. As formalized centers for services, rather than places of intimacy and warmth, synagogues became the last place where people would let down their emotional guard.

The synagogue became so market-oriented that even architecturally it was deployed into zones that reflected discrete market offerings: a school wing with its own entrance and exit; an altogether separate youth lounge; a separate door and foyer that admitted you to the praying space, and a corridor set aside for business dealings with the offices. Only, the inner circle, the regulars, thought the synagogue succeeded at bonding people together as an extended Jewish family—the community that synagogues claimed to be. For them the claim was true. Regulars, remember, are the stalwarts who plan and attend everything; they are the social network facilitated by committees; they travel together to attend synagogue conventions; they are on a first-name basis with the rabbi. For them, the synagogue really is a warm and cozy place. As loyalists, they defend the synagogue by asking, incredulously, why the marginals never show up.

A similar question arose when the synagogue was a civic community, but then the issue was Jewish duty. In the post-war market synagogue, the issue became the quality of programming that the synagogue provided. "Why don't the marginals come?" meant "Why don't they see how wonderful our Jewish programming is?"

The conflict between loyalists and marginals arises from a mutual misunderstanding of the synagogue as community. Loyalists do not see how they themselves have marketed their synagogue beyond their own inner ranks as a market community. But market communities make members into consumers, and consumers do not feel obliged to shop each week just because the department store in town really does carry good merchandise.

The conflict between loyalists and marginals arises from a mutual misunderstanding of the synagogue as community. Loyalists do not see how they themselves have marketed their synagogue beyond their own inner ranks as a market community. But market

communities make members into consumers, and consumers do not
feel obliged to shop each week just because the department store in
town really does carry good merchandise.

Moreover, synagogue "marketing" is aided and abetted by
denominational headquarters:

> Congregations [says Robert Wuthnow] are the most decep-
> tive of all religious institutions. They refer to themselves as
> communities and try to cultivate an atmosphere of collegial-
> ity and informality, yet they are formal institutions through
> and through.... In an earlier time, when hamburgers were still
> being served up by the local mom and pop cafe, most
> churches were already part of vast franchise operations that
> would put McDonalds to shame. Denominational hierarchies
> helped decide where new churches should be located ... and
> in return, these outposts of the soul sent back portions of their
> income to denominational headquarters.[5]

At the level of denominational membership, then, the market model
is at work. Individuals pay dues to synagogues, expecting programs
and services in return; synagogues pay dues to denominations, expecting the same thing. In both cases, members consider leaving when
they no longer need, or decide they cannot afford, what the parent
organization offers.

That became especially true by the 1980s. Raised with a sense of
entitlement, baby-boomers, now grown up, found a panoply of ways
to spend their money on themselves, not on obligatory memberships
and charities, and by the '80s, they were caught up in a national tax-
payers' revolt that came with Reaganomics. They continued to give
money to emergencies—saving Jewish lives abroad and supporting the
State of Israel—but less and less did they feel, as their parents had,
that it was important, as a matter of principle, to sustain the local synagogue; equally, synagogues (now run by the baby-boomers) questioned their financial contributions to denominations. Synagogues
and denominations were not just market communities now; they were
market communities in trouble. Denominations responded first by
urging their member congregations to become "caring congregations"

and, to that extent (though they didn't say so), transcend a market mentality.

Two sets of circumstances combined to make synagogues care about care. First was a weakening of family, Jewish, social, and synagogue ties. In what *Business Week* called "the second war between the states," tax monies were diverted from the rust belt and frost belt to the sun belt, where Jews, like everyone else, were relocating. But moving heralded more than a yen for the sun or the wide open spaces. It announced freedom from old-time family and ethnic obligations, including the mandate to support the Jewish community.

The second contributing factor was the Reaganomic shift of responsibility for supporting the lonely, the sick, and the elderly to local communities without giving those communities money to pay for it. It came just when divorce was on the rise, and baby-boomer parents, if not altogether aging yet, were at least increasingly lonely, separated from children and grandchildren who had moved away. Synagogues, it seemed, might fill the developing vacuum in care.

But the call to become caring communities did not blossom into synagogue transformation. Attempts at making over synagogues into places of care rarely went beyond marketing these initiatives as simply more and better deliverables in return for dues. Transformation is predicated on thinking differently, and that came only in the 1990s, with a generational changeover in rabbinic leadership.

In 1990, a child born in the first of the baby-boom years (1945) turned forty-five. By 1990, then, the earliest-born baby-boomers were attaining senior leadership positions in synagogues. Ever since the '60s, they had opposed their parents' suburban lifestyle—what Riv-Ellen Prell has labeled "Americanized consumers" of denominational bureaucratic religion.[6] Baby-boomer rabbis now found themselves running their parents' synagogues, and in a position to change them. When Synagogue 2000 came upon the scene, we were greeted most warmly by those among this next generation of rabbis who knew their synagogues lacked all but perfunctory community, and needed an ally in transforming them into something more substantial. In response to calls from the national organizations, most had already embraced the idea of being caring communities, but knew that as a program alone, even caring fell short of creating a transformed institution.

But "caring" was spawning "healing," so that (as we saw) one of Synagogue 2000's first concerns was making the still peripheral idea of healing into a genuine constitutive rule of synagogue life.

Healing was just one initiative that sought to change the nature of the market community. The other, which came far easier to Jews (because it tapped traditional values of study), was to create communities of learners, a project undertaken most notably by the Hebrew Union College's Rhea Hirsch School of Education, in its Experiment in Congregational Education (ECE). Like healing, adult study in congregations was conceived only as another program. In her account of the Experiment, Isa Aron went further, faulting the very way we think about synagogue education.

> *U*nimaginative risk-aversive rabbis will take advantage of nothing that comes their way from the outside. Creative rabbis who know their rabbinate is not designed for mediocrity are quick to sign up for everything their unimaginative colleagues do not.

The supplemental synagogue school had been modeled after public education. The 1970s had seen attempts to increase its effectiveness. Now Aron called for a "more radical" solution, "involving the totality of congregational life, rather than being limited to the congregational school as a self-contained entity."[7] Since then, the findings of ECE have been made public,[8] so I need allot no further detail here, except to say that about the same time Synagogue 2000 was undertaking thorough systemic revision of synagogue life, Aron and her colleagues were doing the same thing, but centering on learning. Communities of Jewish learning were an alternative to communities of healing.

Both Synagogue 2000 and ECE appealed to baby-boomer senior rabbis who were looking for guidance in their inchoate striving to make over their synagogues. Unimaginative risk-aversive rabbis will take advantage of nothing that comes their way from the outside. Creative rabbis who know their rabbinate is not designed for mediocrity are quick to sign up for everything their unimaginative colleagues do not.

In retrospect, given what both ECE and Synagogue 2000 were able to offer, I find it striking how unable the denominational movements were to transcend the market paradigm. Though they grasped the need for healing and learning, they are staffed to invent programs, not ideas. Their conventions are filled with "how to do," not "how to think." But changing the nature of a community requires more than an instruction booklet handed out at a workshop. To be sure, at least at the beginning of a paradigm shift, even forward-looking people who sign on need step-by-step guides toward realizing the new vision. But the guides alone do not suffice. Even the finest mechanic's manual will not suffice to fix a car if you have no conceptual model of what it is to drive anything other than a horse.

So synagogues formed caring committees and increased adult classes. But they did not create *communities* of healing and of learning. Synagogue 2000 sought to embed healing and learning in a new form of community, what we called at first a "community of the spirit."

RELIGION AND SPIRITUALITY

Americans are deeply divided over religion, in a way that Europeans are not. In Europe, established churches have become virtually insignificant. Most Europeans, even in places like Italy and Ireland, once bastions of Roman Catholicism, claim no religion at all. The conflict in Europe, therefore, is between religion and its absence. Not so America! Regularly, more than 95 percent of Americans claim belief in God. Since the 1950s, "God" has appeared on our currency and in our Pledge of Allegiance. We open Congress and football games with prayer. Presidents go to church—or they wouldn't be president. The first (and so far, only) Jew to appear on a national presidential ticket was outspokenly religious. As public shows of religion rise, the American divide revolves about the extent to which religion ought to shape the public moral landscape.

But even that divide is not the one I mean here. There is another divide more long-standing and immediately relevant to synagogues: the endemic conflict between institutional and privatized religion. Our values are such that everyone is expected to be religious, and most people say they are. But except for pockets of right-wing religion that are expanding dramatically, Americans increasingly believe in God but not churches and synagogues—which they happily leave, even as they claim they are following religion's inner voice. They differentiate religion from spirituality.

The trend goes deep. It can be traced all the way back at least to the eighteenth century, when "religion of the heart" successfully challenged organized religion in related developments spreading from England to Poland. Hasidism's hero, the Baal Shem Tov, has his Christian parallel in John Wesley, the founder of Methodism; both men preached to illiterate farmers outside official religious structures, telling them God wants the heart.[9] Indeed, some of the stories told about Wesley and the Baal Shem Tov are almost the same.

Individualistic spirituality is therefore nothing new. It may even be innate to the religious enterprise that, on the one hand, institutionalizes the search for God and, on the other, wonders if God shuns institutionalization altogether. But it has been especially evident in American culture, ever since Ralph Waldo Emerson (1803–1882) abandoned his orthodox Unitarian pulpit because he believed that self-reliance, not organized religion, was the key to the kingdom, for "nothing can bring you peace but yourself."[10] The great American poet, prophet, and iconoclast Walt Whitman (1819–1892) concurred. "The flights and sublime ecstasies of the soul," he held, "cannot submit to the statements of any church or any creed."[11]

In 1901–'02, William James popularized the divide in his widely read *Varieties of Religious Experience*. As James saw it, religious insight comes from spiritual geniuses who attract disciples; they, in turn, produce groups of sympathizers, who harden into aspiritual ecclesiastical institutions. "The new church," he cautioned, "can be counted on as a staunch ally in every attempt to stifle the spontaneous religious spirit."[12] Prayer, which is "the very soul and essence of religion," should not be confused with what churches do in their "vain exercise of words" or "mere repetition of sacred formulae." True worship is the "very movement of the soul," and "where this interior prayer is lacking, there is no religion" altogether.[13]

The Great Awakening at the beginning of the nineteenth century had actually tried to reassert the immediacy of religious experience that churches lacked and spiritualists missed. But by midcentury, denominations had tamed evangelical fervor. Then, in the 1890s, old-time religion had given way to the "social gospel," a response to the massive social dislocation of the great migrations that made Poles, Italians, and Jews the backbone of our nation's workforce in slums like New York's Lower East Side. By then another awakening was under way to rescue personal spirituality. But it, too, failed. Until relatively recently, as a result of the latest awakening that began in the 1960s, denominational religion has ruled unchallenged.

Jews emulated the organizational side of American religion. Like Unitarians, Episcopalians, and Presbyterians, we formed denominations. The Christian social gospel of the 1890s had its Jewish parallel in prophetic Reform Judaism, its manifesto appearing as the *Union Prayer Book* in 1894–95.

By the 1920s, evangelical spirituality was distancing itself from mainline church denominations that had begun to coexist with secularism. In 1924, for example, Helen and Robert Lynd began their classic and monumental sociological study of "Middletown" (Muncie, Indiana) and found Sunday being transformed from a Christian Sabbath to a weekend holiday. Mainline churches were leaving personal spirituality far behind—as were American synagogues, which had never really known evangelical fervor to begin with, so fully ethnic was their focus. Judaism was an ethnic identity, not a spiritual hope. By the 1950s, Jews, like Christians, were suburbia bound, franchising the very unspiritual synagogues that Wuthnow describes.

Suburban synagogue life in the making could be seen in a 1947 symposium that gathered together an outstanding panel of architects to pioneer a new kind of synagogue space. No longer structures that revolved about a central sanctuary (the old inner-city model), they would feature massive school wings zoned off from tiny prayer places with expanding walls that open for High Holy Day seating.[14] Those were the glory days for Riv-Ellen Prell's denominational bureaucratic religion, the synagogues that baby-boomer rabbis would someday want to spiritualize.

Emerson and Whitman (in the nineteenth century), James (at the turn of the twentieth century), and Wuthnow (at the turn of the twenty-first) share a common complaint about such organized religion. The difference is that only Wuthnow, himself a churchgoer, imagines things differently. His critique is based on evidence of falling affiliation in mainline churches, but rampant spiritual search everywhere else: nature, support groups, ashrams, yoga, running, bicycling. He champions the megachurch phenomenon, with its small groups, the prototype of Synagogue 2000's Jewish Journey Groups. I said earlier that I first approached the Nathan Cummings Foundation for help with synagogues in 1985, only to be told that synagogues are beyond repair. Tellingly, I can add this detail here: I was offered money instead to establish a series of Jewish sweat lodges, hardly what I thought to be the future of American Judaism. I turned it down.

A decade after that, things had changed enough for the same foundation to support synagogues after all. That implied capitalizing on American trends toward spirituality in general. So Synagogue 2000 sought to remake synagogues into spiritual communities, a trend in mainline churches as well. Summarizing three years of research into denominational, largely liberal churches that parallel our synagogues, Diana Butler Bass reports the steady move to "a God-centered, prayer-centered church, as opposed to a program- and belief-centered church."[15] Imagine a Jewish God- and prayer-centered community instead of a program-centered one. What would that look like?

IN SEARCH OF THE SPIRITUAL

Everyone is in favor of spirituality, one would think. Indeed, lots of Synagogue 2000 participants recognized readily that by concentrating on programming to enhance synagogue busyness, we Jews were missing a spiritual boat that left the dock some time ago. Others, however, rolled their eyes in evident distrust of the very word "spirituality," which is problematic for Jews who were raised with Judaism as their ethnic identity and who built synagogues with institutionalized ethnicity at the center.

We saw in chapter 1 how the word has taken on several meanings, coming eventually, by the 1960s, to denote what Buddhists or Hindus do in the East, as opposed to what Catholics and Protestants do in the West. Most of these usages have been reactive, not proactive; like Emerson, Whitman, and James, they rail against the "aspir-

itual" ways of "established churchiness." But we now have positive
definitions as well. Twelve-step programs use "spirituality" to mean
"connection to a higher power." Catholics relate it to personal and
interior connectedness to God. New age religion uses it for connection
to the earth. In healing circles, it often means inner connectedness, a
sense of personal wholeness. In each of these cases, however, "spirituality" connotes "connectedness," the opposite of the alienated and
fragmented feeling that afflicts us.

At stake are many things we can do nothing about—an expanding information technology, for instance, that keeps most of us working even when we are not technically "at work." But equally at fault
is the virtual monopoly of limited liability market communities—not
just synagogues, but health spas, tennis clubs, community pools, even
neighborhood security organizations—that we patronize for what we
can get from them, not because civic virtue moves us to belong.

Market communities contribute to social fragmentation. More
than a century ago, Emile Durkheim, a founder of modern sociology,
predicted a higher rate of suicide in a market community, because its
citizens would have no experience of solidarity with others. More currently, anthropologist Mary Douglas describes the market community
as a place where we are spun loose from commitments to other people and from assumed rules of conduct; when it comes to other people in the market, you can count on nobody and on nothing. Today's
fascination with spiritual experience is a response to the entrepreneurial loneliness of market society.

As a start, then, Synagogue 2000 adopted the position that whatever authentic Jewish spirituality is, it can find its way into synagogues only if synagogues cease being communities that people join as
consumers, buying services with dues. Yet when we spoke of transforming synagogues into spiritual communities, the word "spiritual"
often proved too big a hurdle to get over. When we mentioned "spirituality," too many Jews looked at us quizzically or even dubiously, as
if we were a Jewish Lewis Carroll inventing a "Jabberwockian" non-
existent substance in an effort to be trendy. I, myself, think spirituality no more vapid a concept than love, duty, conscience, hope, and a
whole lot of other things that we experience rather than define. I continue to use it, to the satisfaction of many. But old ethnic habits die

hard, and it seemed pointless to us to erect conceptual stumbling blocks that only got in the way of temple presidents and even rabbis, sad to say. We needed a word that Jews would more readily adopt as authentic and real. In addition, too many people saw spirituality as the opposite of social justice, as if someone must choose between feeding the poor and nurturing the soul. We wanted a recognizable Jewish concept that covered both. That is how we came to espouse communities of the sacred. But that raises another definitional challenge: what exactly is the sacred?

SACRED CAPITAL

William James was also a founder of American pragmatism, a perspective that trashed most classical philosophical arguments on the grounds that asking about the essence of things is worthless. Instead, James held, we should concentrate on the "cash value" of our ideas, the extent to which they prove useful for the human enterprise. James would have cautioned us against demanding a foolproof delineation of the spiritual altogether. So, too, with the sacred. Instead of requiring a definition, we should ask how a synagogue of the sacred has "cash value," how a particular set of acts, attitudes, and relationships that we call sacred will solve the problems that market communities pose.

James himself makes the intriguing suggestion that religious institutions will succeed only to the extent that "by adopting new movements of the spirit, they can make *capital* out of them and use them for their selfish corporate designs."[16] We can ignore James's polemical language ("selfish corporate designs"). What fascinates is his "cash value" concept of "making capital" out of "movements of the spirit." Substituting "sacred" for "spirit," we can conclude that we do not have to know in advance precisely what the sacred is, so long as we can find Jewish examples of it, and then "capitalize" their existence in ways that are useful for us.

I spoke in chapter 2 about institutional facts and the constitutive rules that make them up. Agreement on what counts as capital (cash or anything else) is such a fact; investing it is such a rule. The capital employed in synagogues as they are now constituted is programs. That is what synagogues "invest in." It is how they measure their worth. Programs attract dues and members. If the synagogue operated with the sacred as its capital, it would still have programs, insofar as programs are the delivery vehicle for what the synagogue does; but the programs would be driven by the capital that the synagogue recognizes: not the money people pay to attend them, but the degree of the sacred that the program embodies.

Capitalism has driven Western society throughout modern times, going back, according to some (founding sociologist Max Weber, for example), all the way to sixteenth-century Protestantism. It fueled England's Industrial Revolution and America's rise to prominence in the nineteenth and twentieth centuries. All attempts to replace capitalism with some other economic system have, so far at least, failed.

Precisely because capitalism has proved so potent, its underlying concepts have provided fertile metaphors for more than just the economy. Capital has come to mean any commodity that we invest, anticipating the generation of more of the same. The most obvious example is monetary currency: dollars, yen, and euros. But there are other kinds of investment capital too: intellectual, social, creative, human, religious, and spiritual, for example. Jewish sources suggest there must be sacred capital too. For synagogues, "sacred capital" is an idea whose time has come.[17]

Discussing all these forms of capital here would prove overwhelming. So for reasons of clarity, I will save *social*, *creative*, and *human* capital for the next chapter. My goal here is to investigate *sacred* capital, and to do that, we need look only at *intellectual* capital (as a model) and then *spiritual* (sometimes called *religious*) capital, which

The value of an organization changes when it recapitalizes with a different form of capital. Synagogues need to substitute "the sacred" for "busyness." With the sacred as its capital, programs would be driven by the capital that the synagogue recognizes: not the money people pay to attend them, but the degree of the sacred that the program embodies.

may sound related to sacred capital, but is really quite different. First,
then, what is intellectual capital?

The idea of intellectual capital emerges out of the economic shift
from production to information.[18] "If you want to know what a business is doing," advises Thomas A. Stewart, "follow the money."[19]
Capital spending for heavy machinery has held more or less steady at
$110 billion a year since 1982. But spending on information machines
went from $49 billion in 1982 to $112 billion in 1991 (when it sur-
passed industrial spending for the first time) and has continued to rise
thereafter. Every modern company is, therefore, increasingly in the
information business nowadays. But for a corporation to count as a
true knowledge company, information must be pursued for its own
intrinsic value, not simply to accomplish something else. The same is true
of capitalism in general. Capitalists pursue money for its own sake, not
simply for what it can buy. Our first lesson, then, is that any form of capital can and will be used to facilitate some further goal, but to be called
capital, it has to be pursued as an end in itself. Sacred communities
will pursue the sacred just for the purpose of pursuing it.

> Any form of capital can and will be used to facilitate some further goal, but to be called capital, it has to be pursued as an end in itself. Sacred communities will pursue the sacred just for the purpose of pursuing it.

Knowledge organizations process information, not inventory;
they hire minds, not hands. But how do you compute intellectual capital? It cannot be quantified, the way inventory can. This becomes a
challenge for traditional accounting. When companies are sold at
something higher than their book value, the discrepancy is put down
(arbitrarily) to "goodwill," which is to say, nothing countable at all.
More and more, however, accountants find it necessary to calculate
intellectual property, which is to say, intellectual capital.

So our second lesson is that the value of an organization changes
when it recapitalizes with a different form of capital. The worth of
sacred communities cannot be computed the same way market commu-

nities are. Separately pursued bar/bat mitzvah training and separately purchased High Holy Day tickets may be valuable for synagogues with limited liability consumers, but worthless in a community of the sacred.

But what exactly is intellectual capital? It turns out (as James and the pragmatists would have predicted) that it is hard to say for sure. Stewart reviews the usual definitions, only to conclude, in good pragmatic fashion, that they function more as descriptions than as definitions. The real question is how information becomes worthwhile as an asset, how it takes on "cash value." Take a list of addresses. The addresses alone are just random data, as useless as a pile of bricks someone leaves in your driveway: if you are building a wall, they are worth a lot; if not, they are junk that you pay to have carted away. Intelligence becomes a capital asset only when it can be put to use. Our example, the list of names, becomes capital only when it is designated as something: a mailing list, a database, or a list of people to be contacted for donations. Knowledge becomes capital only when it becomes useful.

Our third lesson, then, is that without stipulating how acts, attitudes, and relationships become sacred, we are left only with junk. How do these get packaged as useful in a sacred way?

> *The worth of sacred communities cannot be computed the same way market communities are. Separately pursued bar/bat mitzvah training and separately purchased High Holy Day tickets may be valuable for synagogues with limited liability consumers, but worthless in a community of the sacred.*

We now know how the sacred would count as capital. But what is the sacred? Pincer thinking comes in handy here. "Capital" is a secular category; "the sacred" is a Jewish one. We can see what the word "sacred" has entailed in Judaism and then "capitalize" it in measurable fashion.

First, however, we need to look more closely at the idea of "measurable." Measurement depends on what we decide to measure, and ascertaining the total quantity of whatever we decide upon depends on where we look for it. If you audit a factory, you look at hard assets, production costs, replacement value, orders placed versus costs per order, and so on. But what should we look at to audit the *sacred*?

Recent sociological literature is filled with discussions of *spiritual capital* (or, as it is sometimes called, *religious capital*),[20] so we may as well start there. Sacred capital is different, but at least it sounds the same, so understanding capital that is spiritual (or religious) might at least help us understand capital that is sacred.

The concept of religious capital derives from classic economics, which sought to establish what something is worth. From the perspective of the manufacturer, a thing's worth must include the cost of making it: purchasing the raw goods, for example, and buying and maintaining necessary machinery. But cost varies also with labor. Raw goods and machinery can more or less be capitalized precisely—they come with price tags. But labor cost is not so easy to reckon. In a family business, for example, workers may draw no salary at all.

A classic case is the story of Dominick the pizza maker. A pizza chain notices that Dominick makes a spectacular profit and buys him out, only to discover that the profit disappears. That is because Dominick's workers were his two sons, his wife, and a cousin, all of whom worked long hours to realize a family profit, part of which went to the cousin and part to Dominick. The buyer, however, had to pay workers the going hourly rate, whereas Dominick's family had worked "for nothing." So we need a concept beyond mere salaries to arrive at the human cost of production. Hence the idea of "worker capital," which is the additional human output that goes into making or selling anything.

Suppose, similarly, that we were able to capitalize religious behavior—to figure out the cost of producing spectacular worship services, for example. Again, we would compute costs of raw materials (buying prayer books) and upkeep (lighting the sanctuary). We could also figure the labor cost of custodian, rabbi, and cantor. But we would still have an overage of what volunteer time is worth. And even though any two rabbis or cantors might get the same salary, some produce better services than others.

To account for the different cost and value of professionals, we conceptualize something called *religious* capital, what sociologist Laurence Iannacone identifies as the skills, specialized knowledge, and experience that go into successful practice of a religion. For Jews that would include knowledge of Jewish law and custom, cantorial artistry, and the ritual know-how necessary to create worshipful moments. We compensate holders of religious capital with appropriate salaries, but translating religious expertise into monetary payments should not blind us to the fact that what we are paying for is indeed a different sort of capital—religious capital. Of late, the preferred word is "spiritual," a broader term that includes *any* spiritual commitment, not just to established religions.

We can now return to the notion of measurement. The problem here is that there are two ways to think about capitalism: the supply side and the demand side. On the one hand, capitalism is an attitude, the internal drive to use capital to make more capital. It is measured by the extent to which a society builds up capital, not by what its members use their capital to purchase. Since this psychological perspective emphasizes saving for its own sake, we can call it the *supply-side* view of capitalism.

But capitalism need not be motivated by the psychological need to save (the *supply side*); it can also be driven by consumerism, the need to satisfy our desire for buying things (the *demand side*).

Since synagogues as market communities came into being in a period of rampant consumerism, they naturally measure success by the demand side. Hence the accent on programs as capital. Programs are "valuable" to the extent that they attract buyers—measurable in the number of bodies that pass through the front door as dues-paying customers. The bottom line is the number of paying members, a sign of financial capital being passed from congregants to congregation. Synagogues as sacred communities would not have to do that; they could measure success by the sum total of sacred acts and relationships—not by what these acts and relationships buy (the consumer model = the *demand side*), but by how much our investing in them creates more of themselves (the *supply side*). This decision is in keeping with our first lesson mentioned earlier in the chapter: Any form of capital can and will be used to facilitate some further goal, but to call it capital, it has to be pursued as an end in itself. Sacred communities pursue the sacred just for the purpose of pursuing it. We shall see also, in a moment, that the supply-side definition accords perfectly with the Jewish definition of the sacred.

If we cannot measure sacred capital by a listing of programs, we will have to look for it somewhere else. Part of the task will be knowing where to look. It might already be there, but only tacitly and unrecognized. In the case of intellectual capital, for example, much of an organization's knowledge is tacit, but tacit knowledge may never be catalogued, since it is local, housed in people who may not even know they have it. It is the kind of information that is shared informally at the water cooler. Unavailable for large-scale consumption, it lacks immediate large-scale impact. It is like capital squirreled away under a mattress, rather than invested to bear interest. But once recognized, it may be very valuable. It may be miniscule (a handy bit of gossip about the boss) or global (a new way to think about a recurring problem).

Synagogue 2000 regularly found that synagogues had squirreled away sacred capital that was not being unearthed. Synagogues are not spiritual graveyards at all. It is just that, officially, they value (and therefore compute) other forms of capital, namely, programs. They publish them in synagogue bulletins, which can be thought of as institutional balance sheets, adding up programming activities and crediting the people who run them. But tacitly, synagogue resources include many wonderful people who do sacred acts all the time. Part of the challenge is to change the nature of what we publicize, letting people know that our particular synagogue is invested in the sacred, not the programmatic. We might, for example, ask ourselves what a synagogue bulletin dedicated to the sacred would look like.

Having determined that the sacred is measured on the supply side (how sacred acts and relationships multiply, not by how much they are worth in a consumer marketplace), we can turn to the Jewish definition of the sacred, so we know what to look for and invest in, in the first place. More precisely, we need to attend to the following three tasks:

1. Granted that sacred capital is sacred acts and relationships, what counts as sacred? It might mean different things for different religions, so we have to look at what the word "sacred" has entailed in Judaism.

2. We then must "capitalize" it according to specified deliverables (in acts and relationships), so that we can see if it is being invested to create more of itself.
3. Finally, knowing where to look for these specific deliverables, we could change our publicity system to draw people's attention to the synagogue's stock of sacred acts and relationships, rather than a list of its fee-for-service programs.

The first task, examining the word "sacred" in Jewish life and literature, constitutes the Jewish part of pincer thinking. Fortunately, Jewish sources are far from silent on that topic.

Anthropologist Levi Strauss has held that cultures are formulated with a bias toward various binary oppositions. A people living in the forest categorizes itself as lush, green, and verdant, as opposed to the desert that lies beyond the forest—by definition, dry, parched, and arid. Rudyard Kipling's England made its primary distinction Englishmen and natives. Ancient Greeks divided the world into Greeks and barbarians. Evangelicals know the saved and the unsaved. Jews know *kodesh* and *chol*.

Thinkers about Western religion usually translate that dichotomy as sacred and profane. Historian of religion Mircea Eliade, for example, romanticizes "the religious man" of prehistory who lived in close touch with the sacred, even for ordinary activities (like eating) that we normally consider profane.[21] Psychologist C. G. Jung celebrated "medieval man," who knew metaphysical certainty, rather than "modern man," who has replaced that with mere "material security," but at a cost to the psyche.[22] Both Eliade and Jung got their nostalgia from German theologian Rudolph Otto, whose *The Idea of the Holy* was something of a twentieth-century perpetual bestseller,[23] and Otto got it from Emile Durkheim, who had heard it from his father, the Grand Rabbi of Epinal, a town near the Alsatian border. The romanticism of writers after Durkheim mistranslated *chol* into the negative-sounding "profane," whereas the Jewish concept means simply "the everyday."

Sacred community, then, is not something one lives in permanently, and there is nothing wrong with the everyday (*chol*) times, places, and activities that constitute most of our life. There is, however, such a thing as sacred (*kodesh*) to be seen in time (Shabbat, festivals, Yom Kippur), things (Torah), and spaces (the ancient Temple in Jerusalem). The Jewish concept of the sacred is best expressed in an eighth-century prayer recited while lighting Chanukah candles, *Hanerot Ha'eilu* (we know it as *Hanerot Halalu*): "These candles are holy; we are not permitted to make use of them" (*Hanerot ha'eilu kodesh hem v'ein lanu r'shut l'hishtamesh bahem*). The everyday is what we use as means to ends. The sacred exists as its own end. That is why *Pirkei Avot* prohibits us from "using Torah as a spade to dig with" and why, technically, teachers of Torah are not allowed to get paid for what they do (their salary is considered payment for what they would have done had they been free to do something else)—Torah is sacred, after all. That is why, also, we may not use Shabbat as a day to work. Synagogues, too, are sacred, so the Mishnah prohibits using synagogue space as a shortcut. You can't go in the front door and out the back to avoid having to go around the block. And you can't do business in a synagogue either.

> The everyday is what we use as means to ends. The sacred exists as its own end. Sacred communities will pursue the sacred just for the purpose of pursuing it.

That does not mean that a sacred community cannot dedicate itself to further ends. Chanukah candles have an end larger than themselves: *l'farsomei nissa*, in the Talmud's words, "to proclaim a miracle." Torah, too, has an end. Rabbi Gordon Tucker notes that when we say we are studying *Torah lishmah*, we do not just mean Torah for its own sake (as we usually translate the phrase), but Torah for the end to which Torah is intended. Our morning prayer *Elu D'varim* (which comes from the Mishnah) lists a variety of such ends (reserving the corner of our fields for the poor, honoring parents, and so forth), concluding that Torah is equal to them all—that is to say, Torah, though sacred and not to be used for ulterior motives, nonetheless accomplishes these basic goods. Likewise the Temple was intended for sacrifice. Sacred community, then, is dedicated to certain tasks, but these can be realized only in a sacred ambience, not in a market community where people weigh value by the list of limited liability deliverables that they think their dues are buying. The synagogue is a place for pursuing Torah, worshiping God, sacralizing relationships, healing the sick, and feeding the poor. It is a place where we know the presence of God among us and honor each other as made in God's image. It is where we celebrate each other's sacred stories. It is where we emulate God.

Synagogue is not a building; it is the set of sacred relationships that constitute the community and the equally sacred acts that flow from it. I do not make light of the buildings. Father Dick Vosko, our expert in sacred space, who virtually invented his field, taught us much about how space either facilitates or negates relationships. He regularly drew attention to dysfunctional synagogue spaces, everything from the furniture arrangement to the flow

> Sacred community is an organization of relationships and acts by which we emulate God. Synagogue is that set of relationships and acts, not a building.

from the parking lot to the sanctuary. Doors with windows, for example, invite people in. Heavy oak doors give the message "Keep out." High pulpits create social distance between clergy and congregation, to which clergy respond by a formal, even frozen, style of speech— which only further alienates. Appropriately thought-out space is not an envelope into which people fit. It is an architectural representation of a congregation's story; it invites us into the life of the community that lives there. The synagogue building should facilitate the synagogue as a set of sacred relationships and acts.

Going back to the threefold task delineated earlier, we can say:

1. By sacred (*kodesh*), Jewish tradition means "nonutilitarian," even though benefits may accrue from it anyway.
2. We can capitalize the sacred by measuring the number of person-hours engaged in sacred acts.
3. We would look for sacred "deliverables" in the relationships among people and the integrity with which those relationships are directed to emulating God. In that context, we can speak

positively of programming. I have railed against measuring the synagogue's worth by programs, but I am not against programming. I object only to measuring a program's worth by the extent to which it justifies dues. A program may properly be assessed by observing how acts of the sacred are built into the programming fabric of a synagogue's time and budget.

A rabbi in one of our cohorts once described his busy synagogue: people are constantly coming and going for programs, he observed, but "in reality the synagogue is empty." Limited liability communities do not attract personal loyalty. We invest our time there, not ourselves. I may sit next to someone at Shabbat services, but not even know his name. Relationships remain shallow.

By contrast, sacred community reinforces connectedness and overcomes alienation. Its worth is measured in the sacred acts and relations that connect us to one another. These acts are nonutilitarian in their essence—we pursue them for their own sake. But they do have consequences: evoking love, respect, good deeds, mutual care, reverence for each other's stories—the things that provide true connectedness. So important was sacred community for Synagogue 2000 that we developed a curriculum on that subject alone and insisted that all synagogues begin with it before moving on to more specialized areas of our PISGAH vision.

Kabbalah designates the final *s'firah*, or "manifestation of God," as *K'nesset Israel*, "the congregation of Israel." In the experience of the everyday, we experience God and the universe as separate from each other. But that experience is no more real than the mistaken observation that a branch poked halfway into a river is bent. For that matter, most of our ordinary perception is similarly skewed. A heavy oak table, for example, is composed of atoms, so is very largely made up not of the solidity we experience it as, but of the empty space between the atomic particles. The kabbalists accepted our experience of separation as just such a perception—it is real enough, because it is how we feel, but simultaneously, we may intuit ultimate connectedness with God. Since the universe came into being as the end of the process of God's emanating into the void, creation and God are really two sides of the same coin. *K'nesset Israel* is therefore part of creation but also a primal stage in God's self-emanation. The synagogue as sacred community, not as building, is *K'nesset Israel*, connecting us in ultimate ways with God's universe and with God. Sacred community is therefore not just the sum total of sacred acts that the congregation does. It is equally the set of relationships among the members and with God.

Concepts from This Chapter

Loyalists or regulars: The members who sit on the committees, do the work, and attend most of the synagogue's programs. The opposite of loyalists or regulars is watchers or marginals.

Watchers or marginals: The marginal members who merely show up occasionally.

KINDS OF COMMUNITY

Academic communities: Scholarly communities where members demonstrate their right to belong by reading or publishing professional papers, and try their best to prove each other wrong.

Therapeutic communities: Communities for people with common problems, where members offer mutual support and distinctly try not to prove each other wrong.

Market communities: Communities that exist because they promise concrete benefits, not because they are so central to people's lives that their members cannot imagine belonging anywhere else.

Limited liability communities: A particular class of market community, offering specialized services for a fee, and the kind of community that most of us belong to today.

Sacred communities: Communities whose worth is measured in sacred acts and relationships that connect us to one another and to God.

TYPES OF CAPITAL

Intellectual capital: Information pursued for its own intrinsic value, not simply to automate or report on other activities.

Spiritual/religious capital: The extent to which people invest themselves personally in the skills and experiences of their religion with the purpose of providing religious opportunity for others.

Sacred capital: The number of person-hours engaged in nonutilitarian acts dedicated not to everyday pursuits, but to God's own ends.

Activities and Topics for Discussion

1. What would a synagogue look like if it were to operate not with programs but with the sacred as its capital? In thinking this through, determine how many new programs have been introduced at your congregation in the last two years. Look at the synagogue's printed materials that advertise them—newsletters, website, flyers, membership packets. Would someone reading those materials understand their relationship to the synagogue as sacred community?

2. What would a synagogue bulletin dedicated to the sacred look like? What would be on the front page? Who would be acknowledged? How and for what? What would the main headings be, and how would they read? Try your hand at writing copy for Shabbat worship. Would it announce services to come or reflect upon services that have happened? How would it read?

3. How are acts of the sacred built into the programming fabric of your synagogue's time and budget?

4. Consider a single sacred act in which your synagogue currently engages. How could sacred relationships be cultivated and nurtured around that sacred act: Sacred relationships with others? Sacred relationships with God?

5. The next time you attend Shabbat services, an adult education program, or other synagogue event, keep a lookout for "watchers" and pay special attention to their experience. How could they be spotted? What seemed to make them uncomfortable? How could "watchers" be made to feel more at home?

6. Put yourself in a position where you are a "watcher" by attending another synagogue or (better yet) a church where

you are unfamiliar with the local practice, and consider your experience. How did you feel? Where did you sit/stand? What was particularly uncomfortable? Why? Did anyone try to put you at ease? How? Did it work?

6

Sacred Culture, Sacred System

What the synagogue *is*—its people and their relationships—constitutes the community. How the synagogue *works*—the channels by which people communicate—constitutes the system. System determines relationship. Community follows from system.

The synagogue is not just a community; it is also an organizational system that makes the community possible. What the synagogue *is*—its people and their relationships—constitutes the community. How the synagogue *works*—the channels by which people communicate—constitutes the system. System determines relationship. Community follows from system.

TAYLORISM

The system synagogues struggle against is known as "Taylorism," a term deriving from Frederick Taylor, an engineer whose 1911 manifesto for totally rational institutions dictated (among other evils) hierarchical structures of management that have been described as "office factories."[1] They are recognizable by organizational charts that display a pyramid of little boxes, many small ones on the bottom row, occupied by workers who have been trained to do specifically defined tasks, and fewer larger ones toward the top, representing departments or managerial posts, to which the little boxes at the bottom report. At the top is a single large box for the CEO.

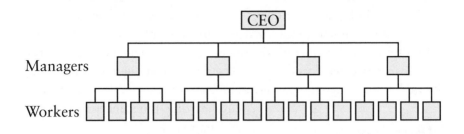

The boxes are properly iconic of reality: tiny cubicles at the bottom for the "lowest" level clerical workers; larger offices just above that for managers; and a penthouse office suite for the CEO, where ultimate responsibility for everything is lodged. Communication flows vertically, never horizontally, since workers are responsible for their own little self-contained tasks alone, so they have no need to know what inhabitants of other cubicles are doing.

Taylorism works reasonably well for organizations designed to do repetitive tasks that can be performed by interchangeable workers, like the proverbial Ford assembly line. It has been abandoned for some time now, in an economy that demands creativity, nimble decision making, and flexibility in a rapidly changing marketplace.

In truth, it should never have been adopted by synagogues—it runs counter to all the values synagogues ought to hold dear. But like everyone else, synagogue leaders of the first half of the twentieth century were certain that Ford's revolution in production was the wave of the future.

I cannot overstate the damage done by Taylor's machine-like bureaucracy. Far worse than its inefficiency at creative problem solving is the competition, suspicion, and distrust that it produces between laypeople and clergy; among clergy and fellow professionals; and among rival synagogues, who fight for turf rather than cooperate for a common Jewish future.

As a not-for-profit with a board and committees, the Tayloresque synagogue actually has two organizational pyramids, one for the volunteers and another for the staff. The former arrays a hierarchy of committees and subcommittees, answerable to the board. Inside the board, there may be an executive board, but, in any case, the board chair is at the top. The board fills the slots for the second hierarchy: a rabbi as CEO, and a variety of other people like a principal, cantor, and executive director, each of whom hires a staff. The rabbi CEO is held responsible for operations; she heads up management. As corporate boards oversee corporate management, synagogue boards evaluate rabbis. Some synagogues go so far as to create a "job description," emphasizing the concept of rabbis as employees.

*I*nstead of creating a shared working relationship, the corporate model creates the expectation that the board pays and rabbi prays.

But synagogues are not corporations. The board of Coca-Cola need not actually drink the stuff they market; synagogue boards, however, are expected to practice Judaism. The bizarre Tayloresque approach to synagogues elects board members who know management or finance, and are expected to be part of an oversight body charged with fiduciary responsibility, but who have no intention of attending services or Torah study. Instead of creating a shared working relationship, the corporate model creates the expectation that the board pays and rabbi prays.

But the synagogue need not turn a profit. How then does the board evaluate the rabbi? The usual measure is overall congregational satisfaction. As every rabbi knows, a thousand happy people rarely advertise their contentment, while one unhappy soul spreads bitterness everywhere. So rabbis are tempted to avoid decisions that might alienate anyone; they play it safe. In Synagogue 2000, we saw many rabbis who hesitated to make changes that would have benefited the majority of members, because they stood in mortal fear of a minority's potential displeasure.

Another measure of success, an objective one, is membership figures. So rabbinic decisions are made with an eye toward retaining old members and attracting new ones. The unsynagogued constitute a huge pool of potential members, which synagogues try to reach, usually as if it were a zero-sum game: a new member for one synagogue means the loss of that member to another. Indeed, when synagogues join movements, they buy the right to prevent "unfair competition" from setting up in the vicinity. To be admitted into a movement, synagogues must demonstrate to a denominational membership committee that they will not eat into a competitor's membership. Movements look askance at breakaway congregations.

Synagogues therefore exist in a steady state of potential competition. Rabbis tend to be loners, doing their CEO job from the top, but not always collaborating with neighboring rabbis doing the same thing. In one city, several congregations established a walk-in storefront address that offered opportunities for the unaffiliated to discover the joy of studying Torah. The coalition broke down when the sponsoring synagogues decided the storefront operation was becoming competitive with the synagogues' own offerings. In another case, a rabbi with two young children moved into town. As a stay-at-home mother, she was uninterested in full-time rabbinic placement. But she wanted to pursue some rabbinic work, perhaps teaching adults one or two nights a week; and she came with a sterling reputation as a teacher. No single congregation had a program large enough to warrant hiring her. But they were unable to band together and pool resources for an advanced Judaica offering that would have reached across congregations and movements, providing what no individual synagogue could offer alone.

In the Taylor system, synagogue dysfunction goes unrecognized, while individual staff members are demonized as the problem. The Taylor model thus prohibits cooperation, inculcates risk aversion, and masks problems by a culture of blame. The default situation wins the day.

When things go wrong in the Taylor system, members of the professional hierarchy blame the people below them. Rarely do all stakeholders in the synagogue—board, rabbi, cantor, educator—

see themselves as equally committed partners facing systemic problems that can be addressed without blaming anyone. Synagogue dysfunction goes unrecognized, while individual staff members are demonized as the problem. The Taylor model thus prohibits cooperation, inculcates risk aversion, and masks problems by a culture of blame. The default system wins the day.

No one consciously holds Taylor's view of synagogues as "bureaucratic factories" anymore, but the leftovers of his system continue to plague us.

SYNAGOGUE AS POLITICAL ARENA

Synagogue insiders frequently refer to a related organizational model that builds on the culture of blame: synagogue as political arena. Sometimes, this view is overlaid with Freudian dynamics—synagogues are not just political minefields; they resemble dysfunctional families as well![2] In this conflict model, it is assumed that players have private interests, either within the synagogue (the budget committee chair wants to become vice-president) or outside of it (the rabbi wants fewer nighttime meetings and more family time). Interests necessarily conflict (the budget committee chair can flex her institutional muscles and become a more credible candidate if she insists that the rabbi show up more, not less). Business requires strategic alliances (the rabbi subtly encourages the ritual committee chair to run against the budget committee chair for the vice presidency). The default position by all the players is wariness. Taylorism teaches the "virtue" of telling others only what they need to know to do their job, nothing more. The same is doubly true in political conflict. Since knowledge is power, players amass information on each other and avoid transparency.

To be sure, synagogues, like other organizations, experience conflict, often deriving from (1) rival role expectations; (2) generational chasms between old and new members—founders, for example, accuse newcomers of thwarting their original vision; (3) rivalry for a share of limited resources; and (4) symbolic issues, usually ritual in nature. By themselves, symbolic issues sound petty. They have been described as "conflict events" that involve "producers and an audience." People use them—even manufacture them—to bring into focus other, underlying issues that have been lying dormant but festering.[3] Secular organizations play this symbolic game also—fighting over who gets a corner office, for example. But religion is by nature more completely ritualized. Such symbols as who gets High Holy Day honors or who sits on the *bimah* are regularized public displays that easily become excuses over which deeper matters are fought.

So the question is not *whether* there are politics in synagogue life; there are politics everywhere. The question is whether the congregational board and professionals think of the system as *essentially* a political arena. If they do, they will develop self-perpetuating oligarchies that harbor power, let no one new in, and protect information from potential rivals.[4] Synagogues *can* become political arenas, but a political arena is only an institutional fact. If the players lay down their cudgels, they can manufacture other institutional facts instead.

The real problem is the conversation of mutual recrimination that Tayloresque and conflict models breed. A rabbi confides that she just cannot stand her educator; a president tells us that the rabbi is overprotective of his turf. In a sacred community committed to the proposition that we are all made in the image of God, the conversation changes—think of meetings that begin with personal check-ins to remind us of our sacred stories.

Political conflict sometimes becomes understandable as a clash in cultures. An example is the relationship between rabbi and cantor, which we found to be almost universally troubling.

CANTORS AND RABBIS IN CONFLICT

As clergy partners occupying a common pulpit, rabbi and cantor should see eye to eye on the worship they facilitate. But we found this frequently not the case. An essential difference in perspective runs deep and cuts across all denominations. It is rarely openly discussed or even acknowledged. Rather, it surfaces quietly behind the scenes. Regularly, rabbis took us aside to say their cantors are prima donnas who want only to hear their own voices. Cantors told us, equally privately, that rabbis neither understand nor value Jewish music. The problem is rooted in the different education the two clergypeople receive, exacerbated by the different levels of professionalization that govern their respective positions.

Professionalization is the socialization process by which personal idiosyncrasies are negated by the imposition of universally agreed upon professional standards. A trial lawyer and a forensic accountant may be altogether different in temperament and have different areas of expertise, but they are equally schooled in confidentiality and the roles of "appropriate" relationships to clients. Their respective schools provide tacit knowledge of professional behavior, so that when they go out to practice, they will obey the canons of their association, not the peculiarities of their own personality. Professionalization levels the playing field by making all doctors or all lawyers more or less the same in the way they view the goals and nature of their work.

In that regard, the rabbinate was professionalized long ago, when the various rabbinic schools were established in America. That is not true of the cantorate. Although some movements do train cantors professionally, it is still not unusual for would-be cantors to study with mentors and join professional organizations without formal cantorial schooling. Someone introduced as "rabbi" is almost always a bona fide graduate of a recognized rabbinic program. People who go by "cantor" may lack a cantorial degree.

After graduation, rabbinic and cantorial education continue in professional organizations, which (among other things) provide tacit knowledge of the values that inform their respective professional cultures, and which reinforce what was taught in school. Rabbinic culture is by now predictable, a result of the many waves of professional graduates taught in seminary and then mentored in the field by other professionals like themselves. It has certain universal qualities—respect for Torah, appreciation of the Jewish heritage, love of Israel, and so forth. It also includes a particularistic commitment to one's movement. Conversations may revolve about "the uniquely Reform approach to social action," "how Reconstructionism balances individual and community," or "the difference between Conservative and Orthodox halakhic process."

Not so cantors. Cantors usually begin their calling as undergraduates attending demanding music programs, singing daily in practice rooms; rabbis-to-be usually specialize in fields like Jewish studies or psychology and spend their discretionary time debating issues of Jewish life at Hillel or on staff at summer camps. So the cultural gap is already formed when the candidates arrive for admission to the seminary. Seminaries highlight rather than heal the rift, since (with few exceptions) the two clergy partners rarely study together. More to the point, rabbinic and cantorial teachers and alumni set different agendas for culture-constituting conversations.

At the New York School of Hebrew Union College, for example, every Wednesday features a public concert of Jewish music, after which the entire cantorial community assembles to discuss the program that has just been heard. Rabbinic classes are not allowed to compete with this sacrosanct community time, so that rabbinic students may attend. But only a handful of rabbinic students do so. More important, even if they want to, they cannot attend the cantorial conversation afterward, since classes resume by then, and in any event, they are not invited. But precisely there, cantorial culture is being formed. Were rabbis present, they would not understand the highly technical conversation at first. But they would see the high level of professionalization to which cantors hold each other responsible. They would grasp the cantors' high regard for the traditional patterns of synagogue music called *nusach*, their love for music of all sorts, and their fears that they may be presiding over a time when sophisticated Jewish music may be dying. These are the topics that animate cantorial conversation not just on Wednesday morning, but everywhere cantors go together for the rest of their cantorial lives. Rabbis are rightly perceived by cantors as knowing a mere smidgen about the music they want to influence.

Similarly, at public worship services every Thursday, a New York Hebrew Union College rabbinic student delivers a "senior sermon," after which the entire community is expected to attend a sermon discussion over lunch. Students give only one such sermon during their entire five years of schooling, and they give it to all their teachers and peers. The pressure to do it well is enormous. If the sermon is good, the conversation following is likely to feature faculty-student dialogue on one of the great issues of our time. But more important than the details of the discussion is its ritual nature designed to socialize students into rabbinic culture. It features the very things that rabbis value most: sermonic delivery and subsequent conversation over the merit of what the sermon said. But just as rabbis absent themselves from the cantorial conversation, so cantors rarely appear at the sermon discussion.

No wonder representatives of the two cultures find themselves in conflict once they share a synagogue *bimah*. To be sure, usually the two colleagues manage well together, either because they really do share certain deeply held values about Judaism and prayer or because the rabbi has already conceded control of services to the cantor (or vice versa). But Synagogue 2000 found that rabbis were overwhelmingly committed to overhauling services in order to make public prayer more participatory, while cantors fought to avoid being relegated to what they considered mere songleaders. When we attended cantorial conventions to explain Synagogue 2000, we discovered how threatening cantors considered us to be. Some cantors see themselves as a dying breed, like animals doomed to extinction; cantors at a Conservative cantorial convention wore badges saying "Chazanasaurus." No matter how often we repeated the message that we were not advocating doing away with the musical heritage that cantors see themselves as safeguarding, it took us eight years even to begin making an inroad into cantorial culture.

We did insist on expanding the cantorial repertoire of music and of skills so as to give congregants their voice; we were convinced that people do not want to be talked at, sung to, and generally excluded from full liturgical participation. And, by and large, we found cantors in the field unable to teach melodies, or even to choose them so as to maximize interactive opportunities for congregations intent on joining in. Only recently has that even been part of the cantorial music curriculum. Cantors counter the demand for participation by saying that listening is a form of participation, and for them it probably is. But I find the claim ingenuous, if only because it skirts the issue.

In actual fact, Synagogue 2000 was by no means opposed to the traditional Jewish musical canon. On the contrary. We preached the validity of Jewish music as authentic Jewish culture; we believed that once congregants find their voice, they are likely to appreciate solos, duets, and choral music. We told rabbis to school themselves in music no less than in midrash.

Enormous disparity in power separates rabbis from cantors. In political infighting, the rabbi usually prevails. Still, we heard horror stories from both sides. Rabbis thought cantors would stab them in the back; cantors said rabbis were out to fire them. In one or two cases, when we taught laypeople to expect participation in services, cantorial soloists, or even cantors themselves, decided to leave (or were asked to leave) their synagogues because they would not (or could not) accommodate the change. We eventually realized the importance of establishing cantorial conversation groups to develop genuine dialogue, but whether we (or anyone else) will successfully bridge the two cultures is still an open question.

Given the experience of America's churches, where engaging worship is becoming more and more important, we can expect issues of synagogue prayer to take on more and more significance, both practically and symbolically. If seminaries do not quickly come to terms with the disastrous split in culture they are perpetuating, rabbinic-cantorial conflict will increase, and we will all be the losers.

Rabbinic-cantorial conflict is endemic to synagogue life, because it reflects an underlying clash in culture, which is more intractable than differences in personalities or personal interests. Personalities come and go, but cultures are continually reinforced by training programs and peer group pressure. So it helps to think of the synagogue as something else again: neither a Tayloresque bureaucracy nor a political arena, but a culture.

SYNAGOGUES AS CULTURAL SYSTEMS

It has long been known that like peoples, tribes, and countries, organizations also have distinctive cultures. Anyone who has changed jobs knows that these cultures are hard to define, but harder to miss, at least for outsiders. Anthropologist Edward T. Hall describes overseeing government contracts with the Navajo in the 1930s. His predecessors had nothing good to say about "the Indians' slothfulness." They would arrive, issue orders, and observe the next day that nothing had gotten done. Hall realized the Navajo had a different view of time than the white government overseers did. The overseers rushed into the field, ordering people about in proper Tayloresque fashion, and then drove off, assuming their Navajo workers would comply. But Navajo culture does not work that way. So Hall changed the routine. He drove up, sat for a while smoking a pipe with the workers, and then, very slowly, discussed what had to be done. They did it.[5]

Cultures control how people think of time, space, relationships, authority—everything. It is simply a fact that people tend to cluster with other people who see the world the way they do. Columnist David Brooks reminds us, "Forty-million Americans move every year, and they generally move in with people like themselves.... Every place becomes more like itself. Crunchy places like Boulder attract crunchy types and become crunchier. Conservative places like suburban Georgia attract conservatives and become more so."[6] What goes for cities goes for congregations. Professor of religion James F. Hopewell chides leaders of congregations who pride themselves on the gamut of beliefs their congregants hold. "They are mistaken," he says. "In no congregation studied so far are world views of members so diverse that one could consider the church a mere aggregate of miscellaneous believers."[7] What Brooks and Hopewell are describing is culture.

Organizations have their own distinctive culture. and where systemic dysfunction persists, it is because it is culturally embedded.

Systemic dysfunction persists because it is culturally embedded. Some synagogues are accident-prone. They are "addictive organizations."[8] They may, for example, attract authoritarian rabbis and build symbiotic relationships that feed other neuroses of board members who do the hiring. Their cultures fill with suspicion and secrecy. Active congregants fall into the morass or leave. Those who stay (perhaps as addictive personalities themselves) attract others like themselves, so that the culture of conflict is constantly rewarded, even though any specific cast of characters (rabbis, presidents, cantors) comes and goes.

It helps to know the kind of culture you have. In size and style, synagogues may be what Alice Mann describes as *corporate* (400–500 members in attendance at any given service) or even larger, as opposed to *program* size (200–350 people in attendance) and *pastoral* (under 150 people there).[9]

A related basic divide is *private* and *public* religion. "Private" congregations cater to the spiritual life of their members. They offer a variety of worship patterns, either within one service or in several parallel *minyanim*. They are likely also to work hard at religious education, for children and for adults. Others pride themselves on connecting members socially and fostering family-like intimacy. People pursue personal needs in the first and make personal friends in the second; both are "private" in orientation. Valuing individuals, they personalize everything. Personal-need synagogues tend to be program size; family-like synagogues prefer pastoral intimacy.

Public synagogues are usually corporate. They stake out public claims in worship style or issues of conscience; they are the place you go to hear sermons on moral topics; they exchange pulpits with the local African American Church; they feature guest speakers on matters of moment. Some become *showplace* synagogues that famous people automatically join (whether or not they actually attend). They pride themselves on specific causes, like being "the social action synagogue" or "the synagogue with great music."

Cultures develop specific styles of governance. Public synagogues (especially of the showplace variety) vest power in senior rabbis, who are encouraged to speak to and for the congregation and to represent Judaism on a communal, interfaith, or even national scale. Showplace congregations may be altogether professionally driven, since they are likely to have the funds from many marginal members, who pay dues but ask nothing in return, and because displaying an appropriate public face may be assumed to be "too much to leave to amateurs." Public synagogues are likely to have very visible worship services, where guests drop in and the public simply knows that this is the place to go.[10]

A related divide is leadership style. Pioneer sociologist Max Weber singled out three leadership styles that are especially apt for congregational life, even today: charismatic, traditional, and rational. *Charismatics* pronounce, and, through the force of their charisma, people follow. All five exemplary synagogues in Sidney Schwarz's study of synagogue life have charismatic rabbis. But what happens for the vast majority of rabbis who lack such charisma?

Some find their way to systems that are *traditional*. Weber had in mind traditional monarchies where the reigning ruler has his way just because he is the monarch. So, too, some synagogues invest their rabbis with authority, no matter who they are personally.

But less and less is that the case. So we are left with Weber's third paradigm, the one that he correctly predicted would be central to modern life: *rational*. Decisions are determined by objective "rules, means, ends, and matter of factness," not by idiosyncratic edicts from all-powerful individuals. Their authority flows from what they are in the system not from who they are personally.[11] Weber was prescient. Rational leadership characterizes successful corporations and democracies. Synagogue transformation depends on how well rabbinic leaders work with laypeople, both of them thrust into leadership by a system of rational authority that Weber foresaw a century and a half ago.

Culture influences and is influenced in return by a congregation's ecological resources. All congregations need members, money, and leaders, says sociologist Mark Chaves.[12] When all is said and done, congregational culture boils down to how the three are attained and allocated—a matter synagogues pay too little attention to. Take just members, as an example. Members may be recruited or just drift in by chance. Once in, they may become active regulars or passive marginals. In either case, they bring monetary resources, but not enough to run the synagogue, which must then decide how to raise more money and how much to raise.

It is universally true that when goods are offered communally, only some people pay for them. In the government sector (sector one), for instance, we all get police and fire departments, but some people cheat on their taxes, while others pay their full assessment and then contribute more besides. If the government couldn't imprison cheaters, taxes would fall stupendously. Fire and police would be like sector three not-for-profits—National Public Radio, for example, which anyone can listen to, but only a few pay for. People who use public resources without paying their fair share are called *free riders*.

Synagogues feature just the opposite, people who pay their fair share but do not use what they pay for. They are *free payers*. Truth be told, then, all our rhetoric to the contrary, we rely upon a majority of members remaining satisfied as marginals, because despite some fixed costs, overall cost rises as more and more people seek counseling, classes, and even prayer books. Synagogue professionals are already stretched too thin to imagine servicing everyone as an active user of programs, and financial assets would not rise enough to hire others. Membership "user hours" (number of members multiplied by average hours of service each member demands) thus impact finances, which in turn determine professional leadership capacity. Good leadership, however, includes volunteer lay members also, and heightened leadership brings in more money and makes broader service to members available.

Culture is all these things—size, style, leadership type, and intake/output of resources—and more. It is the "feel" one gets just by being there. It underwrites everything a synagogue does. And once the culture is established, it is notoriously hard to change, if only because it is so tacit that no one even knows it is there. Additionally, "like attracts like." People join because they like the culture they find there; people who do not like the culture go elsewhere.

Culture is notoriously hard to change because it is so tacit that no one even knows it is there. Additionally, "like attracts like." People join because they like the culture they find there; people who do not like the culture go elsewhere.

Synagogues rarely look at their own culture, which is so embedded that they take it for granted. It is, however, possible to get in touch with who we are. The best way is to invite someone from the outside to spend some time in our synagogue and report on what it feels like. But be prepared for surprises, not all of them pleasant. One synagogue that considered itself warm and inviting asked the neighboring Protestant pastor to be an outside observer. "This is the coldest house of worship I have ever been in!" he exclaimed truthfully. The synagogue board who invited him was not happy.

To make matters worse, we identify with our culture and become defensive about maintaining what it is that we like. We now know what synagogue loyalists are loyal to—not the surface things like liturgical style, sisterhood clothing drives, and Wednesday night book clubs, but to what these symbolize: their local culture, which has become their identity. Changing the synagogue means changing a congregation's implicit identity. No wonder transformative change initiatives are so difficult to pull off.

WHY WE CANNOT REACH ALL THE PEOPLE

We saw earlier in the chapter that no change process reaches all the congregants. In our case, as in all others I know, an inner circle is influenced, as is, perhaps, some committees and the board, but the new way of thinking rarely goes much beyond that. Most congregants remain untouched by whatever changes the synagogue initiates. The reason for this lies in economic theory.

Back in 1776, Adam Smith, who, more than anyone else, founded classical economic theory, faced the troubling problem of value. Shouldn't the value of an object vary with its supply and demand? Water is crucial but plentiful, so costs little. Diamonds, however, "the greatest of all superfluities," are expensive. To explain all this, Smith differentiated "value in use" from "value in exchange." Water has high value in use, low value in exchange. Diamonds have low value in use but high value in exchange. Economics would deal with value in exchange. With the Industrial Revolution, labor became the largest component in this value in exchange, leading another founding father of economics, David Ricardo, to issue the "iron law of wages," which predicted the necessity of leaving workers at subsistence level—a rule against which Marx and Engels struggled.

By the nineteenth century, Smith's value in use as opposed to exchange was questioned as arbitrary. Maybe value should be explained as a question of cost and utility. Accenting cost focuses on the producer—whatever it will cost, especially for labor, to produce an item. Accenting utility spotlights the consumer—how much use the buyer thinks the product has.

In 1871, two economists independently invented the very simple (but also very powerful) concept of marginal utility. Take oil, for example. In good years, without gas guzzlers and plenty of OPEC production, oil is relatively cheap. As production diminishes and usage increases, it goes up in price—by the law of supply and demand. But that law is a simplification. When the supply was high, if my local gas station charged five dollars a gallon, I would go elsewhere and get it for one. The utility of the expensive dealer's gasoline is low because I can get a cheaper gallon of the same thing elsewhere. By contrast, if my local dealer has the last gallon of gas in town, the utility of his gallon skyrockets. Imagine a thousand cars lined up for gasoline. At first, there is lots of it, and we all get it cheaply. As the cars drive away, their owners satisfied with full tanks, fewer and fewer cars stand in line. But word gets out that gas is becoming scarce, and the price of gas goes up with each succeeding customer. Each succeeding sale is further and further on the margins—that is, fewer and fewer people want to buy it. At some point the price escalates so much that drivers will just not pay for it. The last few drivers may pay five dollars; they will balk at a hundred. So even in times of scarcity, the price settles down for what the last few customers will pay. The theory of marginal utility states that the usefulness, or utility, of any good or service diminishes with increasing availability; and it is the utility of the marginal—or least sought after unit—that sets the value for all.

Margin counts not just for utility but for cost as well. Labor is cheap at first but rises in cost as workers are hired and the pool of other workers diminishes. There, too, it is the cost at the margin that sets the cost for all. The result is two intersecting curves, an upward curve of rising cost and a downward curve of falling utility, both based on value at the margins, that can be described jointly as the law of diminishing returns. Marginal costs rise, and marginal utility descends; where the two curves meet, it is no longer prudent to expend capital on desired returns.

We are precisely in that situation when we expend capital to change a congregation's culture. At first, the people who come to us for change are a self-selected group who are at least somewhat dissatisfied with what they have and want what we provide. These are people in search of spiritual experience to start with. Thrilled to see we offer it, the marginal utility is high—they will expend huge amounts of time and effort to get it. Also, since we are working with a small population, which is coming to us, our marginal costs are relatively low. But three years later, in the same congregation, we encounter a more marginal population who is not in search of what we offer. At the new margin, they will invest less and less to get what we have. They are also harder to reach, requiring synagogue volunteers and extra staff. So our marginal costs rise.

Eventually you get to the point where the law of diminishing returns necessarily blocks successful investment in change. It becomes economically unfeasible to invest more effort and resources in trying to reach marginals on the periphery. It follows that much as we wish it were otherwise, we cannot define success as drawing everyone into the synagogue on a meaningful level. Our goal should be embedding a spiritual way of thinking, theological seriousness, a pincer approach to problems, the search for the sacred, a culture of honor, Jewish Journey Groups, uncommittee behavior, the willingness to experiment, and all the other lessons of this book as intrinsic parts of the congregational culture, at least for those we do manage to reach. The good news is that like attracts like. New congregants, at least, will be drawn to (and want themselves to reflect) the new synagogue culture.

Experimentation with these new concepts implies constant learning from success and failure. Hence another model of synagogue life: synagogue as learning organization.

SYNAGOGUE AS LEARNING ORGANIZATION

We all think we know what learning is. We do it all the time, don't we? But synagogues have to learn how to learn, because much of what passes for learning really isn't. In 1972, psychologist Gregory Bateson differentiated "zero-degree learning" from Learning I, Learning II, and Learning III.

- Learning I is memorizing a single rote response to questions or challenges we encounter.
- Zero-degree learning is mindlessly using those rote responses over and over again.
- Learning II is using our intelligence to analyze a problem and select not just a rote response, but the "right" response from a given set of alternatives.
- Learning III equips us to invent new responses and add them to the repertoire from which we select the "right" one.[13]

Take Pavlov's famous dog who salivates when a bell goes off. From hearing the bell, we might say, it learns that food is coming. Actually, however, once the dog has mastered the stimulus–response relationship, new instances of the bell teach it nothing at all. It just reacts. That is zero-degree learning, applying a rote response.

Once upon a time, the dog hadn't known what the bell might mean. Learning to recognize a stimulus and respond the right way was Learning I, mastering a given response that can be repeated ever after by rote.

Most organizations get no higher than Learning I. Workers begin as Pavlovian dogs, learning rote responses to predictable situations. Then they settle down to zero-degree learning, applying them.

Imagine the following scenario. A man arrives at the religious school office to discuss his son's bar mitzvah. A secretarial assistant takes a family history; a bar mitzvah tutor explains the procedure; a financial officer details the tutoring cost; the rabbi describes the service and the parents' role in it. These are rote interviews, where the person across the table has learned the proper response (Learning I) and now performs it pleasantly enough, but mechanically (zero-degree learning).

In response to the interviews, the man reports that he is the child's stepfather and a practicing Methodist. Operating at zero-degree learning, the rabbi learns nothing from the information offered. He hears it as a stimulus for a rule he once learned in Learning I: "If the father is Jewish, say X; if the father is not Jewish, explain Y." So he answers with Y: "You will unfortunately not be able to read prayers from the *bimah* or pass the Torah down to your son." The man leaves.

Learning I has been compared to a thermostat that receives an input on air temperature and either goes on or shuts down in response. There are no other possibilities. By contrast, Learning II encourages the creative application of the available options. A robotic Learning II thermostat would be able to ask why the temperature was set as it is to start with and then adjust its response not only to the information about air temperature at the time, but the nature of the meeting, the psychological state of the people in the room, and the dampness of the air. There are still only two responses: "turn heat on" and "turn heat off." But the robot thinks about the situation before deciding which one to use.

In the synagogue parallel, then, the rabbi might have wondered why the child was presented by the non-Jewish father, not the Jewish mother. Had he asked, he would have been told that the child's mother had converted to Judaism out of convenience, so as to get a rabbi to marry her to her former husband, who was Jewish. When the marriage ended a few years later, she dropped her Judaism altogether. Upon meeting her current husband, the boy's Methodist stepfather, she assumed she and her son would become Christians. The man had objected, however, because he saw her vow to raise the child Jewishly as a binding commitment before God. To the mother's surprise, he agreed to the remarriage only on condition that she keep a Jewish home. As the years dragged on, it became the Methodist father, not the Jewish mother, who took the child's Judaism seriously, insisting (when the time came) on a bar mitzvah. So it was he who presented the child for the bar mitzvah process.

Hearing this, a rabbi with Learning II might have reexamined his response and said, "Maybe you *can* hand the Torah to your son. In a way, you have chosen it for his heritage. You raised him as a Jew, after all." As with the thermostat, there only two fixed responses: "You can" and "You can't." But the rabbi reconstructs the situation creatively and chooses "You can" over "You can't."

Imagine further that the rabbi had graduated to Learning III, which equips people to invent an altogether new set of options. Honoring the father's Christian heritage, he might have invited him to talk briefly to the congregation, explaining how and why he, a Christian, had insisted on Judaism for his stepson; he might have charged the boy to value his Jewish heritage all the more because it had come at so great an effort to himself. This is the kind of advanced learning we can less easily imagine any robotic thermostat doing. It calls for creativity beyond anything ever tried before.

None of that advanced learning occurred in our example. The rabbi had never gone beyond Learning I. Most of his rabbinate happened by rote. When he found himself in situations for which his repertoire was likely to have no available rote response, he panicked. Synagogue 2000 regularly voiced mantras like "It's not about programs; it is about doing synagogue differently." Thinking about a common inscription (in Hebrew) above the ark, "Know before whom

> The highest level of learning (Learning III) equips people to invent new sets of alternatives in response to new information.

you stand," we would remind congregations that it does *not* say, "But we've always done it this way." We were trying to shake up culture, but success demanded comfort with cultural adaptability. Particularly in this era of expressive individualism, synagogue authorities need to be willing to experiment with creative responses.

Another way of looking at it is to differentiate learning into cognitive knowledge (know-what), advanced skills (know-how), systems understanding (know-why), and self-motivated creativity (care-why).[14] Seminaries teach the "know-what" and "know-how"—as a student, our rabbi in question learned what constitutes a bar/bat mitzvah and how to make it happen. As a graduate in a synagogue, the rabbi deepened the "know-how"—mastering the system in place and filling in gaps in his seminary education (like how to interview the father about his son). Also, immersed in the culture of his synagogue, he "knew why"—at least in part, he gave the standard rote response because he feared precedents that would be difficult to apply universally. What he never got to was "care why." It never occurred to him that this situation was altogether unprecedented, demanding an equally unprecedented response to acknowledge the unique role of the stepfather.

Not just individual people, but whole organizations can be stuck at any particular stage of learning. A learning organization has been defined as "skilled at creating, acquiring, and transferring knowledge, and at modifying its behavior to reflect new knowledge and insights."[15] Synagogues that learn work their way all the way up to Learning III, where situations get appraised in wholly novel ways, prompting sets of responses never before imagined, because they "care why."

The "organization as political arena" had one thing right: knowledge is power. In Taylor's bureaucracies, too, information was hoarded at the top. In a learning organization, information is shared, on the assumption that the more people know about the overall goals and challenges, the more they have the power together to solve problems.

Students of organizations have analyzed two successful modes of sharing information. In "companies that produce relatively standardized products to fill basic needs," information is stored in databases to which people throughout the organization have access. But this high-tech answer does not work for organizations that need "highly customized solutions to unique problems." There, "knowledge is shared mainly through person to person contacts." By providing networks of personal interchange, this system surfaces not just official, but also tacit knowledge, the kind of thinking that databases never get to. Mentoring one on one replaces group training and learning from books. Information flows not just vertically, but horizontally across departments, so that knowledge can be shared by people who might otherwise never even meet each other. Hewlett Packard, for example, gives employees access to company airplanes that travel from office to office, so that workers engaged in one division can see what other divisions are doing and, together, work out creative solutions that would never have occurred to them in isolation.[16]

In a learning organization, information is shared, on the assumption that the more people know about the overall goals and challenges, the more they have the power together to solve problems.

Synagogues are clear candidates for the personalization strategy, and some synagogues have gone a long way in applying it. We found places where educators met regularly with clergy, parents, and lay leadership (the education committee and the board), sharing challenges and solving them together. But we also found the opposite: educators who were expected to run the school without interchange with anyone else. We found day schools that were completely zoned off as semi-independent entities, so that even the rabbis had little say about them. In one case, a synagogue board member explained that the synagogue invests in a preschool because parents who enroll their children there might become synagogue members. But the connection was purely technical. No one in the synagogue knew what the children were being taught in the school—about prayer, for example—to make sure that lessons correlated to what was going on inside the synagogue sanctuary.

By emphasizing horizontal communication across programmatic lines, I do not mean to do away with traditional lines of authority and decision making. For some time, our own national Synagogue 2000 team experimented with a flat organization without traditional oversight and accountability. Hearing about trends away from standing committees toward ad hoc teams called pods that meet to solve specific issues as they arise, we assigned people to a variety of such pods, each one designed with a personnel mix that seemed appropriate to the challenge in question. It did not work. People became confused as to what assignments they had; they had trouble thinking in many different directions at once. They preferred a primary assignment in their own specialized area of expertise. And we lost efficient oversight, since everyone seemed responsible to everyone else. We eventually reverted to an executive director, to whom everyone reported. But we did succeed in building an organization where people shared information across channels as well as up and down the organizational ladder.

That is what we advocated for synagogues: systems with porous boundaries where information flows readily among all personnel; where laity and professionals act as information-sharing partners; and where a transparent culture of honor replaces an opaque culture of blame.

Opacity comes from two major sources. There is in general a tendency to avoid even our best theory of openness. Theorist Chris Argyris distinguishes an "espoused theory of action" from an "actual

Synagogues need systems with porous boundaries where information flows readily among all personnel; where laity and professionals act as information-sharing partners; and where a transparent culture of honor replaces an opaque culture of blame.

theory in use."[17] The latter feeds inbuilt psychological needs—to retain control; to maximize winning and minimize losing; to avoid the embarrassment of looking incompetent. Rather than expend effort learning, we work at controlling, winning, and looking good. To make matters worse, organizations build in mechanisms to avoid recognition of the theory in use. People cover up for one another or refuse to acknowledge what is really going on. To become a learning organization, the risk aversion connected to theory in use has to be reversed. People need to be rewarded for taking chances. Failure is not a fault; it may be the best way to find a better solution. Linda Klonsky, our national manager of organizational development, taught us to practice what she called "compassionate truth telling." Build a culture of honor, and you will be supported by your colleagues, even when they suggest you may be wrong.

If there was one leadership failure we found in synagogues that did not manage to achieve transformation, it was risk aversion, especially of clergy, who had been socialized by their culture of blame to fear failure in the eyes of the laity. By contrast, where leaders had worked out relations of honor across the clergy-lay divide, anything seemed possible. Consultant Sam Joseph calls it goodwill. He differentiates Nimitz congregations from healthy adaptive ones. Nimitz congregations get their name from Navy battleships (named after Admiral Nimitz) that are so massively inflexible that it takes them twenty miles just to turn around. What makes congregations adaptive is the enormous amount of good will built into the culture. People take risks because they are not afraid to fail. Everyone will applaud their effort anyway.

As an example, one rabbi with whom we worked became convinced that proper inclusivity requires adding the voices of modern

Jewish men and women to the official canon from which we draw our biblical readings for the morning *haftarah*. He selected poetry, especially by women, for Shabbat morning inclusion, and to emphasize his point that they, too, are sacred, he deposited his modern writings inside the ark, next to the Torah scrolls. The experiment was a disaster! People thought he was desecrating sacred space. But everyone knew it was only an experiment. No one blamed the rabbi. They respected him for the courage to try out a way of inculcating a value the congregation held dear.

> What makes congregations adaptive is the enormous amount of goodwill built into the culture. People take risks because they are not afraid to fail. Everyone will applaud their effort anyway.

I hold fast to the belief that synagogues and their leaders tend to be risk averse. Sociologist Robert Wuthnow diagnoses the problem by noting how programming synagogues depend eternally on demonstrating the merit of their programs. The result is that congregants "are likely to feel it necessary to make public only what they do well … to put on a happy face." They do not admit systemic problems, so find no reason to do things better. Having to do nothing differently and being good at what they do, they are likely to do nothing really wrong either. They just add safe programs, retain dysfunctional relationships, cater to demographically promising areas of Jewish settlement, and settle for being less than excellent. What they do is not bad—they even do it well—but being unable to think beyond what they do, they remain limited.

FROM SYSTEM BACK TO CULTURE

Many of our early congregations arose in the Taylor era, when factories spewed out identical products mass-produced and without surprises. In keeping with that culture, synagogues, too, were all pretty much the same, and congregants were treated as large masses, not individuals with personalities of their own. By the 1950s, industrialism was

giving way to the service economy, making people envision synagogues as just one more service center—the limited liability community for which they exchanged
"dues for services." Now the economy has switched again, to be what
has been called an "experience
economy."[18] Industrial goods are
standardized; services are customized; experiences are personalized. In an experience economy,
people expect synagogues to provide experiences—experiences of
the good and of the spiritual, which
together we are calling the sacred.

*I*ndustrial goods are standardized; services are cus-tomized; experiences are personalized. People now expect synagogues to pro-vide experiences—experiences of the good and of the spir-itual, which together we are calling the sacred.

But the sacred does not exist in
the state of nature, just waiting to
be discovered. It depends on culture. Even Jacob's dream depended
on the culture Jacob inhabited—a
culture where angels were assumed
and where everyone believed that heaven and earth were connected at
nodal points of contact. Jacob's culture was system-driven as well, a
reflection of Middle Eastern patriarchalism, where a single male head
of the clan was expected to see visions and make decisions for everyone else. The sacred is like the beautiful: it exists the way art does, in
and of itself, but produced systemically—through guilds once upon a
time, then through independent artists, who interact with dealers,
museums, showings, and reviewers. The experience economy is
equally a knowledge economy, dependent on experimenting with
strategies that produce an experience of the sacred that responds to
people's lives.[19]

Systemically, synagogues will have to move from Tayloresque
top-down bureaucracies and Machiavellian arenas of political war-
fare to collaborative information sharing and creativity, where no one
person, even the rabbi, knows it all, and where solutions for spiritual
seekers come through deliberation across separate zones of synagogue
life and in dialogue with the seekers themselves.

System creates culture, then, and the fee-for-service synagogue system left over from the service economy just will not let the sacred through. God may be present but may not show up.

How do we cooperate with God to let the sacred surface? It is time to look more carefully at the culture where sacred capital flourishes.

*S*ystem creates culture, and the fee-for-service synagogue system left over from the service economy just will not let the sacred through. God may be present but may not show up.

SACRED AND HUMAN CAPITAL

Some areas of our country enjoy economic growth, while others stagnate. The Midwest "rust belt" has been decaying for decades. New York City's economic woes were reflected on October 30, 1975, when the famous tabloid headline of the *New York Daily News* screamed, "[President] Ford to City: Drop Dead." But now New York is booming; Pittsburgh is not. Why is that?

Some answers appear obvious. New York, one might suppose, is not dependent on manufacturing, whereas Pittsburgh is. But that answer is insufficient. New York, too, was heavily invested in manufacturing until late in the last century. Indeed, its manufacturing falloff is partly what brought it close to bankruptcy in 1975. New York rebounded, however, in part because it had other industries—Wall Street and tourism, for example. But below that reality lies a deeper tale. Urban sociologist Richard Florida has studied areas of economic success in general, places like Boston, Washington, Austin, Raleigh-Durham, and the Bay area.[20] Common wisdom holds that companies create jobs that then attract workers. This turns out not to be the case. True, *manufacturing* plants move to areas with tax incentives and then attract labor; but outside the production sector (which is shrinking), a certain class of workers (which is expanding) is attracted by the area and by its very presence provides what companies need to thrive. Florida calls this the "creative class." It runs on information mastery; it constitutes "human capital."

What attracts this class to one place rather than another? First, its members look for experiences, as we would expect in an experience economy. They deplore boredom. As we would expect too, they like each other and look for a place that attracts a critical mass of others like themselves (like attracts like). They appreciate human difference—they are part of a "live and let live" culture. They avoid places where law and custom define a single "right" lifestyle. They are independent and individualistic. That is what makes them creative.

Sociologist Robert Putnam bemoaned the growing American trend away from joining anything: not clubs, not churches, not political parties—nothing. If people do not see each other regularly, they owe each other less. The result is the loss of social capital—investment in doing things for others.[21] Rabbis too bemoan this loss, hoping to make the synagogue a proper community where people pray together, study together, and work together, thereby restoring social capital.

But the creative class sees that kind of all-embracing community as stifling. Social capital bonds people, but as we all know, when we try to break into a clique, it also creates boundaries that do not admit newcomers easily. The creative class is not interested in that kind of community. It prefers loosely knit communities of choice: a bicycling club, a friendship circle, and tuba playing in a local orchestra. These are people who manufacture their identity by piecing together bits and pieces of work, relationships, and interests, each one connected to a group of like-minded folk; they commute from group to group. What they do not want is the kind of romanticized all-embracing community that rabbis think the synagogue should be.

I am describing Generation X, the phalanx of people who will gradually take the place of the baby-boomers. And their view on the world is not likely to change very much. "Creative class people do not lose their lifestyle preferences as they age. They don't stop bicycling or running, for instance, just because they have children.... They continue to value diversity and tolerance."[22] Whereas baby-boomers identify spirituality with wholeness, wanting to mesh together the disparate parts of their lives, the next generation's creative class lives perfectly well with unconnected experiences, pursued in unconnected communities that they frequent because other people there also believe in piecing together a life. They inhabit multiple communities simultaneously.

Anthropologist Claude Levi Strauss described the way myths are put together as *bricolage*, by which he meant the work a mason does in building a wall out of odd-shaped rocks, stones, and bricks. The wall takes its unique character from the idiosyncratic set of parts that could not have been predicted in advance, obeys no predetermined rule, but becomes a work of art that observers find pleasant to contemplate. Creative identity comes into being in just this fashion. It is never-ending self-*bricolage* by people who locate themselves in an open environment that is rich in opportunity; they pick and choose from the richness of the environment, constantly putting together who they are.[23] Anecdotal evidence suggests that America's young liberal Jews are overrepresented in Florida's creative class. Liberal synagogues should reconsider, then, the kind of community they try to become.

Whereas baby-boomers identify spirituality with wholeness, wanting to mesh together the disparate parts of their lives, the next generation's creative class lives perfectly well with unconnected experiences, pursued in unconnected communities that they frequent because other people there also believe in piecing together a life. They inhabit multiple communities simultaneously.

Not all Jews are liberal. Orthodox Jews cannot be lumped together as a single species, but overall, they tend toward conservative views on things, even sharing some of them with conservative Christians. They want state aid for religious schooling, they tend toward opposition to abortion, and they build all-embracing communities. Indeed, Synagogue 2000 was constantly in awe of the Orthodox communities we saw—where people live in close proximity to each other, walk to *shul*, and take care of one another in a common, halakhically based ambience. We met people who did not actually hold Orthodox commitments but who remained Orthodox just because of the community that embraced them. And we discovered a Conservative congregation where members make a point of living within walking distance and building the tightly knit community of social capital that Putnam misses.

Still, the vast majority of American Jews remain liberal. They are likely not to belong to an Orthodox (or any other) community that stresses a single code of behavior and discourages broad individualistic diversity. Nor will they seek to live in one area, like the small Conservative community I mentioned. We should conceptualize two kinds of synagogue, one conservative and the other liberal. Liberal synagogues will thrive only if they attract the creative class of which Florida speaks.

Keeping our three economies in mind, we can trace synagogues in America through three stages.

1. The "industrial synagogue" discouraged diversity. Reform synagogues throughout most of the twentieth century exercised a strict dress code, eliminated individualistic davening, and made everyone sit, stand, and (mostly) be quiet together. People joined out of civic obligation.

2. The "service synagogue" of the suburbs markets itself as a place for programs, mostly for kids (including bar/bat mitzvah), but also counseling and life cycles (wedding and funerals) for adults. Still, services come preplanned; you take what they give you and pay for it, if you think it worth the price. Neither weddings nor bar/bat mitzvah services get customized. Spirituality is not the point. People join with the cost-benefit analysis that goes into any limited liability community.

3. The "experience synagogue" of the future provides authentic Jewish experiences. On the theological right, these are delivered through intensive all-embracing communities that extract the price of full and total commitment. On the theological left, they arrive through a loose network of relationships and a choice of a Tuesday Kabbalah class, a Sunday meditation *minyan*, a Shabbat morning service of song, and customized life-cycle events to fit the self-*bricolage* of a creative class that is always putting itself together. Synagogue is just one of many things people put into their evolving identity, and like the

other components (the music one likes, the bar one frequents, the friends one makes, the clothes one buys), synagogue, too, is personalized. People come to this, but not to that. The community in attendance varies with the event. Experience synagogues value diversity and encourage personalization.

NOT JUST SPIRITUAL, BUT MORAL

The PISGAH vision had within it a social justice plank that we called "good deeds" (*ma'asim tovim*). From the beginning, then, even before we altered our terminology from "spiritual" to "sacred," we conceptualized synagogues as places where good deeds characterize the way members treat one another and the way they reach out into the world. Synagogue walls, we said, are porous. Unless cries from without are heard within, prayers from within are not heard on high. As I said before, the failure to complete a good-deeds curriculum of study was not due to lack of effort. It was, in part, a result of reconceptualizing the synagogue system so that social justice might have a chance at succeeding. By the time we had figured out how social justice could be embedded in the very fabric of synagogue life, we were overwhelmed with other aspects of our work, and even though we entrusted the curriculum to two different people, we failed to oversee their work sufficiently and make the curriculum a reality.

Especially in the Reform Movement, which identified with prophetic Judaism as far back as the 1890s, synagogues like to think of themselves as places dedicated to social action. Elsewhere, too, however, it is common to have a social justice committee, a *mitzvah* day, food collections, and other opportunities to reach out to others. But in fact, even those synagogues whose identity is closely tied to doing good deeds tend not to do very many of them. The 1998 National Congregation Study (NCS) polled churches and synagogues nationwide, and found a bleak picture of the real social action that churches and synagogues undertake. There are exceptions, of course, and the survey covers so many more churches than synagogues that a somewhat different synagogue trend may be masked by the sample. But that is unlikely. On the whole, churches and synagogues think they are committed to social justice far more than they actually are. "Congregations typically engage in social services in only a minor and peripheral way," involving small groups of volunteers who carry out well-defined tasks on a periodic basis and "in a way that involves minimal contact between congregation members and the needy." Large congregations with more resources to spare do more work than small ones. Liberal congregations do more than conservative ones ("the difference between self-described liberal and self-described conservative congregations is about the same as the difference between a seventy-five person congregation and a thousand-person congregation"). Congregations in poor neighborhoods, but whose members are not themselves poor, volunteer more.[24] Where congregations do make a difference, they feed into established noncongregational programs in a minor way, the most common being a couple of days' work by a few volunteers on Habitat for Humanity.

Nor were congregations historically more actively engaged in social action. In Muncie, Indiana, for example, following the 1893 economic panic, an "Associated Church Charities" had arisen, fueled by the social gospel in vogue at the time. But by 1900, with the great migrations under way, the churches were unable to handle the demand. Studies from the 1920s and '30s paint the same picture. A relatively small amount of money was given and only a tiny fraction of clergy time applied to social justice work—then as now.

Given this stark reality, which has not changed in over a century, we are entitled to look for systemic causes running deep within the congregational system—a clear instance of synagogue dysfunction. Early on, Synagogue 2000 identified the problem as a leftover of the Taylor bureaucracy's love of compartmentalization.

Congregational departments are called committees. In most synagogues, social action is entrusted to a committee. When anyone thinks of a project worth doing, it gets dumped in the agenda of that already overworked committee. Success is hijacking another member for the committee, for what seems better described as a life sentence than a term appointment. Social action committees regularly complain of being overworked and undersupported by the congregation as a whole. Thanks to the NCS data, we can see how both claims are true. But they are not more true of the social action committee than they are of other committees. The difference lies in the fact that social action requires extracting time and money from congregants, more than say, the ritual, budget, or school committee does. Social action is more like adult education; both are program committees, inventing opportunities for congregational involvement and then marketing the opportunities to synagogue members. But we've seen how synagogues are limited liability market communities. On the whole, people do not join with social justice and continuing education on their list of demands. It would be unlikely indeed for them to turn out in droves for either one.

Overall, social justice in the synagogue context succeeds when it is done with some other rationale in mind and when it is easy to accomplish. Spending a day building a home for Habitat may be glamorous and fun, attending *mitzvah* day as a family constitutes quality time together, bringing cans of food to services is easy to do, and sending kids to religious school with some minor amount of *mitzvah* money helps educate children to give *tz'dakah*. Otherwise, like adult education, social justice appeals to a small number of people who happen to have it on their list of things they want from the synagogue. Its failure is built into the system—the fee-for-service culture and the committee organizational scheme.

That does not mean that people do not want to help others. They do. But they are highly selective about their causes. My wife's mother died of leukemia, and for years (when neighborhood canvassing was commonplace) she took time to canvas door-to-door for money to fight the disease. Fighting hunger is a cause that appeals to both of us, so we give large amounts of money to organizations that provide food for the hungry. But there are any number of important causes that we do not particularly support, not because they are not worthy, but because we, like others, pick and choose the things to occupy our social justice commitment. Except for projects with temporary high visibility (like raising money for victims of 9/11, the Tsunami of 2004, and New Orleans a year later), no committee-sponsored cause is likely to attract more than a tiny percentage of congregants. And the problem is, with only a single committee doing the work, no congregation is likely to have time for more than a tiny number of projects.

We therefore reconceptualized the work of social justice as a set of Jewish Journey Groups. Rather than a single social justice committee puzzling out a handful of opportunities that another handful of members would find marginally appealing, why not organize the synagogue according to affinity groups that revolve around passions that already exist in people's hearts and souls? Everyone has at least one such passion that is shared by others; they just don't know who the others are. Put people together according to causes they share as passions, and you would have constant social justice going on everywhere.

So our proposed social justice curriculum was to be designed less as a study guide to Jewish values than as a means of social organization, modeled after the work of Saul Alinsky. Originally a criminologist, Alinsky was an unabashed radical of the 1960s, who organized communities to fight for their rights. "Power," he is rumored to have said, "goes to those who've got money and those who've got people." He generated power by organizing people. At first, then, we sought a curriculum that would organize people around causes they already held dear.

Rabbi Joel Soffin eventually created a Social Justice Jewish Journey Guide, but I consider not producing the larger curriculum our biggest failure. That curriculum would have done more than fill synagogues with social action. It would have changed the entire synagogue culture, facilitating Jewish Journey Groups of other kinds as well. It would have reorganized the synagogue away from the systemic dysfunction that prevents synagogues from reaching the majority of their members.

Social justice is part of the synagogue's "foreign affairs;" spirituality is its "domestic policy. Taking seriously their covenant with God, members look for the spiritual and the just, which together constitute the sacred.

As a community, synagogues must look both inward and outward. Social justice is its agenda facing outward, part of the synagogue's "foreign affairs," as opposed to its "domestic" policy, which we labeled "spirituality." By adopting the word "sacred," we were able to conceptualize both. The synagogue as sacred community invests sacred capital in the way members treat each other and in the acts of social concern with which they treat the world. Taking seriously their covenant with God, they look for the spiritual and the just, which together constitute the sacred.

SYNAGOGUE AS LIVING ORGANISM

To complete our task of understanding synagogues differently, we need one final metaphor from organizational studies: not synagogue as machine, political arena, culture, or learning organization, but synagogue as living organism.

An organism is the exact opposite of a machine. Thought of as machines, synagogues work by inbuilt algorithms controlling every decision and action with efficient and predictable specificity. They feature systems that are closed. As organisms, synagogues interact with an environment with considerable unpredictability. Their systems are open. They are flawed, the way people are. And they build what we call "identities."

Identities are what we think of as our "self," meaning we are beings with sufficient depth and complexity to be struggling to discover a larger picture of who we are, a conception that integrates our daily finite actions into an overall meaningful whole. We develop a self-image that we value morally, caring that others see us in as good a light as we ourselves do. We are selves only in the sense that certain issues matter. Some things are right and good, others wrong and evil. We cannot have an identity, then, without orienting ourselves to the fundamental notion of what we call morality. Our selves exist in *virtual moral space*. To explain who we are, moreover, we need a story, a narrative of how our life unfolds.[25]

As organisms, then, synagogues also require a fundamental orientation to the good, without which they have no identity. They are not soulless machines. They interact with the neighborhood, the church next door, the causes that come and go, and the human lives they encounter. As machines, congregations need only be efficient; as organisms, they must strive for authenticity in whatever they consider the good. Synagogues require regular and ongoing conversations not just on what they do, but on who they are and who they want to be.

In becoming a sacred community, we may also recapture the promise of civic community, the synagogue as a place that people automatically join in the belief that its moral compass completes their personal self-image. The word "civic" comes from the Latin *civitas*, meaning "city," which historian Lewis Mumford describes as "a kind of religious theater in which eternal values might be represented and the favor of the gods secured." It was a public place where people practiced civic virtue and met to pray. A synagogue, then, can be a place where Judaism's "eternal values are represented" through the sacred drama we call prayer. Just as a city's values get played out by its citizens, so Jewish values are put into action in social justice, the good deeds that synagogue members perform in their community.

"I read somewhere," says a character named Ouisa in John Guare's play *Six Degrees of Separation*, "that everybody on this planet is separated by only six other people.... I am bound to everyone on this planet by a trail of six people. It's a profound thought." Indeed it is. All of creation is connected and we are part of the "all." This is the ultimate religious truth that a transformed synagogue reveals: the profound mystery of the universe in which we are connected to each other, to the cosmos, to eternity, and to God.

Concepts from This Chapter

Professionalization: The socialization process by which personal idiosyncrasies are negated by the imposition of professional standards.

Private synagogues: Synagogues that exist for the sake of the spiritual life of their members. Members pursue personal needs and make personal friends.

Public synagogues: Synagogues that stake claims in issues of worship style or public conscience.

LEADERSHIP TYPES

Charismatic leaders: Leaders who simply pronounce and, through the force of their charisma, people follow.

Traditional leaders: Leaders who have inherent authority as a result of their position, no matter who they are personally.

Rational leaders: Leaders who work with others not by virtue of who they are but of what role they play in the system.

Kinds of Learning

Learning I: Learning that demonstrates the mastery of a given response from an unchanging set of responses.

Zero-degree learning: The mindless use of rote responses from Learning I, used over and over again to respond to questions and challenges we encounter.

Learning II: Learning that lets us not just apply the same old rote response all the time, but encourages us to apply the available options creatively.

Learning III: Learning that equips us to actually invent an altogether new set of alternative responses.

TYPES OF KNOWLEDGE

Cognitive knowledge: Know-what.

Advanced skills: Know-how.

Systems understanding: Know-why.

Self-motivated creativity: Care-why.

Learning organization: An organization that is skilled at creating, acquiring, and transferring knowledge, as well as modifying its behavior to reflect new knowledge and insights. The new *creative class* of individuals runs on information mastery, is attracted by area, and as *human capital*, provides by its very presence what organizations need to thrive.

AMERICAN SYNAGOGUE BY PERIOD

Industrial synagogues: Synagogues in the period of mass production of goods, which discouraged diversity and treated individuals as part of the mass. People joined out of *civic obligation*.

Service synagogues: Synagogues in the post-World War II era of a service economy, which provide "services" to members, who join after cost-benefit analyses to get programs (mostly for kids), rabbinic counseling, and life-cycle officiation.

Experience synagogues: The personalized synagogues of the future, providing authentic Jewish experiences that appeal to those in search of identity—the larger picture of "who we

think we are." To articulate and explain our identity, we need
a story, a narrative of how our life unfolds.

Activities and Topics for Discussion

1. Conduct an informal survey by asking if people view your synagogue as a "private synagogue" or "public synagogue." Be
   sure to ask professionals, "regulars," "watchers," and those
   who only know the congregation by reputation. Are there differences among the responses? What do you think accounts
   for those differences?

2. Consider how information is shared in your synagogue. Is the
   business accomplished at synagogue board and committee
   meetings made public? Are minutes published? If information
   is available to congregants, are they aware of what they can
   learn and how they can access it? How are congregants able to
   share their own information with leaders in the congregation?
   What procedures are there for collecting, storing, and utilizing
   a catalogue of the many different skills, talents, and expertise
   in the congregation?

3. Evaluate your synagogue's kinds of learning. Where do you
   use Learning I, even though Learning II or III would be most
   appropriate? Is your synagogue a learning organization?

4. What kind of leaders does your synagogue value: charismatic,
   traditional, or rational/bureaucratic?

5. Look at your synagogue's organization charts. How much of
   Taylor's dysfunctional system is still in place?

6. Discuss your synagogue's culture. What would an outsider say
   you are "like"?

7. Does your synagogue have a culture of honor or a culture of
   blame?

7
Synagogues in Context: The Larger Picture

Sometime in the late 1990s, I spoke to a national gathering of Jewish leaders, nearly all of them active in their local Federations, pleading the case for synagogues. The response was telling: one after another found what I was saying barely credible. Campaigns against intermarriage? Yes. Day schools? Certainly. Trips to Israel? For sure. Hillels rejuvenated? Great idea. But synagogues transformed? Impossible. The synagogue was too far gone for that.

Given this attitude, it is not surprising to find that synagogues are rarely on Federation agendas. By contrast, every single one of the alternative initiatives mentioned above has received enormous attention. In 1997, a large and impressive coalition of donors established a Partnership for Excellence in Jewish Education (PEJE) to further day schools. In 1999, a similar philanthropic coalition founded "Birthright Israel" to provide every Jew between the ages of eighteen and twenty-six with a free trip to Israel. The scope of funding involved comes from a report in *Ha'aretz* of May 25, 2005 (recommended by the Birthright Israel website). The American partners raised $71 million for the project. My third example is Hillel—in 1988, new President Richard Joel raised the annual budget from $14 million to $51 million.

I applaud all these efforts. But in the end, we have to remember the "hand-off" effect (chapter 3). Imagine a Jewish child who receives the best education day schools can offer, joins Hillel, and visits Israel

via Birthright. Then what? What institution, other than the synagogue, is likely to satisfy the spiritual search that is abundantly docu-
mented in America today? To be sure, spirituality alone is insufficient
for Jews, who are historically not just a religion but a people. But the
once-surprising question from the young couple at camp, "Why be
Jewish?" has become commonplace. The synagogue alone is outfitted
to inculcate and celebrate the transcendent purpose for which the
People Israel lives. My thesis here is, first, that synagogues are largely
failing at that; but, second, if they think differently, they will succeed.
Synagogues are wanting not because they are religious, but because
they are not, or at least not *spiritually* so.

Every survey in the last decade has demonstrated the pervasive
search for spirituality. Newspapers and magazines as diverse as the
Wall Street Journal and *The New Republic* have headlined it. On
November 28, 1994, the cover story of *Newsweek* trumpeted "The
Search for the Sacred: America's Quest for Spiritual Meaning," and
again eleven years later (September 5, 2005) it heralded "Spirituality
in America: What We Believe, How We Pray, Where We Find God."

As the leading indicator of Jewish identity and the most frequented gateway to Jewish life, synagogues remain our best asset. You don't have to like synagogues to want to fix them, and you don't have to appreciate spirituality to want synagogues to have it.

I noted in chapter 1 that many Jews find the word "spiritual" difficult. If we have any doubt, however, that Jews are seeking it, we need only follow Hillel's advice: *Puk chazi ma'i ama d'var*, "Go out and see what the people are doing."

It turns out also that Jews who belong to synagogues are more Jewishly engaged elsewhere as well—"communally, ritually, philanthropically, [and] culturally."[1] As the leading indicator of Jewish identity, the only institution with which Jews come in contact during life-cycle crises, and the most frequented gateway to Jewish life, synagogues remain our best asset. You don't have to like synagogues to want to fix them, and you don't have to appreciate spirituality to want synagogues to have it. A broad coalition of all Jews should be fighting for a renewed synagogue as our most promising destination for the end of the hand-off phenomenon and the most likely route to a Jewish future—especially now, in the window of opportunity provided by a genuine religious awakening.

ANOTHER RELIGIOUS AWAKENING

American society is bewilderingly religious. No other industrial or postindustrial country is like it. Churches in Europe have devolved into museums reminiscent of Shakespeare's "bare ruined choirs." There are those who would apply that description to all of Western religion and, ultimately, to religion everywhere, as other societies evolve the way Europe has. They assume it is only a matter of time until the natural world is demystified, religious beliefs discredited, and once-official religions dismissed by the majority of people.[2] A particularly interesting version of this "secularization thesis" (as it is called) holds that religious institutions flourish only when they have some ulterior social function beyond providing religion.[3] Catholicism remained strong in Poland, for example, as long as Poland was occupied by the USSR, because it provided a nationalistic rallying point against the occupiers. It thrives among Latino immigrants in the United States, because it protects ethnicity, nurtures nostalgia, and provides comfort in the natural hardship of being a stranger in a strange land. When the secondary function is no longer needed, the benefits of religion are trumped by those of secularization. Right-wing religion will retain a tiny enclave of holdouts, but liberal religion is doomed, since liberals prefer the freedoms of secular society to the strictures of religion.

When philosophical skeptics questioned the existence of an external, material, and actual world, philosopher G. E. Moore is said to have held out his hands, as if to say, "Look! Here's proof that you are wrong." So, too, secularization theorists have attracted opponents who simply point to the world as obvious proof that religion is growing, not declining.[4] But proponents respond that what has grown is right-wing religion, which indeed does provide a benefit other than itself. In the Arab world, it insulates old-guard interests against democracy and change. Here in the United States, it perpetuates a culture of class and gender interests against freedoms that a secular society would bring.

I think the secularization theorists are wrong on other grounds. Their theory may indeed hold for those societies where religion has been allied to a regressive state in the fight against modernity. That was very largely the case throughout Europe, where established religion supported the conservative interests of entrenched monarchies and their allied ruling classes. The best example is the infamous Dreyfus case. In 1894, Alfred Dreyfus, the only Jewish captain in the French army, was falsely charged with treason. His trial, imprisonment, and eventual release symbolized a larger battle for the soul of France. Dreyfus's supporters were the liberals pitted against conservative monarchists in league with the Catholic Church. Now, except for Muslim immigrants (for whom religion plays a clear ulterior immigrant role), France is largely a secular society.

But America remains an anomaly. Constitutional fiat here left religion unprotected by the state, thereby forcing it to compete in the free market of ideas. It has had to learn to change with the times in order to retain consumer loyalty in a fluctuating spiritual marketplace.

Throughout this book, I have alluded to the impact of religious awakenings, periods when religion has impacted particularly powerfully on American culture.[5] The first awakening came in the colonial period, when Calvinist churches squelched in Europe broke free here. The second featured public evangelical meetings from about 1800 to 1840. A third arrived near the turn of the twentieth century, when revivalist preachers like Billy Sunday drew masses to harangues against "hog-joweled, weasel-eyed, sponge-columned, mushy-fisted, jelly-spined, pussy-footing and four-flushing liberals."[6] The current awakening (which began in the 1960s and '70s), thoroughly American, is personalist, spiritual, and experiential. It features new church forms, including the megachurch (which we have looked at) and emergent churches (which I will discuss presently). Its Jewish variety includes Shlomo Carlebach, Zalman Schachter-Shalomi, Jewish renewal, JuBus (Jews who adopt Buddhism as their spiritual practice), Aish Hatorah, and a resurgence of Chabad.[7]

Historians point to a change in temperament following Napoleon. Hitherto, European intellectuals had championed an age of reason, which held that beneath all national and cultural differences, human beings are alike in having reason at their core. Moses Mendelssohn (1729–86) could therefore argue the case for Jewish civil rights on the grounds of universal reason. But the French Revolution culminated in the Napoleonic Wars, after which European intellectuals reacted by denying any universal substratum and stressing cultural, national, and religious specificity. As the grounds for claiming Jewish rights, the old argument of universal reason wouldn't work anymore. Jewish strategy for claiming civic liberties shifted, therefore, from citing universal reason to celebrating specifically Jewish culture. Germans had history, texts, and traditions; so, too, did Jews.

Not everyone was able to shift strategies. David Friedlaender (1750–1834), a follower of Mendelssohn, persisted in claiming universal reason as the Jewish right to civic equality. He failed. History largely ignores him except as an example of a leader petrified in his past.

We stand at just such a turn in culture. We are threatened only to the extent that we emulate Friedlaender's inability to adapt. Prior to nineteenth-century romanticism, no one had thought to present Judaism as a distinctive culture with a textually based history of its own. But of course Judaism has such a thing, or to be more precise, it could legitimately be reinvented with one. So, too, until the 1990s, no one thought of Judaism as a tradition rife with spirituality. Now we know better.

To last, however, ideas need to be embedded in institutions. Judaism as a culture took hold because it was studied in German universities and taught in modern synagogues. American spirituality also requires institutional support. It is nurtured through publishers, journals, meditation centers, and even *Newsweek*, which saw fit to recognize it. *Jewish* spirituality, however, has so far been nourished only on the margins, and the problem with the margins is that they are undisciplined. Half a dozen aficionados of almost anything can dance up a storm on top of a mountain and call it Kabbalah. Where spirituality should have been nurtured—seminaries and synagogues—it has been dismissed. Where it should have been heavily funded—Federations—older, safer policies (day schools, Israel, cultural secularism) prevailed. If we do not save our synagogues as places of the spirit, we will have let history pass us by.

Quantum leaps in Jewish culture do not appear by chance; they are plotted, supported, and institutionalized. They derive from people who know the Jewish People is still here because we dared to adapt to changing circumstances. We saw in chapter 2 that whenever we have found ourselves in a welcoming host society, those quantum leaps derive from patterning our Judaism after the positive waves of change that the host society offers. We should ask what window of opportunity we now have to move Judaism forward.

The answer is clear: the anomaly with which I started, American religion. Churches of the spirit are a growth industry. Synagogues of the spirit are the Jewish parallel, moving Jewish spirituality from the margins to the center, where it can thrive. Nothing is more pressing, for Jews will seek spirituality anyway, and if they cannot find it in synagogues, they will go elsewhere—to dancing aficionados, whether Jewish or not.

One persistent critique of the new spirituality is its presumed disregard for social justice. People in search of the spiritual turn inward, it is said, to meditate, try out yoga, and the like. By contrast, social justice requires outreach beyond the self. Spirituality, therefore, breeds selfishness at the expense of caring for others. But that critique turns out to be false. When the Union for Reform Judaism was seeking its current president, newspapers featured articles about the two finalists. One had directed the social action desk; the other was known for leadership in matters of prayer. One article described the moment by saying, "Reform Judaism chooses between social action and spirituality." The social action candidate won but then proved the article false by dedicating his leadership to worship, spirituality, and prayer.

Historically, too, spirituality has not dampened social action. Much larger societal changes are at fault. In chapter 6, we looked briefly at the Lynds' classic study of Muncie, Indiana. In other cities, too, the complexity of the great migration at the turn of the twentieth century necessitated governmental intervention beyond the paltry amount of social action of which religious institutions are capable. By

1935, the Depression forced direct governmental intervention on not just the local but the national level, and since then, given the complexity of poverty, congregations have been even less efficient purveyors of social services altogether. None of this can be laid at the door of spirituality, which was barely in the American lexicon back then.

The real issue for congregations is that the nature of social justice is changing. Less and less are religious organizations, including synagogues, quite as united about political policy as they once were. In the 1960s, religion took a decided turn to the left. During the '70s, a conservative reaction set in. Denominations became splintered internally, as liberals and conservatives formed warring alliances across religious lines. During anti-abortion campaigns, for example, Protestant evangelist Pat Robertson shared his mailing list with like-thinking Catholics, who recruited some Orthodox rabbis as well. In cases where denominational governance remained liberal, conservative churches spun off independently or waited patiently for new leaders to emerge. In many cases, those new leaders now in power hold their denominations intact by avoiding politically controversial claims.

What is left are local people-to-people services that the national government advocates as faith-based initiatives. But urging synagogues and churches to step in where government has left the field is not likely to be very successful on any but a very tiny and local level. The religious revival rooted in spirituality does not preclude social justice. It is just that we are surrounded by massive and intractable issues like poverty, the high cost of health care, and homelessness. Seeing spirituality as the culprit behind synagogue powerlessness to change society is a convenient fiction.

In any event, seeing synagogues as "sacred centers" allows us to view spirituality and social justice as two sides of the same coin.

GENERATIONAL TRANSITION

Baby-boomers were born between 1946 and 1964. Generation X was born between 1964 and 1983. The oldest Gen-X members are now in their forties, and their parents, the oldest baby-boomers, are turning sixty. In ten years, the two groups will be fifty and seventy, making

Gen X, not baby-boomers, the population that makes or breaks our congregations. How will synagogues prepare for that eventuality?

Significant differences separate Gen X from their elders. The boomers lived through heady times: the post–World War II economic boom, then the Kennedy Camelot and the Johnson Great Society. They knew what it was to change the world, even to end an unjust war. Gen Xers grew up to suspect the political process. Trust is everything for a generation where government promises less and less and business leaders are unmasked as scoundrels. Gen Xers have replaced messianic expectations with local friendships—boomers watched *MASH*; Gen X watched *Friends*.

Having invented an entitled self, boomers thrive on therapy and on style—the unfettered use of unlimited goods to express individuality.[8] But they recall their parents' admonitions to be responsive to Jewish causes like Israel. For the boomers, the Holocaust is not ancient history. They remember the Six-Day War. They have some latent ethnic Jewish loyalty.

By contrast, Gen X has little ethnic memory. It knows nothing first hand of the Shoah. Israel appears less like pioneers who clear swamps and more like an army that bulldozes homes. Intermarriage is a given. Organizations in general are suspect, especially impersonal and distant ones like Federation and national congregational denominations.

High on the Gen-X agenda is the creation of an evolving self rooted in personal choice. Indeed, boomers take them to task for being selfish, a judgment Gen X hardly bothers even to debate, so irrelevant is it in its nonjudgmental world of personal laissez faire. Sociologist Ann Swidler identifies the core concern of the self-made self as the fear of self-depletion in pursuit of self-endowment. That is why new religions "attempt to tap sources of energy within the self, or to remove 'blockages' to a flow of energy. Scientologists, weekend Buddhists, trendy Kabbalists, meditators and Goddess worshipers are united in attempting to find new sources of personal, psychic energy."[9]

Conservative religion targets this condition as debilitating, demanding all-embracing community and religious certainty. It energizes the depleting self by framing human foibles as addictions or weaknesses that can be healed by God's love. Liberal religion agrees on the human condition; it, too, promises authenticity and connection with God. But rather than summon people to community that is all-embracing (which it sees as stifling), it celebrates synagogue as just the most significant community of many that contribute to the ongoing self-bricolage of identity creation. Theologically, it reserves the right to pass judgment on the others. Cooking classes Monday night? Fine. Ku Klux Klan revivals Tuesday nights? Never. Catholic Mass Sunday morning? Fine, if you are a Catholic, but not if you claim to be Jewish.

Gen-X members recall little childhood experience of ties that last—50 percent of their parents' marriages ended in divorce. Their parents married younger than any prior American generation; Gen X marries late, and only after trying out relationships that are not expected to prove lasting. Gen X is experimental, gifted with the possibility of moving from job to job or school to school for a decade or more, before settling down to a career and family—which may give way to other careers and families in the course of time. But Gen X is the victim of education inflation. Every change of goal demands more years in schools that up tuition as often and as much as they can. Gen-X lifestyle, moreover, demands experimentation with excellence, rather than economizing. Gen X has amassed the largest personal debt of any generation ever.

Spirituality is key to both the boomers and Gen X, but in different ways. Boomers want to integrate the disparate sectors of their lives. "How does it all fit together?" they ask. Gen Xers live segmented lives and like it that way. One Gen Xer said, "I am a father, a husband, a lawyer, and a bicycler. I put aside time for each." This is a generation that lives several coterminous lives, switching choices all the time, as they try things out—jobs, schooling, activities, live-in mates, and marriages. Gen X does not look for metaphysical wholes to justify a set of ongoing experiments.

Boomers are the ultimate print generation; Gen X is electronic. Growing up in the solitude of reading books is an exercise in closure: a plot begins; you stay with it, and it resolves. Patterning life on multitasking while logging on to an endless series of changing websites with no linear order or satisfying end may alter the narrative we tell about ourselves. Rather than narrative, it may be isolated vignettes that define a Gen-X life. Given a world of websites that may be purely private opinion or outright shams, Gen X looks for authenticity. Growing up in an era where nothing was trustworthy—not the government, not the Jewish power structure, not even (in many cases) their parents' marriages—Gen X appreciates the authentic, not the kitsch. Synagogues that cannot provide authentic Jewish sustenance are in trouble. Rabbis who substitute image for substance will not see many Gen Xers cross their portals—not twice in a row, anyway. Seminaries, rabbinic organizations, denominations, and synagogue leaders still largely think of Gen X (if they think of it at all) as their problematic children. They need to think differently.

Crucial to that new way of thinking is the issue of membership. Gen X samples; it does not belong. Sociologists Steven Cohen and Ari Kelman are studying Jewish culture on the sidelines, a plethora of cultural offerings that spring up in bars, parks, and neighborhoods—a Jewish film festival, perhaps, or a klezmer concert. The Jews who go there are the creative Gen-X class in search of experiences, excellence, and relationships. They find these also at New York's B'nai Jeshurun and synagogues that feature Craig Taubman's "Friday Night Live"—but they do not join them. A Gen-X rabbinic student commented, a few years back, "Why should we expect people to make the synagogue the center of their lives? I go to the dentist and attend movies; neither is my life's center." Gen X has no life's center. It is worth repeating an insight from chapter 6: "Creative class people do not lose their lifestyle preferences as they age. They don't stop bicycling or running, for instance, just because they have children."[10] It is therefore unlikely that today's thirty-year-olds will ever see lifelong synagogue membership as an ideal. Synagogues need to rethink membership. And some have—albeit uneasily, and incompletely.

> Synagogues that cannot provide authentic Jewish sustenance are in trouble. Rabbis who substitute image for substance will not see many Gen Xers cross their portals—not twice in a row, anyway.

A first step was acknowledging the high cost of joining a synagogue.[11] Several congregations now offer "free membership" for a year, in the hope that people will see the cost of synagogue as worthwhile. Temple Emanu-El in San Francisco, for example, initiated such a program in 2000–2001. In their first year, members are asked for voluntary donations. About 65 percent come through, with 39–40 percent paying more than the suggested figure. The program has been expanded now to invite *all* members to make voluntary contributions rather than be assessed dues. Between 2000 and 2005, the membership roll grew from 1,700 to 2,300.[12]

Synagogue 2000 advocated appealing to a single "passion" that would draw Gen Xers to the synagogue—parenthood, for example. We recommended a Jewish Lamaze experience whereby couples expecting children would learn not just how to have the baby, but how to be Jewishly concerned and spiritually fulfilled parents, while also exploring more thorny Jewish questions like relationships to non-Jewish grandparents and the problematic issue of circumcision. Couples would then receive two years of free membership and be targeted for the specific experience of class reunions as their children grew into their first two years of life. In effect, synagogues would have formed a Jewish Journey Group around the difficult but potentially spiritual experience of starting a family. It seemed inconceivable to us that after two satisfying years together, at least some of these young people would not opt to continue membership of some sort.

New conceptions of membership are probably just around the corner. Temple Micah in Washington, D.C., for instance, uses new nomenclature. Drawing on the biblical account of Abraham and Sarah, Rabbi Daniel Zemel describes it as "the souls we gather around us." We are at a turning point in redefining synagogue theologically, not just organizationally. We are back to speaking differently once again.

SYNAGOGUE POVERTY AND COMPETITION FOR EXCELLENCE

Synagogue membership has remained relatively steady over the last twenty years and is, if anything, growing. The affiliation rate from the

1990s was about 37 percent. By 2000–2001, it had risen to 40 percent.[13] But raw figures can be deceptive. For one thing, the growth in the last decade reflects a rise in Orthodoxy alone. It would be a mistake to allow Orthodox success to cloud the question of the liberal movements' future.

When Jews identified themselves by movements in 1970, 42 percent said they were Conservative, 32 percent Reform, and 11 percent Orthodox (Reconstructionism was not a survey option). Conservative Judaism dominated, a holdover from eastern European ethnicity. Reform Judaism, widely seen until the 1960s as cold, sterile, anti-Israel, and unresponsive to Jewish Peoplehood, had languished. The Orthodox numbers were impressive, but many people reporting Orthodox affiliation neither attended Orthodox synagogues nor lived Orthodox lives. Orthodoxy had been their parents' preference and it remained theirs in theory. They were comfortable with it, not committed to it.

The figures are quite different, however, if we look at third-generation Jews alone, where Reform and Conservative figures were virtually reversed. Extrapolating from third-generation figures, one would have predicted that Reform Judaism would thrive, while Conservative Judaism would shrink. By 1990, however, that prediction had only partly materialized. Reform had indeed grown, but Conservative had not lost in equal measure, and Orthodoxy had been cut in half. The new figures were Orthodox 5.5 percent, Conservative 40 percent, Reform 40 percent, and Reconstructionism (which appeared for the first time) 1 percent. Orthodoxy shrank, it seems, because it moved further to the right, staking out its serious claims on practicing *halakhah*; purely nominal Orthodox Jews therefore moved to Conservative ranks, making up the Conservative loss to Reform. Reform therefore approached the predicted third-generation 1970 level of 42 percent, but Conservative did not fall to 32 percent because in-migration from Orthodoxy halted the skid at 40 percent.

It is the 2000–2001 figures that surprise. The Orthodoxy figure is 10 percent, Conservative 27 percent, Reform 35 percent, and Reconstructionism 2 percent. By 2000, Orthodox losses had been reversed; Conservative losses continued, but without dissident Orthodox Jews to make them up. Reform became the preferred address for a plurality of American Jews. But Reform Judaism has not really grown. Its "market share" of Jews has shrunk from 40 percent in 1990 to 35 percent in 2000. Other troubling trends for liberals include the graying of their ranks. The median age of Conservative Jewish adults is fifty-two and Reform fifty, compared to Orthodoxy's forty-four. But fully one-third of Orthodox adults are under the age of thirty-five.

When we translate self-identification into synagogue membership, we find that of those who belong to synagogues, 20 percent are Orthodox, 33 percent are Conservative, 41 percent are Reform, and 3 percent are Reconstructionists. But not all who belong attend. It is hard to say with certainty what the weekly figure is, because if asked, churchgoers, at least, over-report attendance by 100 percent.[14] We have no independent studies of Jews. Still, anecdotal evidence is at least suggestive. Many Orthodox Jews live in walking distance from a synagogue, and the entire neighborhood heads out to synagogue every Shabbat. Among liberal Jews, however, any given service will draw only 10–15 percent of the population, mostly over the age of fifty.

In addition, we are seeing a rise in "post-denominational" congregations who join none of the movements. That incipient trend both explains and is fed by (1) new and independent seminaries taking root across the country; (2) the coming of age of Gen X, for whom labeled affiliation is anathema; and (3) computer technology (to which I will return in the next section). For denominations, all this spells trouble.

To make matters worse, denominationally affiliated synagogues face staggering fiscal problems: dilapidated plants, soaring energy prices, demographic shifts that empty out old buildings and require construction of new ones, changing technology, security procedures, and massive investments in health care for the people who work there. In addition, the salary for rabbis and cantors is significant, and rising. It was mostly insufficient finances that prevented the synagogues we worked with from hiring staff to develop Jewish Journey Groups, for instance. One executive director remarked wryly, "Sure. It's a great idea. But who's going to do it? My plate is completely full."

Under the burden of fiscal pressure, the first thing to go is investment in technology, and given the changing nature of our constituency, that is proving disastrous. Gen X has grown up enwrapped in the excellence of virtuality. Boomers remember faded copies from mimeograph machines; they have patience with poor sound, grainy images, and overhead visuals projected off-center. Spending hours a day surfing the web, Gen X finds this quaint. Boomers recall settling for the relative best of three major TV networks, a couple of local newspapers, and Macy's or Bloomingdales. What you chose was not necessarily excellent; it was just the best you could find.

Synagogues still operate as just "the best you can find." They are often among the least excellent experiences an average person encounters. Their websites are amateurish, sanctuary lighting is poor, staffing is insufficient, and sound systems are antediluvian. A typical story comes from a speaker at a national synagogue body meeting in a large synagogue. The planners knew in advance that he needed an overhead projector. When he got to the room, no projector had been found, and when the projector did arrive, there was still no screen. He spent much of his time finding a wall onto which to project the images. By the time his presentation began, he had lost most of his audience. He shouldn't have used overhead at all, of course; the whole thing should have been converted to computer technology. But here we encounter a related failure, not just *technological* but *organizational* incompetence, in this case a system in which the speaker had not been taught PowerPoint (or its equivalents) and had no support network to prepare the presentation for him. Synagogues just do not use technology well.

The most obvious foil is the megachurch evangelicals, who turn out electronic copies of the pastor's sermon before the worshipers even leave church and then use advanced organizational competence to market and sell it worldwide. Sunday morning seeker services themselves are plotted with technology at their core. Already in the 1980s, for instance, Menlo Park Presbyterian Church, a relatively tiny example and still denominationally allied, had on staff an entire team to devise worship that rivals television for its carefully planned integration of music, movement, and script into a service that is beamed onto congregational screens in segments timed to the minute.

Craig Taubman, a professional at technological delivery and a Synagogue 2000 Fellow, showed us what could be done with sufficient funding and sophistication when he produced *Hallelu*, a Synagogue 2000 Los Angeles "spectacular" that brought six thousand people to the Universal Amphitheater in celebration of synagogues. I stood backstage talking to singer Rick Recht, who observed, "If synagogues delivered this, I'd go. But most things in synagogues are mediocre: bad lighting, messy rooms, poor acoustics, just a sense of things being shabby. My generation is used to the best. We look for excellence, and can usually find it, somewhere. Synagogues have to compete by being more than mediocre."

That was, in effect, our own version of a seeker service, which we wanted to follow up by bringing Synagogue 2000 to Los Angeles and launching a campaign to sign up the unaffiliated. But the Los Angeles Jewish community lacked the organizational competence needed to capitalize on the event. The most logical sponsor of an effort to organize Jews in building Jewish community, the Federation, split into warring factions, each one unwilling to aid the other. By contrast, megachurches have a *Hallelu* every Sunday, then follow the performance with food courts, mass baptisms, an army of greeters who get new names and addresses while inviting people to return, and neighborhood organizations that arrange rides to bring would-be members back to church the next week.

Synagogue excellence demands a focused, ongoing, and concerted effort to incorporate technological and social competence into everything a synagogue does.

Synagogue excellence, then, demands a focused, ongoing, and concerted effort to incorporate technological competence into everything a synagogue does. Providing that excellence is one more task synagogues cannot now afford, but cannot afford to be without. Few synagogues have interactive websites that encourage members (and others) to log on, sign in, and volunteer for committees, projects, and classes. Fewer still can draw selectively on members through updated information about them—to select out, for instance, all parents with learning-disabled children for a targeted approach to helping them. Most synagogues still use hard-copy or, at most, e-mail bulletins that may look like electronic communication but are really just the old print medium delivered on computers. Bulletins untargeted as to readership and dependent on being read like a book from cover to cover will be received as little more than spam. New technology is more than a new delivery system; it is a new way of interacting with the world. Automobiles are not just horses that eat gasoline rather than oats; photography is not just a better kind of painting; print is a whole lot more than talk written down; a "web page" is not really a page. As long as new technology is used the way the old one was, the people using it miss the point.

FROM THE CENTER TO THE PERIPHERY: THE FUTURE OF MOVEMENTS

Post-denominationalism is the second of three stages of revolt against denominational labeling. Stage one featured the 1970-style *chavurot* breaking free from what they saw as their parents' "consumer" religion. But *chavurot* were hard to organize and harder still to maintain. Their principled objection to synagogue professionals meant that members had to master the skills of organization and service leadership. Moreover, *chavurot* were the opposite of welcoming; they were frequently doctrinaire, even elitist. In the end, synagogues co-opted them by renaming their standing program groups *chavurot*. An ordinary book club (for example) became the "Book *Chavurah*." Meanwhile, the independent *chavurot* had trouble sustaining membership much beyond their revolutionary founders. They eventually joined the Reconstructionist Movement to avoid being marginalized as unimportant islands in the evolving Jewish world.

A second trend, post-denominationalism, is epitomized by New York's B'nai Jeshurun (BJ). A Synagogue 2000 study of BJ demonstrated its affinity to megachurches. Both feature something akin to seeker services, both depend on strong clergy presence, and both are driven ideologically. BJ is just the opposite of *chavurot*, which preached radical democracy among its members and eschewed professional clergy altogether. *Chavurot* were tiny groups of true believers that bordered on a clique; BJ features crowds of visitors attracted by a professionally run service that borders on spectacle.

Of late, a third stage of independence has emerged. As with other religious trends, this one, too, has its Christian counterpart that goes by the name "emergent church" and is popularly linked not to the usual institutional seeding, but to what is simply called "a conversation," initiated in the 1990s among Gen Xers who found the boomer megachurches alienating.

Distinctive Gen-X churches arose in the 1980s. They were modeled after megachurches but with music and style that fit the aesthetic taste of the younger generation—"loud passionate worship, irreverent banter, raw narrative preaching, and *Friends* (the TV series) type relationships.[15] Some Gen-X Christians found a place in megachurches themselves, which built youth and young adult churches within the larger church structure. Emergent churches are revolts against that structure. As we saw, the megachurches work because of their reliance on small groups. Some emergents, sometimes called "home churches" because of their intimacy, are the small groups without the "mega" superstructure.[16]

It is, however, hard to pin down a definition of "emergent" except to say that it is what it sounds like: "emerging." Emergents purport to be an expression of postmodernism, which is equally hard to describe. The part of postmodernism that emergents seize upon is the claim that there are no certainties anymore. As one emergent put it, "I needed to trust God more than my theology of God."[17] This is not to say the emergents do not theologize; they do. But more important than what they believe is what they do. They try to live the gospel directly, modeling the life of Jesus. Labels are out; ritual is in. They meet in spaces reminiscent of coffeehouses, informally, in an ambience of family. Worship is flexible, apt to use videos, paintings, icons, television clips, almost anything.

The emergents communicate through an informal network of blogs. Since labels are considered irrelevant, gatherings mix liberals with conservatives, believing that postmodernism allows them to transcend old liberal-conservative differences. Emergent leader Brian McLaren explains, "Conservatives tend to be rigid theologically and promiscuous pragmatically, and liberals tend to be rigid methodologically and a lot more free theologically. Maybe we could trade."[18]

Unlike denominations, emergent churches are no single thing. Rather than a model, they are a mind-set—a mind-set that largely accords with the principles of Synagogue 2000. Except for the specifically Christian theology, what Dan Kimball, an emergent pastor and theorist, describes as characteristic of emergents could have been taken from this book:

> The emerging church must redefine how we measure success: by the characteristics of a kingdom-minded disciple of Jesus produced by the Spirit, rather than by our methodologies, numbers, strategies, or the cool and innovative things we are doing.[19]

What would a Jewish equivalent of "kingdom-minded disciple of Jesus produced by the Spirit" be? Until synagogues can answer that question, they will be unable to speak to the next generation. It really is about theology, not programs.

The description of Christian emergents sounds very much like the informal Jewish gatherings studied by Cohen and Kelman. A good illustration is Brooklyn Jews, a loosely knit organization with a website that describes itself as "a living room conversation" that became "a launching pad for a fresh new approach to creating Jewish community." Both emergent church and synagogue are marked by loose organization and an aversion to all-inclusive community. This is in keeping with what we saw in chapter 6 regarding the creative class's preference for loosely knit communities of choice. New York, for example, is awash in small *minyanim* that pop up as if out of nowhere.[20] Jews in search of alternative but traditional worship make their way first to one and then to another of these "worship scenes," which are a far cry from long-term institutional synagogues as we have known them.

It is too early to predict all-out success for the Jewish emergents. Like *chavurot*, they may prove unsustainable over the long run. The people they attract have little long-term investment in them, since they are looking for a network of attractive places, not a single spiritual home. They depend on foundation grants to pay the people they hire. While they work well for the "not-yet marrieds" (in sociologist Steven Cohen's terminology),[21] their very lack of structure may prevent their supplying what their adherents will someday want when they are "familied." But emergents are, at the very least, another step in the hand-off process. Will emergent members someday join denominational synagogues? Perhaps, but only if those synagogues live up to Gen X's expectations regarding authenticity, depth, and seriousness, becoming the "spiritual and moral centers" that Synagogue 2000 advocates.

More than emergents, it is computer technology that threatens denominations as they exist today. As long as synagogues had no independent access to resources, movements provided curricula, publications, prayer books, and information in general. Since information is power, power resided with the movement headquarters. The web now allows synagogues to go worldwide to access program resources by any number of religious entrepreneurs. So after two centuries of denominational centralization, the power is shifting from the center (movement headquarters) to the periphery (individual synagogues). The emergents are just the extreme cutting edge, living entirely on the margins, nurtured by the web, and commuting easily from one *minyan* to another.

The movements have reason to be unnerved. They face "taxpayer" revolts, distrust of the center, technology that empowers the margins, and "post-denominational" synagogues. But there is a solution: theological thinking. That is what drives Orthodox success—not a surfeit of programs, but a clarion call of principle. The same is true of emergents, not just Christian, but Jewish as well. Without clear and compelling spiritual visions, denominations will fight an increasingly uphill battle, especially as Gen X comes of age, replacing baby-boomers in cultural power.

I said before that Gen X, too, will eventually seek synagogues. But

> Synagogues with spiritual responses to human joys and crises will become addresses to which Gen X will be drawn

which ones? Gen X demands authenticity and ritual. Its members will favor places that are serious about religious quest and ritual fullness. A young professional woman suffering from chronic depression made the rounds of synagogues and therapists until she found a rabbi who took her into the sanctuary, opened the ark, and prayed with her. The rabbi's response would have been virtually unthinkable a decade ago, when rabbis were taught to psychologize, not to pray. Synagogues with spiritual responses to human joys and crises will become addresses to which Gen X will be drawn.

CONGREGATIONAL ATOMISM

I began by saying that synagogues should adopt theological standards for what they do. I can now expand that notion by saying there are actually three "ologies" that matter: not just *theology*, the doctrine of God, but also *anthropology*, our religious doctrine of human nature, and *cosmology*, our metaphysical notion of the nature of the universe. Affirming a culture of honor, not of blame, is a logical extension of a positive anthropology, a view of human nature that assumes, all things being equal, that people prefer to act morally and responsibly. The relationship a single congregation has relative to other synagogues and institutions is a question of cosmology.

When I say "a metaphysical notion," I do not mean some prescientific view of the universe, like the speculative descriptions of reality that characterized philosophic thought from Aristotle (who thought stones fall because it is the nature of stoniness) to Hegel (who characterized human history as the unfolding of universal reason, or spirit). I mean a view of the universe beyond what science can address—the value of that universe and how human beings are a part of it. What is the role of the individual within the totality? We say, for example, that although individuals have freedom of speech, they may not falsely yell "Fire!" in a crowded theater. A parallel question is the extent to which any individual institution is separate from any other. Individualist Walt Whitman wrote, "I celebrate myself." John Donne's assessment was, "No man is an island." Should synagogues "celebrate themselves" or consider "no synagogue an island"?

Americans lean toward Whitman, in what I will call social atomism. In physics, atomism is the theory that all reality consists of bedrock entities that exist independently but come together to constitute the universe. To be sure, we now recognize subatomic particles, but the principle remains the same. Ultimate reality is a set of bedrock particles.

Organizational systems must decide whether its parts are atomistic, bouncing around at will, or whether they owe allegiance to the greater whole of which they are a part. The answer is "both," but at the moment, the emphasis is unduly on atomism. At the highest level, *denominations* pursue their atomistic interests without regard for one another. One level below that, congregations take themselves to be independent of, and even rivals of, other synagogues in the vicinity. Finally, on the micro level, individual members presume the right to demand personalized services without regard for the rest of the congregation—a privatized bat mitzvah ceremony, perhaps, that chases out the regulars who would otherwise be praying there on Shabbat morning.

Congregational atomism is the legacy of a Reformation that fought bitterly for independence from the corporate Church of Rome. It thrived in colonial America, where it both fed on and created American individualism. Synagogues here happily followed suit.

But congregational atomism is limiting. There are exceptions— very large synagogues in wealthy areas with enough "free payers" to cover programming costs and a fundraising rabbi at the helm—but otherwise, fiercely atomistic synagogues are likely never to have enough money to master excellence. They will always remain understaffed. New members will join and never be heard from again. Old members will leave because no one attends to them. There will be no Jewish Journey Groups, no advanced websites, no state-of-the-art technology, and no one to operate it even if the synagogue had it. Overworked rabbis will have no time to think differently.

Synagogues need to pursue finances more aggressively. But synagogue development requires rabbinic moral suasion, and most rabbis have never been taught development skills. They are further hampered by the fact that fundraising requires cultivating potential givers, and rabbis do not want to be perceived as catering to the wealthy. Overworked and understaffed, they are also limited by time. Wealthy congregants, meanwhile, have been trained to give large donations to Federation and only afterward to support the synagogue. There are limits to the funding that most synagogues on their own are likely to find.

Atomism with excellence is found in the larger Christian population that supports entirely self-sufficient magnet churches like Willow Creek and Saddleback. But salaries there are much smaller than what synagogues pay; and the ten thousand (or so) members who tithe do not have to contribute to Federation first. Most important (except in rare exceptions, like New York), Jewish demographics make truly excellent go-it-alone megasynagogues unlikely. Take Houston, for instance, with its estimated 2004 population of 2,012,625 residents, but only 45,000 Jews. A megachurch that attracts 10,000 attendees every Sunday actually touches only 0.049 percent of the total population. A synagogue drawing an equal percentage of Jews would bring 22 people to services.

Synagogues unable to pursue large-scale development are left with the current system of dues. The result is the high cost of membership that limits access to Jewish institutions other than the synagogue. A woman in New York tells me she pays $4,000 a year, not counting a building fund pledge. That probably takes up the entire extent of the income she can afford to spend on being Jewish. Joining a synagogue as if it is the only Jewish community necessary but then having no expenditure left for other Jewish experiences is hardly forward thinking by a Jewish community intent on Jewish continuity. It is a predictable fallout from atomism, which has managed also to occasion synagogue infrastructural poverty at precisely the point where synagogues need more than ever to compete in the market of excellence.

Jewish demographics make mega-syna-gogues unlikely. Large cities can afford "magnet" synagogues, like New York's B'nai Jeshurun, which attracts the specialized population of Manhattan's Upper West Side as well as like-minded Jews from across the metropolitan area. Most cities have too few Jews to do that successfully.

We have reached the point, then, where the Jewish community can no longer afford to operate atomistically. In the mid-1990s, a JCC in Washington, D.C., proposed holding High Holy Day services for young adults who were likely not to attend synagogues; the synagogues, in any case, were already filled to capacity and had no extra seating available. Vociferous and universal rabbinic outrage scuttled the idea. How much better it would have been if all the synagogues had jointly sponsored the JCC plan and sent some of their rabbis, other synagogue workers, and young members to meet the ad hoc JCC congregation to demonstrate how welcoming synagogues can be. What was missing was the relationship of trust. Rabbi Andy Bachman, who reaches out to unaffiliated Jews in Brooklyn, envisions a "passport to Jewish life," which would allow people to belong to the community as a whole, moving easily from one institution to another with a single "ticket."

Engrained atomistic thinking is like a cold war. No single party can afford to give up the competitive game without seeing some benefit accruing in return. If institutions are to cede some of their autonomy, they will require funding incentives. Enter Federations at their best! Federations have organizational ability but no discernible theology. That is to say, Federations are in the business of raising money and forging community, but avoiding theological principles in order to do so. What we need is a merger of interests: the theological positions of the movements with the economic and organizational capacity of Federations. Is it conceivable that Federations—the very institutions that gave me an audience of radical doubters (the story with which I began this chapter)—can see their way to supporting synagogues not just tangentially, but as partners with the synagogue community? The requisite money is there. To cite but one example, between 2000 and 2005, Chicago's Centennial Campaign alone raised $400,000,000 in pledges. From donor-advised funds, it allocated $43,300,000 in fiscal 2005–06. Interest this year from endowment came to $10,184,288. And that is just Chicago.

Synagogue 2000 successes are indebted to many donors, but our cohort work depended almost universally on Federations, our de facto Jewish government after all. They saw synagogues as the lynchpin for a communal Jewish future. They knew, too, that by supporting synagogue excellence, Federation will have access to the next generation that otherwise has no clear rationale for keeping Federation going. (In the year 2000, 39 percent of Jews aged fifty-five to sixty-four contributed to Federation campaigns, while only 22 percent of Jews aged thirty-five to forty-four did so.)

Martin Buber tells the well-known Hasidic tale of a man lost in the woods. He comes across a second traveler and they move on together, not because they know the way out, because they know they will be much worse off if they continue as they are. Synagogues and Federation are two such travelers, who struck out independently in the twentieth century but cannot afford that luxury anymore, lest we lose Jewish community altogether.

We need an alternative model of Jewish communal life, a model that respects individuality but also demands cooperative communal thinking; a model, moreover, that retains the individual at its core, even as it directs the individual to higher purposes. I want to call that model a "web of sacred relations."

A WEB OF SACRED RELATIONS

I have said, more than once, that Jewish continuity requires strong Jewish addresses all along the spectrum of synagogue identity. I am therefore worried about the fact that only among the Orthodox do we see synagogue growth. Since the 1970s, the trend toward "strictness" and away from liberal religion has characterized churches as well. Debate has therefore raged on the issue of whether strict churches necessarily grow while liberal ones necessary fail, a hypothesis first advanced in 1972[22] and pursued with a twist in 1994.[23] One version of the theory holds that where people feel obliged to attend worship regularly, the religious fervor and satisfaction thereby produced accrue to all present, who are then more likely to return. That enormous satisfaction comes with social barriers to member involvement with people farther to the left on social and theological issues, thus building up social capital among members and further increasing the probability of even more church involvement. By contrast, liberal churches that foster relativism and encourage dialogue with religious alternatives can hardly demand singleminded participation in their own affairs. In liberal churches a larger percentage of marginals will give nothing to the production of religious satisfaction, but take whatever they want whenever they feel like it.

Here economics enters, not just in the form of money, but of commitment. Members of a strict church must adopt a strict regimen of practice, limit outside social contact, and commit ever more time and resources to the church. Too much strictness, then, can make the cost of belonging prohibitive. For most liberal church members, there is almost no personal cost at all, but there is equally very little reward. For the most part, life as a marginal goes on as it did before joining.

But the strict-church hypothesis may not, in fact, be directly relevant to strictness, if by strictness one means such things as proclaiming an exclusive truth while condemning deviants, outsiders, and nonbelievers. Even members of strict churches are increasingly likely to be influenced by countervailing trends of modernity. If they are well educated, they are used to reasonable debate, and they enjoy a wide circle of friends, not all coming from the same social-religious group. Even strict churches therefore, nowadays, accept adherents with different levels of commitment and engage in dialogue with the outside world.

It is not strictness per se, then, that makes churches grow, but what has been called "authoritativeness" in the way the religious message is delivered. People value religious leaders who show confidence in what they preach.[24] If that is the case, there seems no reason to believe that, given the right leadership, liberal religion could not grow as quickly and as well as its conservative parallel. Indeed, the churches that Diana Butler Bass called "Practicing Congregations" are just that—liberal churches that embody authoritative certainty of religious message. The successful recipe for liberal success is a combination of four factors:

- *Retraditioning*: Reaching back into the past for traditions that have proved sustaining, and recontextualizing them for the present.
- *Reflexivity*: Willingness to change through engagement with tradition and an equal willingness to change the tradition through engagement.
- *Reflection*: Thoughtfulness about practice and belief.
- *Risk taking*:[25] If we always think the way we always thought, we'll always get what we always got.

These are precisely the characteristics Synagogue 2000 sought to instill in the synagogues with which we worked. We found also that strong rabbinical leadership, intent on going beyond programming, was best able to accomplish them. We can now give a name to the kind of visionary leader we sought: *authoritative*—not authoritarian (!) mind you, but authoritative—rooted in Jewish tradition, willing to take risks, and able to encourage reflection among members, who become moved by their rabbi's insistence on talking and thinking spiritually.

In the past, synagogues in America have needed no theological seriousness; they were ethnic enclaves. They have also often been civic communities that Jews joined unquestioningly as "simply what one does." But only 40 percent of American Jews are now affiliated, and in some places, the figure is less than a third. Most members are marginals who join only to buy services in exchange for dues. Without authoritative leadership rooted in a religious rationale, and without changes throughout the system—seminaries, movements, Federations, individual funders—Jewish community will further be eroded. But it doesn't have to be that way. We are not just at the end of one era; we are equally at the beginning of another.

*F*our "R"s of congregational success:
Retraditioning: Reaching into the past to recontextualize authentic sustaining traditions.
Reflexivity: Engaging tradition but willing to change it.
Reflection: Thoughtfulness about practice and belief.
Risk taking: If we always think the way we always thought, we'll always get what we always got.

Students of ritual call this state of being betwixt and between "liminal," an adjective implying standing on the threshold (in Latin, *limen*). Liminal existence can be frightening, since old understandings prove increasingly irrelevant, while new ones have yet to take their place. It is like being about to join a wedding banquet, after mixing and mingling in a cocktail hour. Before actually entering the ballroom, people pause in the doorway to reconnoiter the situation, at the very least to find out where they should sit. But once the new sit-down rules are clear, they are apt to have a wonderful time. Who can blame us, then, for pausing at the doorway of the future, feeling nostalgia for what was and anxiety for what will be?

But liminal existence has the greatest potential for creativity. If the old rules are null and void, we are free to make up new ones without the old restraints that once kept us in check. Anticipating the future is exciting enough to attract metaphors of having a baby: stopping to consider a new idea is a pregnant pause; good ideas are pregnant with meaning; ideas are conceived before we give birth to them. Liminality is that intermediate zone of pregnancy, when we do not yet know what baby will be born. Between conception and birth, the most wonderful imaginings are possible.

Jewish tradition concurs, so let us undertake one final piece of pincer thinking, moving from the anthropological theory of liminality to a pair of Jewish texts, one from our High Holy Day liturgy and another from the ceremony of inducting a child into the covenant. As the new year, Rosh Hashanah is the liminal moment par excellence, appropriately filled with anxiety: we urge *t'shuvah* (repentance)—what if we do not get inscribed in the book of life? But simultaneously, the day is filled with joy: honey and apples, new clothes, and a phrase repeated three times as the shofar announces the new year—*Hayom harat olam*—"This is the day of the world's conception." As old gives way to new, we are invited to remember how God once conceived a universe—and to conceive ourselves of the universe that we will create in the year ahead.

Then, too, boys, and now increasingly girls as well, have ceremonies that welcome them into the covenant. It occurs eight days after birth. During that time, the child does not yet even have a name, is not yet a social being, not yet part of the ongoing Jewish project. Those eight days are liminal. But when the eighth day finally arrives, we start the covenant ceremony by designating a chair as *kisei shel eliyahu hanavi*, "the chair of Elijah the prophet." We then place the child temporarily in that chair, as if to say, "Little one, maybe you are Elijah the prophet, who, tradition says, will announce the coming of the Messiah. You may even be the Messiah. Who knows?" Medieval Jews in Italy recognized that connection explicitly, by welcoming the child as a descendant of David.

We live in an age of possibility. Who knows what ideas we may conceive, what new era we may give birth to? We should picture

ourselves in the eight days preceding our own admission to a newly
formed covenantal community where synagogues will be central.
Sitting at our endless meetings on the subject, when the chair gets
uncomfortable, we should consider that perhaps we are perched on
kisei shel eliyau hanavi. Who knows what greatness we are capable of!

Concepts from This Chapter

Congregational atomism: The assumption that synagogues, like
atoms, are autonomous entities, rather than parts of a larger
whole, the community.

Four "R"s of congregational success: Clear and certain religious
message emanates from congregations that succeed at the following:

Retraditioning: Reaching back into the past for traditions that
had proved sustaining, and recontextualizing them for the
present.

Reflexivity: Willingness to change through engagement with tradition and an equal willingness to change the tradition
through engagement.

Reflection: Thoughtfulness about practice and belief.

Risk taking: If we always think the way we always thought, we'll
always get what we always got.

Activities and Topics for Discussion

1. With the temple board or other congregational group, list synagogues, communal organizations, and other Jewish institutions (both locally and beyond) that might be partners in
   reaching out to Jewish households in your community. Then
   ask everyone to write down three assumptions they hold about
   working with those potential partners. Have participants
   share their lists aloud and then discuss the assumptions as a
   group.
2. Agree together to take a risk. Pick an idea and run with it, not
   because you are convinced it will work, but because you feel
   strongly that it is worth trying. If it is helpful to do so, label
   the effort as an "experiment" rather than a "change," to communicate its provisional nature, and set a timeline for the

activity and soliciting feedback. As you evaluate the results of the particular idea, be sure to reflect upon the process of risk taking, as well.

3. Identify one way in which your congregation currently finds itself at a liminal threshold. What is the substance of the change? Why is it necessary? What do you hope the new frontier will hold? Create a ritual to accompany your congregation's passage into this new space.

Acknowledgments

My thanks go, first and foremost, to the members of our Synagogue 2000 national team. It was a blessing to work with each and every person I name here. Merri Lovinger Arian was our original director of programming, then director of music. She knows more about music, worship, and teaching people to sing in a spiritual vein than any person I know. She provided not just music for our conferences, but wisdom and leadership for us all. Dr. Adrianne Bank provided early and critical organizational judgment, educating me while I was still a novice in the field. Cantor Ellen Dreskin provided not just musical skill, but organizational talent in following Merri Arian as director of programming. Rabbi Robyn Tsesarski and Ellen Franklin joined us from the start as wonderful enablers of everything. Robyn left to have and take care of her children; Ellen stayed on as the vital center of all we did, aided by a wonderful soul, Rhonda Slater. Two other pioneers were Karen Lustig and Rabbi Randy Sheinberg. Karen ran the New York office, epitomizing excellence in every way. Randy was a student at the time, but came with a consultancy background that was enormously helpful to us. Harriet Lewis was our conference coordinator, but after Karen left, became also the center and the soul of the New York office and an amazingly talented administrator, on whom I relied entirely. She was aided by Fran Heller, an equally wonderful person, who, along with Harriet, made the New York office a pleasure to be in. From the beginning, Dr. Joel Hoffman added his enormous talents and creativity to develop our computer capacity; but more, he photographed conferences, ran sound systems, presented at conferences, and provided academic wisdom that often guided what I did. I am quite in awe of all that he does well. Rabbi Yoel Kahn developed curricula for us; he conceived them, wrote them, and taught them at our conferences. So, too, did Rabbi Joel Soffin, whose passion is social justice. Rabbi Ruth Zlotnick worked assiduously on programs, but also presented at conferences; when she left to take a congregational pulpit, we were fortunate to find Rabbi Leora Kaye, who picked up where she left off. Linda Klonsky guided our organizational development efforts with incredible diligence and care. I owe a great deal to Linda for her insights in general and for teaching me a tiny fraction of what she knows. When we grew to need an executive director, we found Judy Mann, who understood our mission and shared our passion. Dr. Amy Sales of Brandeis University evaluated our work, helping us see where we had succeeded and where we had fallen short.

From the outset, we were blessed with farsighted funders, each with true passion for our work: Rabbi Rachel Cowan at the Nathan Cummings Foundation, Rachel Levin and Marge Tabankin at the Righteous Persons Foundation, and Bruce Whizin at the Whizin Foundation. We relied also on local funders, usually Federations. In Detroit we worked with Harlene Appelman, Julie Falbaum, Dale Rubin, and Steven Posen; in Denver, Lisa Farber Miller, Shere Kahn, Susan Spero, and Ros Begun. In New York, Elliott Forchheimer, Deborah Joselow, and Alisa Kurshan; and in Washington, D.C., Vickie Marx. Lisa Farber Miller funded most of the Denver project through the Rose Family Foundation and remained a valuable advisor to me throughout the Synagogue 2000 years. Rabbis Danny Freelander, Elliot Kleinman, Sue Ann Wasserman, and Kim Geringer more than ably represented the Union for Reform Judaism as part of the worship initiative begun by Rabbi Eric Yoffie. I am grateful also to Dr. Ruth Durchslag, Don Friend, Peter and Julie Gale, Lee Hendler, and Melanie Sturm, who generously funded important projects for us.

Barry Schrage, who directs the Combined Jewish Philanthropies of Boston, deserves enormous credit in general for his generous support of synagogues. So, too, does John Ruskay, the director of UJA Federation in New York and Bob Aronson, then director of the Federation of Metropolitan Detroit.

We were privileged to develop the field of spiritual leadership training. Barry Schrage's initiative resulted in a magnificent team: Dr. Carl Scheinbaum, Dr. Carl Sloan, Dr. Todd Jick, Rabbi Jeff Sirkman, and Rabbi Gordon Tucker—and, especially, David Trietsch, who directed the effort with great love and diligence. A seminary course in leadership was generously financed by Linda and David Glickstein.

Then, too, there was our board, and what a board it was. It stays on now as the board of Synagogue 3000. Unlike most organizations, we shared everything with board members, valuing their wisdom and guidance. Thanks are due to Larry Akman, Marion Blumenthal, Lili Bosse, Rabbi Ed Feinstein, Don Friend, Lee Hendler, Rabbi Rick Jacobs, Terry Rosenberg, Mark Schlesinger, Steve Silberman, Larry Smith, Melanie Sturm, Bruce Whizin, and Shelley Whizin.

This book is the richer for all the people who have helped me write it. Student Rabbis Howard Goldsmith, Todd Markley, and Stephanie Kolon helped with research. Rabbi Stephanie Alexander supplied the summaries of concepts and suggested activities and discussion topics at the end of the chapters. I especially thank the members of an alumni class I have had the privilege of teaching for over twenty years, each of whom took time out of their busy rabbinic lives not just to read the manuscript, but to gather in New York for an entire day to critique it with me. I may work *with* congregations, but they work *in* them. I take pride in listing the names of the rabbis who are changing the synagogue landscape: Rabbis Danny Freelander, Elyse Frishman, Robert Goldstein, Linda Henry Goodman, Debbie Hachen, Rick Jacobs, David Katz, Jackie Koch, Shira Milgrom, Jim Prosnit, Amy Schwartzman, Bonnie Steinberg, Maggie Wenig, Marjorie Yudkin, Debbie Zecher, and Daniel Zemel.

My cofounder of Synagogue 2000 (now renamed Synagogue 3000), Dr. Ron Wolfson, always thoughtful and honest, read it too, of course. We were an ideal partnership and remain best friends. Rabbi Aaron Spiegel, a Synagogue 3000 board member, read it also, bringing unique expertise from his work at the Center for Congregations in Indianapolis. Dr. Shawn Landres, Synagogue 3000's director of research, on his way to a doctorate in religious studies, added wonderful suggestions. From a cantorial perspective, Cantor Ellen Dreskin provided her always insightful comments. From a synagogue lay leader point of view, I was overwhelmingly fortunate to receive critiques from Terry Rosenberg and Lee Hendler, past and present chairs of the Synagogue 2000/3000 board, and synagogue past presidents as well—one Reform, the other Conservative. Finally, I am indebted to Dr. Steven M. Cohen, who corrected my sociological data, advised me on various academic matters, engaged me in debate, and helped me make the book much better conceptually.

I cannot find an adequate way to describe the work of our Fellows, the stellar models for synagogue life who taught at our conferences and advised Ron and me at every step along the way. I wish I had records sufficient to list everyone who helped us even once. This list represents only those who presented regularly at our conferences and who, thereby, entered our formal list of "Fellows." They enriched my life enormously: Karen Barth, Cantor Rosalie Boxt, Rabbi/Cantor Angela Warnick Buchdahl, Rabbi Rachel Cowan, Penny Dannenberg, Rabbi Elliot Dorff, Rabbi Paula Mack Drill, Rabbi Amy Eilberg, Rabbi Helaine Ettinger, Rabbi Ed Feinstein, Rabbi Nancy Flam, Karen Frank, Rabbi Danny Freelander, Debbie Friedman, Rabbi Elyse Frishman, Dr. Joel Grishaver, Dr. Carol Hausman, Rabbi Rick Jacobs, Risa Jaroslow, Rabbi Sam Joseph, Dr. Elliot Kranzler, Rabbi Larry Kushner, Amichai Lau Lavie, Liz Lerman, Danny Maseng, Rabbi Roly Matalon, Cantor Jack Mendelson, Rabbi Kerry Olitsky, Chazan Ari Priven, Rabbi Jonathan Rosenblatt, Cantor Benjie Ellen Schiller, Rabbi Ron Shulman, Rabbi Alan Silverstein, Rabbi Jonathan Slater, Rabbi Joel Soffin, Craig Taubman, Fr. Dick Vosko, Rabbi Elaine Zecher, and Rabbi Daniel Zemel.

For over fifteen years I have enjoyed the luxury of working with Jewish Lights Publishing. As usual, Emily Wichland, vice president of Editorial, has closely attended to every step that goes into publishing a book. I have come to depend on her in very many ways. My thanks go also to Debra Corman, who copyedited the manuscript with her usual care. Added thanks go to Sara Dismukes, who designed the cover; Kristi Menter who typeset the book; and Karyn Slutsky, who proofread the manuscript. Above all, I express gratitude to Stuart M. Matlins, publisher of Jewish Lights, a gifted visionary of what Jewish life can be. Jewish Lights was founded to make such a vision real. I am grateful to be associated with this remarkable experiment in creating a spiritual future.

My greatest thanks go, however, to my wife, Sally, and not just by way of the usual "To Sally" that typifies dedication pages. I include such a page, but I enlarge on it here. My work with Synagogue 2000 took me away from home countless weekends and weekdays: to the many Synagogue 2000 conferences (up to ten a year); to board and internal administrative meetings; to constant fundraising opportunities; to communities to meet with synagogue leaders (lay and clergy) and to hammer together alliances with Federations and private funders; and more and more and more. No one should be away from home that frequently. I once left early on a Sunday morning after just getting in the mail the announcement that I had joined the American Airlines "million mile club." At the airport, I asked the receptionist in that airline's Admirals Club if I received any tangible reward for so much travel. "You get a divorce!" she replied, only halfheartedly "joking" with me. "That's what you get." Instead of a divorce, I got love and support from my wife of forty-two years, who understood my passion for the future of Jewish life and allowed me to pursue it. Sally, I love you.

Notes

CHAPTER 1: THE THEORY IN SHORT

1. Peter Wonnacott, "Zoroastrians Turn to Internet Dating to Rescue Religion," *Wall Street Journal*, February 6, 2006.

2. Richard Rorty, *Philosophy and Social Hope* (London: Penguin Books, 1999), pp. 63, 64.

3. George A. Theodorson and Achilles G. Theodorson, *A Modern Dictionary of Sociology* (New York: Thomas Y. Crowell, 1969).

4. Lawrence A. Hoffman, "Ethics and Ritual: Lessons from Freud," in *Finding Voice to Give God Praise: Essays in the Many Languages of the Liturgy [Festchrift in Honor of Gilbert Ostdiek, O.F.M.]*, ed. Kathleen Hughes (Collegeville, MN: Liturgical Press, 1998). My most significant source there is Yosef Yerushalmi, *Freud's Moses: Judaism Terminable and Interminable* (New Haven: Yale University Press, 1991).

5. "Jewish civilization" is, of course, the by now famous construction of Judaism by Mordecai Kaplan. I borrow much from Kaplan, even as I claim we have moved beyond the Jewish world that he knew.

6. Lawrence A. Hoffman, "A Rendezvous of Ancestors: Wrestling for Ritual Truth," *Proceedings of the North American Academy of Liturgy*, 2004, pp. 18–40.

7. Joel M. Hoffman, *In the Beginning: A Short History of the Hebrew Language* (New York: New York University Press, 2004).

CHAPTER 2: THINKING SPIRITUALLY

1. Cf. Margaret Gilbert, *On Social Facts* (Princeton: Princeton University Press, 1985); John R. Searle, *Speech Acts* (Cambridge: Cambridge

University Press, 1969); John R. Searle, *The Construction of Social Reality* (New York: Free Press, 1995); Ian Hacking, *The Social Construction of What?* (Cambridge, MA: Harvard University Press, 1999); Charles Taylor, "Interpretation and the Human Sciences," *Review of Metaphysics* 25, no. 1 (1971): 3–51; reprinted in Charles Taylor, *Philosophy and the Human Sciences*, Philosophical Papers 2 (New York: Cambridge University Press, 1985), pp. 15–58.

2. L. Emmet Holt, *Care and Feeding of Children* (New York: Cable, 1975), pp. 166–67.

3. John B. Watson, *Psychological Care of Infant and Child* (New York: W. W. Norton, 1928), pp. 9–10.

4. *The School Journal* 54:3 (January 16, 1897), pp. 77–80.

5. As reported in www.caderbooks.com/best40.html.

6. *Kol Kitvei Ramban*, vol. 2, p. 42; Tosafot, BK 85a, d.h. *shenitnah*.

CHAPTER 3: TELLING THE STORY

1. Barbara Hardy, "Towards a Poetics of Fiction," and C. Linde, *Life Stories*, cited by Peter Collins, "Congregations, Narratives and Identity: A Quaker Case Study," in Matthew Guest, Karin Tusting, and Linda Woodhead, eds., *Congregational Studies in the U.K.* (Aldershot: Ashgate Publishing, 2004), pp. 100–1.

2. Cited by Laura Miler, "Far from Narnia," *The New Yorker*, December 26, 2005–January 2, 2006, p. 52.

3. Tim Celek and Dieter Zander with Patrick Kampert, *Inside the Soul of a New Generation* (Grand Rapids: Zondervaan Publishing, 1996), p. 67.

4. Appropriating Philip Rieff's "psychological man;" Yerushalmi, *Freud's Moses*, p. 10.

5. Shoshanah Feher, "Managing Strain, Cointradictions and Fluidity: Messianic Judaism and the Negotiation of a Religious-Ethnic Identity," in *Contemporary American Religion: An Ethnographic Reader*, ed. Penny Edgell Becker and Nancy L. Eiesland (Walnut Creek, CA: AltaMira Press, 1997), pp. 29–30.

6. Lauren F. Winner, *Girl Meets God: On the Path to a Spiritual Life* (Chapel Hill: Algonquin Books, 2002), pp. 59–60.

7. Ibid., p. 99.

8. Beverly Rose, *Mothers Never Die* (Nashville: Integrity Publishers, 2002), pp. 160, 162.

9. Robert Wuthnow, *Producing the Sacred* (Urbana: University of Illinois Press, 1994), p. 67.

10. Sidney Schwarz, *Finding a Spiritual Home* (2000; repr., Woodstock, VT: Jewish Lights Publishing, 2003), pp. 247, 248.

11. *Willow Creek Community Church*, Harvard Business School case study, #9-691-102, rev. January 23, 1996.

12. Data taken from Willow Creek Association website, www.willow-creek.com/wca, November 2004.

13. Rick Karlgaard, *"Purpose Driven,"* *Forbes*, February 16, 2004.

14. Martin E. Marty, *Pilgrims in Their Own Land* (New York: Penguin Books, 1984).

15. Steven M. Cohen, "Non-Denominationalims and Post-Denominationalism: Two Tendencies in American Jewry," *Contact*, Summer 2005, pp. 7–8.

16. Bethamie Horowitz, *Connections and Journeys: Assessing Critical Opportunities for Enhancing Jewish Identity* (New York: UJA–Federation of New York, 2000).

17. Ibid., p. 28.

18. Steven M. Cohen, "Engaging the Next Generation of American Jews: Distinguishing the In-married, Inter-married and Non-married" (paper prepared for the World Conference of Jewish Communal Service Jerusalem, June 2006).

19. Daniel J. Elazar (1976), revised as *Community and Polity: The Organizational Dynamics of American Jewry* (Philadelphia: Jewish Publication Society, 1995).

20. Ibid., pp. 218–19.

21. Robert Wuthnow, *Sharing the Journey* (New York: Free Press, 1994).

22. Warren Bird, "The Great Small-Group Takeover," *Christianity Today*, February 7, 1994, p. 27.

23. Wuthnow, *Sharing the Journey*, pp. 45, 46, 48, 51.

24. Ibid., pp. 55, 33.

25. Rick Warren, *The Purpose Driven Church* (Grand Rapids: Zondervan Publishing House, 1995).

26. See summary of literature with regard to churches specifically in Laurence R. Iannoccone, "Why Strict Churches Are Strong," in *Sacred Companies: Organizational Aspects of Companies and Religious Aspects of Organizations*, ed. N. J. Demerath III, Peter Dobkin Hall,

Terry Schmitt, and Rhys R. Williams (New York: Oxford University Press, 1998), pp. 272–3.

27. John P. Kotter and Dan S. Cohen, *The Heart of Change* (Boston: Harvard Business School Press, 2002), p. 15.

28. Sue Fishkoff and Alexandra J. Wall, "Nonprofit Steers Unaffiliated Through Maze of Jewish Options," *Northern California Jewish News Weekly*, January 13, 2006.

CHAPTER 4: CRAFTING THE VISION

1. Rick Warren, *The Purpose Driven Church* (Grand Rapids: Zondervan Publishing, 1995), p. 364.

2. Ronald A. Heifetz, *Leadership Without Easy Answers* (Cambridge, MA: Harvard University Press, 1994).

3. For detail, see Ron Wolfson, *The Spirituality of Welcoming: How to Transform Your Congregation into a Sacred Community* (Woodstock, VT: Jewish Lights Publishing, 2006).

4. Sidney Schwarz, *Finding a Spiritual Home* (2000; repr., Woodstock, VT: Jewish Lights Publishing, 2003), pp. 76, 113, 161–3, 195–6.

5. Jackson W. Carroll and Wade Clark Roof, *Bridging Divided Worlds: Generational Cultures in Congregations* (San Francisco: Jossey-Bass, 2003), p. 36.

6. Ibid., p. 85.

7. Steven M. Cohen and Arnold M. Eisen, *The Jew Within* (Bloomington: Indiana University Press, 2000), p. 24.

CHAPTER 5: SACRED COMMUNITY

1. Stephanie Coontz, *The Way We Never Were* (New York: Basic Books, 2000), p. 10.

2. Cf. Robert N. Bellah, "Civil Religion in America," *Daedalus* 96, no. 1 (1967): 1–21; W. Lloyd Warner, *American Life* (Chicago: University of Chicago Press, 1962).

3. Robert Wuthnow, *Producing the Sacred* (Urbana: University of Illinois Press, 1994), p. 44.

4. Jack Wertheimer, "The American Synagogue: Recent Issues and Trends," *American Jewish Year Book, 2005*, p. 11.

5. Wuthnow, *Producing the Sacred*, p. 152.

6. Riv-Ellen Prell, *Prayer and Community: The Havurah in American Judaism* (Detroit: Wayne State University Press, 1989), p. 31.

7. Isa Aron, "Learning Congregations," in *A Congregation of Learners*, ed. Isa Aron, Sara Lee, and Seymour Rossel (New York: UAHC Press, 1995), p. 68.

8. Isa Aron, *Becoming a Congregation of Learners: Learning as a Key to Revitalizing Congregational Life* (Woodstock, VT: Jewish Lights Publishing, 2000).

9. Ted A. Campbell, *The Religion of the Heart* (Columbia: University of South Carolina Press, 1991): pp. 130–51.

10. Ralph Waldo Emerson, "Self-Reliance," *Essays First Series*.

11. Walt Whitman, *Leaves of Grass*.

12. William James, *The Varieties of Religious Experience* (New York: Modern Library Edition, 1994), pp. 366, 369.

13. Ibid., p. 506.

14. See Lawrence A. Hoffman, "Synagogues and American Spirituality," in *Synagogue Architecture in America*, ed. Henry Stolzman and David Stolzman (Australia: Images Publishing, 2004), pp. 80–1.

15. Diana Butler Bass, "Vital Signs," *Sojourners*, December 2005.

16. James, *Varieties*, p. 367.

17. I have omitted Pierre Bourdieu's "cultural capital." See his *Language and Symbolic Power* (Cambridge: Harvard University Press, 1991). I think it closely allied to Florida's "creative capital," which I use instead.

18. Thomas A. Stewart, *Intellectual Capital: The New Wealth of Organizations* (New York: Doubleday, 1997).

19. Ibid., p. 20.

20. On which, see Laurence R. Iannocone, "Religious Practice: A Human Capital Approach," *Journal for the Scientific Study of Religion* 29 (1990): 297–314; and on-line papers by the working group of *The Spiritual Capital Project*: Peter L. Berger and Robert W. Hefner, "Spiritual Capital in Comparative Perspective," n.d.; Theodore Roosevelt Malloch, "Social, Human and Spiritual Capital in Economic Development," 2003; Robert W. Woodberry, "Researching Spiritual Capital," n.d.; Roger Finke, "Spiritual Capital: Definitions, Applications, and New Frontiers," 2003.

21. Mircea Eliade, *The Sacred and the Profane* (New York: Harcourt Brace, 1959); Bryan S. Rennie, *Reconstructing Eliade* (New York: SUNY Press, 1996), chaps. 1–3.

22. C. G. Jung, *Modern Man in Search of a Soul* (New York: Harcourt Brace, 1933), p. 204.

23. Rudolf Otto, *The Idea of the Holy* (London: Oxford University Press, 1917).

CHAPTER 6: SACRED CULTURE, SACRED SYSTEM

1. Gareth Morgan, *Images of Organization* (Newbury Park, CA: Sage Publications, 1986), p. 31.
2. Edwin H. Friedman, *From Generation to Generation* (New York: Guilford Press, 1985).
3. Penny Edgell Becker, *Congregations in Conflict* (Cambridge: Cambridge University Press, 1999), p. 36.
4. Morgan, *Images of Organization*, chap. 6.
5. Edward T. Hall, *An Anthropology of Everyday Life: An Autobiography* (New York: Anchor Books, 1992), pp. 104–7.
6. *New York Times*, op-ed, August 10, 2005.
7. James F. Hopewell, *Congregation: Stories and Structures* (Philadelphia: Fortress Press, 1987), p. 95.
8. Anne Wilson Schaef and Dianne Fassel, *The Addictive Organization* (San Francisco: HarperSanFrancisco, 1988).
9. Alice Mann, *The In-Between Church* (Washington, DC: Alban Institute, 1998).
10. Based, in part, on Becker, *Congregations in Conflict*.
11. Cited in a classic collection of Weber's writings, by H. H. Gerth and C. Wright Mills, *From Max Weber* (New York: Oxford University Press, 1958), p. 244.
12. Mark Chaves, *Congregations in America* (Cambridge: Harvard University Press, 2004), pp. 36–43.
13. Learning typology is from Gregory Bateson, *Steps to an Ecology of Mind* (New York: Ballantine Books, 1972), pp. 283–306.
14. James Brian Quinn, Philip Anderson, and Sydney Finkelstein, "Managing Professional Intellect: Making the Most of the Best," *Harvard Business Review on Knowledge Management* (Cambridge: Harvard Business Review Paperback, 1999), pp. 183–4.
15. David A. Garvin, *Harvard Business Review on Knowledge Management*, p. 51.
16. Morton T. Hansen, Nitin Nohria, and Thomas Tierney, "What's Your Strategy for Managing Knowledge?" *Harvard Business Review*, March/April 1999.
17. Chris Argyris, "Good Communication That Blocks Learning," *Harvard Business Review*, July/August 1994.
18. B. Joseph Pine and James H. Gilmore, "Welcome to the Experience Economy," *Harvard Business Review*, July/August 1998, pp. 97–105.
19. Etienne Wenger, Richard McDermott, and William M. Snyder, *Cultivating Communities of Practice* (Boston: Harvard Business School Press, 2002).

20. Richard Florida, *The Rise of the Creative Class* (New York: Basic Books, 2002).

21. Robert Putnam, *Bowling Alone: The Collapse and Revival of American Community* (New York: Simon & Schuster, 2000).

22. Florida, *Creative Class*, pp. 296–7.

23. See Wade Clark Roof, "Religion and Narrative," *Review of Religious Research* 34, no. 4 (June 1993): 14. For an application specifically regarding Jewish identity, see treatment of "the sovereign self," in Steven M. Cohen and Arnold M. Eisen, *The Jew Within* (Bloomington: Indiana University Press, 2000), pp. 13–42.

24. Chaves, *Congregations in America*, pp. 46, 52–3.

25. Charles Taylor, *Sources of the Self* (Cambridge: Harvard University Press, 1989).

CHAPTER 7: SYNAGOGUES IN CONTEXT: THE LARGER PICTURE

1. Jonathon Ament, *American Jewish Religious Denominations* (A United Jewish Communities report, 2005), p. 34.

2. The range of theories can be easily accessed from Grace Davie, "Europe: The Exception," in *The Desecularization of the World*, ed. Peter L. Berger (Grand Rapids: William M. Eerdman's Publishing, 1999), pp. 73–82. For application of the thesis to Jews and Judaism, see David Ellenson, *After Emancipation* (Cincinnati: Hebrew Union College Press, 2004).

3. Cf. Steve Bruce, *Religion in the Modern World* (Oxford: Oxford University Press, 1996); Steve Bruce, ed., *Religion and Modernization* (Oxford: Oxford University Press, 1992).

4. See set of essays in Peter Berger, ed., *Desecularization of the World* (Grand Rapids: Wm. B. Eerdmans, 1999), particularly chapter by Berger himself, "The Desecularization of the World: A Global Overview," pp. 1–18.

5. The description and dating that follow come from Robert William Fogel, *The Fourth Great Awakening and the Future of Egalitarianism* (Chicago: University of Chicago Press, 2000).

6. Cited in Sydney E. Ahlstrom, *A Religious History of the American People* (New Haven and London: Yale University Press, 1972), p. 748.

7. Summarized briefly, but effectively, in Jack Wertheimer, "The American Synagogue: Recent Issues and Trends," *American Jewish Year Book, 2005*, pp. 59–60. For detail, see Yaakov Ariel, "Hasidism in the Age of

Aquarius: The House of Love and Prayer in San Francisco, 1967–1977," *Religion and American Culture: A Journal of Interpretation* 13, no. 2 (2003): 139–65.

8. See Virginia Postrel, *The Substance of Style* (New York: HarperCollins, 2003).

9. Ann Swidler, "Saving the Self: Endowment Versus Depletion in American Institutions," in *Meaning and Modernity: Religion, Polity and Self*, ed. Richard Madson, William M. Sullivan, Ann Swidler, and Steven M. Tipton (Berkeley: University of California Press, 2002), p. 44.

10. Richard Florida, *The Rise of the Creative Class* (New York: Basic Books, 2002), pp. 296–7.

11. Wertheimer, "The American Synagogue," pp. 24–7.

12. Personal conversation with Gary Kohn.

13. Forty-six percent is the figure for the core Jewish population only (Jonathon Ament, *American Jewish Religious Denominations* [A United Jewish Communities report, 2005]). If we include the marginals, the figure falls to 40 percent (Steven M. Cohen, personal communication, February 2, 2006).

14. Cf. C. Kirk Hadaway, Penny Long Marler, and Mark Chaves, "What the Polls Don't Show: A Closer Look at U.S. Church Attendance," *American Sociological Review* 58 (1993): 741–52; C. Kirk Hadaway and Lenny Long Marler, "How Many American Attend Worship Each Week? An Alternative Approach to Measurement," *Journal for the Scientific Study of Religion* 44 (2005): 307–22.

15. Eddie Gibbs and Ryan K. Bolger, *Emerging Churches* (Grand Rapids: Baker Academic Press, 2005), p. 30.

16. Rita Healy and David van Biema, "There's No Pulpit Like Home," *Time Archive: 1923 to the Present* [website], March 6, 2006.

17. Gibbs and Bolger, *Emerging Churches*, p. 34.

18. Scott Bader-Saye, "The Emergent Matrix: A New Kind of Church?" *The Christian Century*, November 30, 2004.

19. Dan Kimball, *The Emerging Church* (Grand Rapids: Zondervan, 2003), p. 15.

20. Jay Michaelson, "A Prayer Group of Their Own," *The Forward*, November 14, 2003.

21. Steven M. Cohen, "Engaging the Next Generation of American Jews: Distinguishing the In-married, Inter-married, and Non-married" (paper prepared for the World Conference of Jewish Communal Service, Jerusalem, June 2006).

22. Dean Kelley, *Why Conservative Churches Are Growing: A Study in the Sociology of Religion* (Macon, GA: Mercer University Press, 1972).

23. Laurence R. Iannaccone, "Why Strict Churches Are Strong," *American Journal of Sociology* 99, no. 5 (1994): 1180–1211.

24. Joseph B. Tamney and Stephen D. Johnson, "The Popularity of Strict Churches," *Review of Religious Research* 39, no. 3 (March 1998): 209–23.

25. Diana Butler Bass, *The Practicing Congregation* (Washington, DC: Alban Institute, 2004), p. 50.

Meditation

The Handbook of Jewish Meditation Practices
A Guide for Enriching the Sabbath and Other Days of Your Life
By Rabbi David A. Cooper
Easy-to-learn meditation techniques. 6 x 9, 208 pp, Quality PB, ISBN 1-58023-102-0 **$16.95**

Discovering Jewish Meditation: Instruction & Guidance for Learning an Ancient
Spiritual Practice *By Nan Fink Gefen, PhD* 6 x 9, 208 pp, Quality PB, ISBN 1-58023-067-9 **$16.95**

A Heart of Stillness: A Complete Guide to Learning the Art of Meditation
By Rabbi David A. Cooper 5½ x 8½, 272 pp, Quality PB, ISBN 1-893361-03-9 **$16.95**
(A SkyLight Paths book)

Meditation from the Heart of Judaism: Today's Teachers Share Their
Practices, Techniques, and Faith *Edited by Avram Davis*
6 x 9, 256 pp, Quality PB, ISBN 1-58023-049-0 **$16.95**

Silence, Simplicity & Solitude: A Complete Guide to Spiritual Retreat at Home
By Rabbi David A. Cooper 5½ x 8½, 336 pp, Quality PB, ISBN 1-893361-04-7 **$16.95**
(A SkyLight Paths book)

The Way of Flame: A Guide to the Forgotten Mystical Tradition of Jewish
Meditation *By Avram Davis* 4½ x 8, 176 pp, Quality PB, ISBN 1-58023-060-1 **$15.95**

Ritual/Sacred Practice/Journaling

The Jewish Dream Book: The Key to Opening the Inner Meaning of
Your Dreams *By Vanessa L. Ochs with Elizabeth Ochs; Full-color illus. by Kristina Swarner*
Instructions for how modern people can perform ancient Jewish dream practices
and dream interpretations drawn from the Jewish wisdom tradition. For anyone
who wants to understand their dreams—and themselves.
8 x 8, 120 pp, Full-color illus., Deluxe PB w/flaps, ISBN 1-58023-132-2 **$16.95**

The Jewish Journaling Book: How to Use Jewish Tradition to Write
Your Life & Explore Your Soul *By Janet Ruth Falon*
Details the history of Jewish journaling throughout biblical and modern times,
and teaches specific journaling techniques to help you create and maintain a vital
journal, from a Jewish perspective. 8 x 8, 304 pp, Deluxe PB w/flaps, ISBN 1-58023-203-5 **$18.99**

The Book of Jewish Sacred Practices: CLAL's Guide to Everyday & Holiday
Rituals & Blessings *Edited by Rabbi Irwin Kula and Vanessa L. Ochs, PhD*
6 x 9, 368 pp, Quality PB, ISBN 1-58023-152-7 **$18.95**

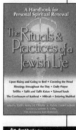

Jewish Ritual: A Brief Introduction for Christians
By Rabbi Kerry M. Olitzky and Rabbi Daniel Judson
5½ x 8½, 144 pp, Quality PB, ISBN 1-58023-210-8 **$14.99**

The Rituals & Practices of a Jewish Life: A Handbook for Personal Spiritual
Renewal *Edited by Rabbi Kerry M. Olitzky and Rabbi Daniel Judson*
6 x 9, 272 pp, illus., Quality PB, ISBN 1-58023-169-1 **$18.95**

Science Fiction/
Mystery & Detective Fiction

Mystery Midrash: An Anthology of Jewish Mystery & Detective Fiction
Edited by Lawrence W. Raphael. Preface by Joel Siegel.
6 x 9, 304 pp, Quality PB, ISBN 1-58023-055-5 **$16.95**

Criminal Kabbalah: An Intriguing Anthology of Jewish Mystery & Detective Fiction
Edited by Lawrence W. Raphael. Foreword by Laurie R. King.
6 x 9, 256 pp, Quality PB, ISBN 1-58023-109-8 **$16.95**

Wandering Stars: An Anthology of Jewish Fantasy & Science Fiction
Edited by Jack Dann. Introduction by Isaac Asimov.
6 x 9, 272 pp, Quality PB, ISBN 1-58023-005-9 **$16.95**

More Wandering Stars: An Anthology of Outstanding Stories of Jewish Fantasy and
Science Fiction *Edited by Jack Dann. Introduction by Isaac Asimov.*
6 x 9, 192 pp, Quality PB, ISBN 1-58023-063-6 **$16.95**

Life Cycle
Marriage / Parenting / Family / Aging

Jewish Fathers: A Legacy of Love
Photographs by Lloyd Wolf. Essays by Paula Wolfson. Foreword by Harold S. Kushner.
Honors the role of contemporary Jewish fathers in America. Each father tells in his own words what it means to be a parent and Jewish, and what he learned from his own father. Insightful photos. 9½ x 9⅞, 144 pp with 100+ duotone photos, Hardcover, ISBN 1-58023-204-3 **$30.00**

The New Jewish Baby Album: Creating and Celebrating the Beginning of a Spiritual Life—A Jewish Lights Companion
By the Editors at Jewish Lights. Foreword by Anita Diamant. Preface by Sandy Eisenberg Sasso.
A spiritual keepsake that will be treasured for generations. More than just a memory book, *shows you how—and why it's important*—to create a Jewish home and a Jewish life. 8 x 10, 64 pp, Deluxe Padded Hardcover, Full-color illus., ISBN 1-58023-138-1 **$19.95**

The Jewish Pregnancy Book: A Resource for the Soul, Body & Mind during Pregnancy, Birth & the First Three Months
By Sandy Falk, MD, and Rabbi Daniel Judson, with Steven A. Rapp
Includes medical information, prayers and rituals for each stage of pregnancy, from a liberal Jewish perspective. 7 x 10, 208 pp, Quality PB, b/w illus., ISBN 1-58023-178-0 **$16.95**

Celebrating Your New Jewish Daughter: Creating Jewish Ways to Welcome Baby Girls into the Covenant—New and Traditional Ceremonies
By Debra Nussbaum Cohen 6 x 9, 272 pp, Quality PB, ISBN 1-58023-090-3 **$18.95**

The New Jewish Baby Book, 2nd Edition: Names, Ceremonies & Customs—A Guide for Today's Families *By Anita Diamant* 6 x 9, 336 pp, Quality PB, ISBN 1-58023-251-5 **$19.99**

Parenting As a Spiritual Journey: Deepening Ordinary and Extraordinary Events into Sacred Occasions *By Rabbi Nancy Fuchs-Kreimer* 6 x 9, 224 pp, Quality PB, ISBN 1-58023-016-4 **$16.95**

Judaism for Two: A Spiritual Guide for Strengthening and Celebrating Your Loving Relationship *By Rabbi Nancy Fuchs-Kreimer and Rabbi Nancy H. Wiener*
Addresses the ways Jewish teachings can enhance and strengthen committed relationships. 6 x 9, 208 pp, Quality PB, ISBN 1-58023-254-X **$16.99**

Embracing the Covenant: Converts to Judaism Talk About Why & How
By Rabbi Allan Berkowitz and Patti Moskovitz 6 x 9, 192 pp, Quality PB, ISBN 1-879045-50-8 **$16.95**

The Guide to Jewish Interfaith Family Life: An InterfaithFamily.com Handbook
Edited by Ronnie Friedland and Edmund Case 6 x 9, 384 pp, Quality PB, ISBN 1-58023-153-5 **$18.95**

Introducing My Faith and My Community
The Jewish Outreach Institute Guide for the Christian in a Jewish Interfaith Relationship
By Rabbi Kerry M. Olitzky 6 x 9, 176 pp, Quality PB, ISBN 1-58023-192-6 **$16.99**

Making a Successful Jewish Interfaith Marriage: The Jewish Outreach Institute Guide to Opportunities, Challenges and Resources
By Rabbi Kerry M. Olitzky with Joan Peterson Littman 6 x 9, 176 pp, Quality PB, ISBN 1-58023-170-5 **$16.95**

The Creative Jewish Wedding Book: A Hands-On Guide to New & Old Traditions, Ceremonies & Celebrations *By Gabrielle Kaplan-Mayer*
Provides the tools to create the most meaningful Jewish traditional or alternative wedding by using ritual elements to express your unique style and spirituality. 9 x 9, 288 pp, b/w photos, Quality PB, ISBN 1-58023-194-2 **$19.99**

Divorce Is a Mitzvah: A Practical Guide to Finding Wholeness and Holiness When Your Marriage Dies *By Rabbi Perry Netter. Afterword by Rabbi Laura Geller.*
6 x 9, 224 pp, Quality PB, ISBN 1-58023-172-1 **$16.95**

A Heart of Wisdom: Making the Jewish Journey from Midlife through the Elder Years
Edited by Susan Berrin. Foreword by Harold Kushner. 6 x 9, 384 pp, Quality PB, ISBN 1-58023-051-2 **$18.95**

So That Your Values Live On: Ethical Wills and How to Prepare Them
Edited by Jack Riemer and Nathaniel Stampfer 6 x 9, 272 pp, Quality PB, ISBN 1-879045-34-6 **$18.99**

Holidays/Holy Days

Yom Kippur Readings: Inspiration, Information and Contemplation
Edited by Rabbi Dov Peretz Elkins with section introductions from Arthur Green's These Are the Words
An extraordinary collection of readings, prayers and insights that enable the modern worshiper to enter into the spirit of the Day of Atonement in a personal and powerful way, permitting the meaning of Yom Kippur to enter the heart.
6 x 9, 348 pp, Hardcover, ISBN 1-58023-271-X **$24.99**

Leading the Passover Journey
The Seder's Meaning Revealed, the Haggadah's Story Retold
By Rabbi Nathan Laufer
Uncovers the hidden meaning of the Seder's rituals and customs.
6 x 9, 208 pp, Hardcover, ISBN 1-58023-211-6 **$24.99**

Reclaiming Judaism as a Spiritual Practice: Holy Days and Shabbat
By Rabbi Goldie Milgram
Provides a framework for understanding the powerful and often unexplained intellectual, emotional, and spiritual tools that are essential for a lively, relevant, and fulfilling Jewish spiritual practice. 7 x 9, 272 pp, Quality PB, ISBN 1-58023-205-1 **$19.99**

7th Heaven: Celebrating Shabbat with Rebbe Nachman of Breslov
By Moshe Mykoff with the Breslov Research Institute
Explores the art of consciously observing Shabbat and understanding in-depth many of the day's spiritual practices. 5⅛ x 8¼, 224 pp, Deluxe PB w/flaps, ISBN 1-58023-175-6 **$18.95**

The Women's Passover Companion
Women's Reflections on the Festival of Freedom
Edited by Rabbi Sharon Cohen Anisfeld, Tara Mohr, and Catherine Spector
Groundbreaking. A provocative conversation about women's relationships to Passover as well as the roots and meanings of women's seders.
6 x 9, 352 pp, Quality PB, ISBN 1-58023-231-0 **$19.99**; Hardcover, ISBN 1-58023-128-4 **$24.95**

The Women's Seder Sourcebook
Rituals & Readings for Use at the Passover Seder
Edited by Rabbi Sharon Cohen Anisfeld, Tara Mohr, and Catherine Spector
Gathers the voices of more than one hundred women in readings, personal and creative reflections, commentaries, blessings, and ritual suggestions that can be incorporated into your Passover celebration.
6 x 9, 384 pp, Quality PB, ISBN 1-58023-232-9 **$19.99**; Hardcover, ISBN 1-58023-136-5 **$24.95**

Creating Lively Passover Seders: A Sourcebook of Engaging Tales, Texts & Activities
By David Arnow, PhD 7 x 9, 416 pp, Quality PB, ISBN 1-58023-184-5 **$24.99**

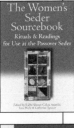

Hanukkah, 2nd Edition: The Family Guide to Spiritual Celebration
By Dr. Ron Wolfson. Edited by Joel Lurie Grishaver.
7 x 9, 240 pp, illus., Quality PB, ISBN 1-58023-122-5 **$18.95**

The Jewish Family Fun Book: Holiday Projects, Everyday Activities, and Travel Ideas
with Jewish Themes *By Danielle Dardashti and Roni Sarig. Illus. by Avi Katz.*
6 x 9, 288 pp, 70+ b/w illus. & diagrams, Quality PB, ISBN 1-58023-171-3 **$18.95**

The Jewish Gardening Cookbook: Growing Plants & Cooking for
Holidays & Festivals *By Michael Brown* 6 x 9, 224 pp, 30+ illus., Quality PB, ISBN 1-58023-116-0 **$16.95**

The Jewish Lights Book of Fun Classroom Activities: Simple and Seasonal
Projects for Teachers and Students *By Danielle Dardashti and Roni Sarig*
6 x 9, 240 pp, Quality PB, ISBN 1–58023–206–X **$19.99**

Passover, 2nd Edition: The Family Guide to Spiritual Celebration
By Dr. Ron Wolfson with Joel Lurie Grishaver 7 x 9, 352 pp, Quality PB, ISBN 1-58023-174-8 **$19.95**

Shabbat, 2nd Edition: The Family Guide to Preparing for and Celebrating the Sabbath
By Dr. Ron Wolfson 7 x 9, 320 pp, illus., Quality PB, ISBN 1-58023-164-0 **$19.95**

Sharing Blessings: Children's Stories for Exploring the Spirit of the Jewish Holidays
By Rahel Musleah and Michael Klayman
8½ x 11, 64 pp, Full-color illus., Hardcover, ISBN 1-879045-71-0 **$18.95** *For ages 6 & up*

Spirituality

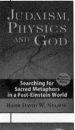

Does the Soul Survive? A Jewish Journey to Belief in Afterlife, Past Lives & Living with Purpose   *By Rabbi Elie Kaplan Spitz. Foreword by Brian L. Weiss, MD*
Spitz relates his own experiences and those shared with him by people he has worked with as a rabbi, and shows us that belief in afterlife and past lives, so often approached with reluctance, is in fact true to Jewish tradition.
6 x 9, 288 pp, Quality PB, ISBN 1-58023-165-9 **$16.99**; Hardcover, ISBN 1-58023-094-6 **$21.95**

First Steps to a New Jewish Spirit: Reb Zalman's Guide to Recapturing the Intimacy & Ecstasy in Your Relationship with God
By Rabbi Zalman M. Schachter-Shalomi with Donald Gropman
An extraordinary spiritual handbook that restores psychic and physical vigor by introducing us to new models and alternative ways of practicing Judaism. Offers meditation and contemplation exercises for enriching the most important aspects of everyday life.   6 x 9, 144 pp, Quality PB, ISBN 1-58023-182-9 **$16.95**

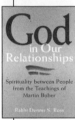

God in Our Relationships: Spirituality between People from the Teachings of Martin Buber   *By Rabbi Dennis S. Ross*
On the eightieth anniversary of Buber's classic work, we can discover new answers to critical issues in our lives. Inspiring examples from Ross's own life— as congregational rabbi, father, hospital chaplain, social worker, and husband— illustrate Buber's difficult-to-understand ideas about how we encounter God and each other. 5½ x 8½, 160 pp, Quality PB, ISBN 1-58023-147-0 **$16.95**

Judaism, Physics and God: Searching for Sacred Metaphors in a Post-Einstein World   *By Rabbi David W. Nelson*
In clear, non-technical terms, this provocative fusion of religion and science examines the great theories of modern physics to find new ways for contemporary people to express their spiritual beliefs and thoughts.
6 x 9, 352 pp, Quality PB, ISBN 1-58023-306-6 **$18.99**; Hardcover, ISBN 1-58023-252-3 **$24.99**

The Jewish Lights Spirituality Handbook: A Guide to Understanding, Exploring & Living a Spiritual Life   *Edited by Stuart M. Matlins*
What exactly is "Jewish" about spirituality? How do I make it a part of my life? Fifty of today's foremost spiritual leaders share their ideas and experience with us.
6 x 9, 456 pp, Quality PB, ISBN 1-58023-093-8 **$19.95**; Hardcover, ISBN 1-58023-100-4 **$24.95**

Bringing the Psalms to Life: How to Understand and Use the Book of Psalms
By Dr. Daniel F. Polish
6 x 9, 208 pp, Quality PB, ISBN 1-58023-157-8 **$16.95**; Hardcover, ISBN 1-58023-077-6 **$21.95**

God & the Big Bang: Discovering Harmony between Science & Spirituality
By Dr. Daniel C. Matt 6 x 9, 216 pp, Quality PB, ISBN 1-879045-89-3 **$16.99**

Godwrestling—Round 2: Ancient Wisdom, Future Paths
By Rabbi Arthur Waskow 6 x 9, 352 pp, Quality PB, ISBN 1-879045-72-9 **$18.95**

One God Clapping: The Spiritual Path of a Zen Rabbi   *By Rabbi Alan Lew with Sherril Jaffe*
5½ x 8½, 336 pp, Quality PB, ISBN 1-58023-115-2 **$16.95**

The Path of Blessing: Experiencing the Energy and Abundance of the Divine
By Rabbi Marcia Prager 5½ x 8½, 240 pp, Quality PB, ISBN 1-58023-148-9 **$16.95**

Six Jewish Spiritual Paths: A Rationalist Looks at Spirituality   *By Rabbi Rifat Sonsino*
6 x 9, 208 pp, Quality PB, ISBN 1-58023-167-5 **$16.95**; Hardcover, ISBN 1-58023-095-4 **$21.95**

Soul Judaism: Dancing with God into a New Era
By Rabbi Wayne Dosick 5½ x 8½, 304 pp, Quality PB, ISBN 1-58023-053-9 **$16.95**

Stepping Stones to Jewish Spiritual Living: Walking the Path Morning, Noon, and Night   *By Rabbi James L. Mirel and Karen Bonnell Werth*
6 x 9, 240 pp, Quality PB, ISBN 1-58023-074-1 **$16.95**; Hardcover, ISBN 1-58023-003-2 **$21.95**

There Is No Messiah ... and You're It: The Stunning Transformation of Judaism's Most Provocative Idea   *By Rabbi Robert N. Levine, DD*
6 x 9, 192 pp, Quality PB, ISBN 1-58023-255-8 **$16.99**; Hardcover, ISBN 1-58023-173-X **$21.95**

These Are the Words: A Vocabulary of Jewish Spiritual Life   *By Dr. Arthur Green*
6 x 9, 304 pp, Quality PB, ISBN 1-58023-107-1 **$18.95**

Spirituality/The Way Into... Series

The Way Into... Series offers an accessible and highly usable "guided tour" of the Jewish faith, people, history and beliefs—in total, an introduction to Judaism that will enable you to understand and interact with the sacred texts of the Jewish tradition. Each volume is written by a leading contemporary scholar and teacher, and explores one key aspect of Judaism. *The Way Into...* enables all readers to achieve a real sense of Jewish cultural literacy through guided study.

The Way Into Encountering God in Judaism   *By Neil Gillman*
6 x 9, 240 pp, Quality PB, ISBN 1-58023-199-3 **$18.99**; Hardcover, ISBN 1-58023-025-3 **$21.95**

Also Available: **The Jewish Approach to God: A Brief Introduction for Christians**
By Neil Gillman 5½ x 8½, 192 pp, Quality PB, ISBN 1-58023-190-X **$16.95**

The Way Into Jewish Mystical Tradition   *By Lawrence Kushner*
6 x 9, 224 pp, Quality PB, ISBN 1-58023-200-0 **$18.99**; Hardcover, ISBN 1-58023-029-6 **$21.95**

The Way Into Jewish Prayer   *By Lawrence A. Hoffman*
6 x 9, 224 pp, Quality PB, ISBN 1-58023-201-9 **$18.99**; Hardcover, ISBN 1-58023-027-X **$21.95**

The Way Into Judaism and the Environment   *By Jeremy Benstein, PhD*
6 x 9, 225 pp (est.), Hardcover, ISBN 1-58023-268-X **$24.99**

The Way Into *Tikkun Olam* (Repairing the World)   *By Elliot N. Dorff*
6 x 9, 320 pp, Hardcover, ISBN 1-58023-269-8 **$24.99**

The Way Into Torah   *By Norman J. Cohen*
6 x 9, 176 pp, Quality PB, ISBN 1-58023-198-5 **$16.99**; Hardcover, ISBN 1-58023-028-8 **$21.95**

Spirituality and Wellness

Aleph-Bet Yoga
Embodying the Hebrew Letters for Physical and Spiritual Well-Being
By Steven A. Rapp. Foreword by Tamar Frankiel, PhD, and Judy Greenfeld. Preface by Hart Lazer
7 x 10, 128 pp, b/w photos, Quality PB, Layflat binding, ISBN 1-58023-162-4 **$16.95**

Entering the Temple of Dreams
Jewish Prayers, Movements, and Meditations for the End of the Day
By Tamar Frankiel, PhD, and Judy Greenfeld
7 x 10, 192 pp, illus., Quality PB, ISBN 1-58023-079-2 **$16.95**

Jewish Paths toward Healing and Wholeness: A Personal Guide to Dealing with Suffering *By Rabbi Kerry M. Olitzky. Foreword by Debbie Friedman.*
6 x 9, 192 pp, Quality PB, ISBN 1-58023-068-7 **$15.95**

Minding the Temple of the Soul
Balancing Body, Mind, and Spirit through Traditional Jewish Prayer, Movement, and Meditation   *By Tamar Frankiel, PhD, and Judy Greenfeld*
7 x 10, 184 pp, illus., Quality PB, ISBN 1-879045-64-8 **$16.95**
Audiotape of the Blessings and Meditations: 60 min. **$9.95**
Videotape of the Movements and Meditations: 46 min. **$20.00**

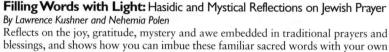

Spirituality/Lawrence Kushner

FillingWords with Light: Hasidic and Mystical Reflections on Jewish Prayer
By Lawrence Kushner and Nehemia Polen
Reflects on the joy, gratitude, mystery and awe embedded in traditional prayers and blessings, and shows how you can imbue these familiar sacred words with your own sense of holiness. 5½ x 8½, 176 pp, Hardcover, ISBN 1-58023-216-7 **$21.99**

The Book of Letters: A Mystical Hebrew Alphabet
Popular Hardcover Edition, 6 x 9, 80 pp, 2-color text, ISBN 1-879045-00-1 **$24.95**
Collector's Limited Edition, 9 x 12, 80 pp, gold foil embossed pages, w/limited edition silkscreened print, ISBN 1-879045-04-4 **$349.00**

The Book of Miracles: A Young Person's Guide to Jewish Spiritual Awareness
6 x 9, 96 pp, 2-color illus., Hardcover, ISBN 1-879045-78-8 **$16.95** *For ages 9–13*

The Book of Words: Talking Spiritual Life, Living Spiritual Talk
6 x 9, 160 pp, Quality PB, ISBN 1-58023-020-2 **$16.95**

Eyes Remade for Wonder: A Lawrence Kushner Reader *Introduction by Thomas Moore*
6 x 9, 240 pp, Quality PB, ISBN 1-58023-042-3 **$18.95;** Hardcover, ISBN 1-58023-014-8 **$23.95**

God Was in This Place & I, i Did Not Know
Finding Self, Spirituality and Ultimate Meaning 6 x 9, 192 pp, Quality PB, ISBN 1-879045-33-8 **$16.95**

Honey from the Rock: An Introduction to Jewish Mysticism
6 x 9, 176 pp, Quality PB, ISBN 1-58023-073-3 **$16.95**

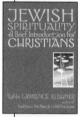

Invisible Lines of Connection: Sacred Stories of the Ordinary
5½ x 8½, 160 pp, Quality PB, ISBN 1-879045-98-2 **$15.95**

Jewish Spirituality—A Brief Introduction for Christians
5½ x 8½, 112 pp, Quality PB Original, ISBN 1-58023-150-0 **$12.95**

The River of Light: Jewish Mystical Awareness 6 x 9, 192 pp, Quality PB, ISBN 1-58023-096-2 **$16.95**

TheWay Into Jewish MysticalTradition
6 x 9, 224 pp, Quality PB, ISBN 1-58023-200-0 **$18.99;** Hardcover, ISBN 1-58023-029-6 **$21.95**

Spirituality/Prayer

Pray Tell: A Hadassah Guide to Jewish Prayer
By Rabbi Jules Harlow, with contributions from Tamara Cohen, Rochelle Furstenberg, Rabbi Daniel Gordis, Leora Tanenbaum, and many others
Enriched with insight and wisdom from a broad variety of viewpoints.
8½ x 11, 400 pp, Quality PB, ISBN 1-58023-163-2 **$29.95**

My People's Prayer Book Series

Traditional Prayers, Modern Commentaries *Edited by Rabbi Lawrence A. Hoffman*
Provides diverse and exciting commentary to the traditional liturgy, helping modern men and women find new wisdom in Jewish prayer, and bring liturgy into their lives. Each book includes Hebrew text, modern translation, and commentaries from all perspectives of the Jewish world.

Vol. 1—The *Sh'ma* and Its Blessings
7 x 10, 168 pp, Hardcover, ISBN 1-879045-79-6 **$24.99**
Vol. 2—The *Amidah*
7 x 10, 240 pp, Hardcover, ISBN 1-879045-80-X **$24.95**
Vol. 3—*P'sukei D'zimrah* (Morning Psalms)
7 x 10, 240 pp, Hardcover, ISBN 1-879045-81-8 **$24.95**
Vol. 4—*Seder K'riat Hatorah* (The Torah Service)
7 x 10, 264 pp, Hardcover, ISBN 1-879045-82-6 **$23.95**
Vol. 5—*Birkhot Hashachar* (Morning Blessings)
7 x 10, 240 pp, Hardcover, ISBN 1-879045-83-4 **$24.95**
Vol. 6—*Tachanun* and Concluding Prayers
7 x 10, 240 pp, Hardcover, ISBN 1-879045-84-2 **$24.95**
Vol. 7—Shabbat at Home
7 x 10, 240 pp, Hardcover, ISBN 1-879045-85-0 **$24.95**
Vol. 8—*Kabbalat Shabbat* (Welcoming Shabbat in the Synagogue)
7 x 10, 240 pp, Hardcover, ISBN 1-58023-121-7 **$24.99**
Vol. 9—Welcoming the Night: *Minchah* and *Ma'ariv* (Afternoon and Evening Prayer) 7 x 10, 272 pp, Hardcover, ISBN 1-58023-262-0 **$24.99**

Theology/Philosophy

Aspects of Rabbinic Theology
By Solomon Schechter. New Introduction by Dr. Neil Gillman.
6 x 9, 448 pp, Quality PB, ISBN 1-879045-24-9 **$19.95**

Broken Tablets: Restoring the Ten Commandments and Ourselves
Edited by Rachel S. Mikva. Introduction by Lawrence Kushner. Afterword by Arnold Jacob Wolf.
6 x 9, 192 pp, Quality PB, ISBN 1-58023-158-6 **$16.95**; Hardcover, ISBN 1-58023-066-0 **$21.95**

Creating an Ethical Jewish Life
A Practical Introduction to Classic Teachings on How to Be a Jew
By Dr. Byron L. Sherwin and Seymour J. Cohen
6 x 9, 336 pp, Quality PB, ISBN 1-58023-114-4 **$19.95**

The Death of Death: Resurrection and Immortality in Jewish Thought
By Dr. Neil Gillman 6 x 9, 336 pp, Quality PB, ISBN 1-58023-081-4 **$18.95**

Evolving Halakhah: A Progressive Approach to Traditional Jewish Law
By Rabbi Dr. Moshe Zemer
6 x 9, 480 pp, Quality PB, ISBN 1-58023-127-6 **$29.95**; Hardcover, ISBN 1-58023-002-4 **$40.00**

Hasidic Tales: Annotated & Explained
~~...~~ *...hapiro. Foreword by Andrew Harvey, SkyLight Illuminations series editor.*
~~...~~ *0 pp, Quality PB, ISBN 1-893361-86-1* **$16.95** *(A SkyLight Paths Book)*

A Heart of Many Rooms: Celebrating the Many Voices within Judaism
By Dr. David Hartman 6 x 9, 352 pp, Quality PB, ISBN 1-58023-156-X **$19.95**

The Hebrew Prophets: Selections Annotated & Explained
Translation & Annotation by Rabbi Rami Shapiro. Foreword by Zalman M. Schachter-Shalomi
5½ x 8½, 224 pp, Quality PB, ISBN 1-59473-037-7 **$16.99** *(A SkyLight Paths book)*

Keeping Faith with the Psalms: Deepen Your Relationship with God Using the
Book of Psalms *By Daniel F. Polish* 6 x 9, 320 pp, Quality PB, ISBN 1-58023-300-7 **$18.99**
Hardcover, ISBN 1-58023-179-9 **$24.95**

The Last Trial
On the Legends and Lore of the Command to Abraham to Offer Isaac as a Sacrifice
By Shalom Spiegel. New Introduction by Judah Goldin.
6 x 9, 208 pp, Quality PB, ISBN 1-879045-29-X **$18.95**

A Living Covenant: The Innovative Spirit in Traditional Judaism
By Dr. David Hartman 6 x 9, 368 pp, Quality PB, ISBN 1-58023-011-3 **$20.00**

Love and Terror in the God Encounter
The Theological Legacy of Rabbi Joseph B. Soloveitchik
By Dr. David Hartman
6 x 9, 240 pp, Quality PB, ISBN 1-58023-176-4 **$19.95**; Hardcover, ISBN 1-58023-112-8 **$25.00**

The Personhood of God: Biblical Theology, Human Faith and the Divine Image
By Dr. Yochanan Muffs; Foreword by Dr. David Hartman
6 x 9, 240 pp, Hardcover, ISBN 1-58023-265-5 **$24.99**

The Spirit of Renewal: Finding Faith after the Holocaust
By Rabbi Edward Feld 6 x 9, 224 pp, Quality PB, ISBN 1-879045-40-0 **$16.95**

Tormented Master: *The Life and Spiritual Quest of Rabbi Nahman of Bratslav*
By Dr. Arthur Green 6 x 9, 416 pp, Quality PB, ISBN 1-879045-11-7 **$19.99**

Your Word Is Fire: The Hasidic Masters on Contemplative Prayer
Edited and translated by Dr. Arthur Green and Barry W. Holtz
6 x 9, 160 pp, Quality PB, ISBN 1-879045-25-7 **$15.95**

I Am Jewish
Personal Reflections Inspired by the Last Words of Daniel Pearl
Almost 150 Jews—both famous and not—from all walks of life, from all around
the world, write about Identity, Heritage, Covenant / Chosenness and Faith,
Humanity and Ethnicity, and *Tikkun Olam* and Justice.
Edited by Judea and Ruth Pearl
6 x 9, 304 pp, Deluxe PB w/flaps, ISBN 1-58023-259-0 **$18.99**; Hardcover, ISBN 1-58023-183-7 **$24.99**
Download a free copy of the *I Am Jewish Teacher's Guide* at our website:
www.jewishlights.com

About Jewish Lights

People of all faiths and backgrounds yearn for books that attract, engage, educate, and spiritually inspire.

Our principal goal is to stimulate thought and help all people learn about who the Jewish People are, where they come from, and what the future can be made to hold. While people of our diverse Jewish *itage are the primary audience, our books speak to people in the Christian vell and will broaden their understanding of Judaism and the roots of the_

We bring to you authors who are at the forefron experience. While each has something different to say, they all say i that you can hear.

Our books are designed to welcome you and then to engage, stimulate, and inspire. We judge our success not only by whether or not our books are beautiful and commercially successful, but by whether or not they make a difference in your life.

For your information and convenience, at the back of this book we have provided a list of other Jewish Lights books you might find interesting and useful. They cover all the categories of your life:

Bar/Bat Mitzvah	Life Cycle
Bible Study / Midrash	Meditation
Children's Books	Parenting
Congregation Resources	Prayer
Current Events / History	Ritual / Sacred Practice
Ecology	Spirituality
Fiction: Mystery, Science Fiction	Theology / Philosophy
Grief / Healing	Travel
Holidays / Holy Days	Twelve Steps
Inspiration	Women's Interest
Kabbalah / Mysticism / Enneagram	

Stuart M. Matlins, Publisher

Or phone, fax, mail or e-mail to: **JEWISH LIGHTS Publishing**
Sunset Farm Offices, Route 4 • P.O. Box 237 • Woodstock, Vermont 05091
Tel: (802) 457-4000 • Fax: (802) 457-4004 • www.jewishlights.com
Credit card orders: (800) 962-4544 (8:30AM–5:30PM ET Monday–Friday)
Generous discounts on quantity orders. SATISFACTION GUARANTEED. Prices subject to change.

For more information about each book, visit our website at www.jewishlights.com